VULCAN
GOD OF FIRE

TIM McLELLAND

VULCAN

GOD OF FIRE

The History Press

First published 2012

The History Press
The Mill, Brimscombe Port
Stroud, Gloucestershire, GL5 2QG
www.thehistorypress.co.uk

British Library Cataloguing in Publication Data.
A catalogue record for this book is available from the British
Library.

ISBN 978 0 7524 6379 7

Typesetting and origination by The History Press
Printed in India
Manufacturing managed by Jellyfish Solutions Ltd

CONTENTS

INTRODUCTION

Britain's long history of innovative military aircraft design and construction has produced some truly outstanding designs. Often driven by the expediencies of war, classic aircraft such as the Spitfire and Lancaster have become familiar names in the nation's vocabulary. It would be fair to say that it is these (and other) aircraft from the days of the Second World War that have become the most familiar icons. The decades which followed certainly produced a wider range of exciting and unusual aircraft that generated a great deal of attention whenever they emerged, but they inevitably faded into history as even more advanced and capable machines replaced them. However, one aircraft could perhaps be described as a true exception. Its unorthodox, graceful lines were somehow merged with a menacing stature belying its true purpose. Although designed for warfare, it captured the imagination and emotions of almost everyone who saw it. Built not for beauty, this sleek, shining machine was created to kill. It was a wholesale murderer, a true weapon of mass destruction.

1

THE BOMB

During the dark, austere years immediately after the Second World War the euphoria of wartime victory did not last for long. There was little to celebrate in Britain. Food rationing was still a daily source of misery for every household across the land and the government struggled to rebuild a nation that had been crippled both emotionally and financially. The war with Germany was over and the brutal war with Japan had been brought to a dramatic conclusion, but there was no sense of peace or security to comfort Britain's long-suffering citizens while the country slowly began the task of rebuilding itself. A new threat had emerged and it held a menacing promise of more misery and more warfare. The Soviet Union might have been a wartime ally, but it quickly became obvious that Stalin's friendship had been only a temporary convenience that had swiftly turned sour, and as the joy of Japan's surrender slowly faded into history, Britain was faced with a future that often looked even more terrifying than the grim days of the Second World War. The Soviet Union's increasingly aggressive attitude could not be separated from the very clear knowledge that if Britain and her allies were forced into another military confrontation, such a war would not merely be a question of achieving victory. This time, the inevitable outcome would be complete devastation for both the victor and vanquished. Britain had entered the nuclear age.

It was against this background that the Vulcan bomber was created. British industry's output of fighting machines for the Royal Air Force – which had begun as a result of Britain's first conflict with Germany – reached a peak of excellence during the Second World War. In addition to the creation of classic fighter aircraft such as the Spitfire and Hurricane, a whole series of bombers had been designed and manufactured, all of which were vital to Britain's efforts to take the war back to skies over Germany. In this field the immortal Avro Lancaster represented the pinnacle of Britain's technical expertise, but as the Second World War reached its conclusion, even the mighty Lancaster was already beginning to show signs of obsolescence. During the 1940s designs emerged with remarkable speed and by the time that the Second World War ended, America had already created the superlative Boeing B-29 Superfortress, which had demonstrated its potential over Japan. However, with meagre resources and a stifling lack of forward thinking, Britain's offensive capabilities diminished with astonishing speed. The Royal Air Force was destined to replace its Lancaster, Halifax and Stirling bombers with the Lincoln, an aircraft that was, in effect, little more than an improved version of the Lancaster. However, circumstances quickly shaped the RAF's future and the lumbering Lincoln was in fact the last of a distinguished line of piston-engined bombers. The jet age had dawned and it was inevitable that this new technology would enable the RAF to re-equip with fighters and bombers that would achieve speeds and altitudes almost beyond imagination just a few years previously. Indeed, the jet engine would ultimately lead to the creation of a completely new RAF bomber that would represent a seismic shift in technology and thinking, a radical new design that was so revolutionary and advanced that it often seemed like an impossible dream. But the dream was, in fact, a nightmare. Britain's new bomber would be designed to perform only one mission against only one target. It would be tasked with the carriage and delivery of just one, deadly, atomic bomb.

To understand the reasons why and how the Vulcan bomber was created, it is important to understand the circumstances that prevailed at the time of the project's conception. Unlike any other British bombers that preceded it, the Vulcan and the V-force was inextricably linked to a specific weapon and one fundamental role. The aircraft and the weapon it was designed to carry were equal parts of one incredibly expensive project on which Britain's very existence effectively relied.

Far left: Avro 698 prototype VX770 pictured over Hampshire en route to the Farnborough SBAC show. (BAE)

Oddly, the full story of the Vulcan requires some knowledge of the complicated world of particle physics. The tale begins with Otto Frisch, an Austrian scientist who was engaged in studies at the Institute of Theoretical Physics in Copenhagen (he'd been forced to leave Nazi Germany because of his nationality). He was invited to relocate to England in order to continue his molecular physics studies at the University of Birmingham. Having worked in Denmark under the leadership of fellow physicist Niels Bohr, he had established the basic principles of what became known as nuclear fission while spending a Christmas holiday with Lise Meitner (who happened to be his aunt), herself a respected scientist who had been conducting experiments with two other physicists, Otto Hahn and Fritz Strassman. Together, they had produced a detailed report, which had described how barium was created as a result of the collision of uranium nuclei and neutrons. They made a series of tests and with calculations based on the first report, Frisch and Meitner concluded that in order to have created barium, somewhere in the microscopic process the impact of a neutron upon a uranium atom must have actually elongated the shape of its nucleus. Nuclei contain protons that (because of their electrical charge) normally try to repel each other, but strong surface tension normally holds these protons together. Frisch and Meitner discovered that if the nucleus became elongated into a 'peanut' shape, it ought to enable the electrical forces to overcome this surface tension, allowing the nucleus to split into two similarly sized portions. Frisch concluded that this must have been what had actually happened and he described this theory as 'nuclear fission'. However, this in itself was not the most important point. He also calculated that the mass of the two halves created by the fission process was slightly less than that of the original nucleus, and this tiny shortfall of mass therefore represented (if Einstein's theories were correct) an output of energy produced during the creation of the two fragments. Frisch and Meitner calculated that even though the actual amount of energy involved in this fission process would obviously be only microscopic in size, in proportional terms it would be 'surprisingly large'. They had discovered the fundamentals of nuclear power.

Physicist Niels Bohr continued to investigate the new research data and his experiments led him to conclude that this uranium fission process was created by the presence of uranium 235, a rare isotope that is present in relatively small quantities within the more common uranium 238 that every chemistry student is familiar with. Bohr established that during the fission process, secondary neutrons were created and if these same neutrons were then able to initiate further fissions, a self-sustaining 'chain reaction' would then occur, creating more and more fission and, therefore, a huge release of energy. As the process applied only to the rare uranium 235, this chain reaction process never occurred naturally, either because of the slow rate of radioactive decay or because of the isotope's relative scarcity when compared to the more common uranium 238 isotope (it normally occurs at a rate of little more than just one in 140 parts). Frisch agreed with this conclusion, but he couldn't help wondering just how much uranium 235 would actually be needed to start this theoretical chain-reaction process. Working with Rudolf Peierls (Professor of Physics at Birmingham University), Frisch was astonished to find that the required amount was remarkably small ('only about a pound' he subsequently recalled).

Clearly, this discovery had great potential and could form the basis of a very efficient source of power if the basic theory was correct and the process could be translated into a practical application. Although their thoughts inevitably turned towards the possibilities of creating what could be an almost limitless source of commercial power, they also suddenly realised that the concept would also have a more sinister potential. Frisch and Peierls submitted their research to Henry Tizard, who at that time was Chairman of the Committee on the Scientific Survey of Air Defence. It is ironic to note that Tizard had recently championed the development and introduction of radar, a subject that both Frisch and Peierls had also been keen to explore, but they had been forbidden to study it at the University of Birmingham, because of their nationalities. It was fortuitous that no such restrictions had been placed on the study of particle physics. However, their report was given to Tizard in March 1940 and it outlined a number of important issues:

The attached detailed report concerns the possibility of constructing a 'super bomb' which utilises the energy stored in atomic nuclei as a source of energy. The energy liberated in the explosion of such a super bomb is about the same as that produced by the explosion of 1,000 tons of dynamite. This energy is liberated in a small volume in which it will, for an instant, produce a temperature comparable to that in the interior of the sun. The blast from such an explosion would destroy life in a wide area. The size of this area is difficult to estimate, but it will probably cover the centre of a big city. In addition, some part of the energy set free by the bomb goes to produce radioactive substances, and these will emit very powerful and dangerous radiations. The effect of these radiations is greatest immediately after the explosion, but it decays only gradually and even for days after the explosion any person entering the affected area will be killed. Some of this radioactivity will be carried along with the wind and will spread the contamination; several miles downwind this may kill people.

Perhaps understandably, Tizard was both excited and impressed by the findings and he immediately made arrangements to set up a committee to explore the matter in more detail. Meeting for the first time in April 1940, this 'Maud Committee' (the unusual code name was derived from Maud Rey, the former governess of Niels Bohr's children) explored the findings thoroughly, and tried to establish whether the discovery could possibly be translated into some form of destructive power. Their revised 1941 report included the following remarks:

> Work to investigate the possibilities of utilizing the atomic energy of uranium for military purposes has been in progress since 1939, and a stage has now been reached when it seems desirable to report progress. We should like to emphasise at the beginning of this report that we entered the project with more scepticism than belief, though we felt it was a matter which had to be investigated. As we proceeded we became more and more convinced that release of atomic energy on a large scale is possible and that conditions can be chosen which would make it a very powerful weapon of war. We have now reached the conclusion that it will be possible to make an effective uranium bomb which, containing some 25lb of active material, would be equivalent as regards

Classic Charles Brown photograph of the Avro 698 prototype VX770. Brown photographed the aircraft from the rear turret of a Lancaster. *(BAE)*

> destructive effect to 1,800 tons of TNT and would also release large quantities of radioactive substance, which would make places near to where the bomb exploded dangerous to human life for a long period. The bomb would be composed of an active constituent (referred to in what follows as U) present to the extent of about a part in 140 in ordinary uranium. Owing to the very small difference in properties (other than explosive) between this substance and the rest of the uranium, its extraction is a matter of great difficulty and a plant to produce 2–4lb per day (or three bombs per month) is estimated to cost approximately £95,000,000, of which sum a considerable proportion would be spent on engineering, requiring labour of the same highly skilled character as is needed for making turbines.

> In spite of this very large expenditure we consider that the destructive effect, both material and moral, is so great that every effort should be made to produce bombs of this kind. As regards the time required we estimate that the material for the first bomb could be ready by the end of 1943. This of course assumes that no major difficulty of an entirely unforeseen character arises.

The mighty Vulcan thrilled air show spectators for more than three decades. Four Waddington-based aircraft are pictured here performing a scramble demonstration from RAF Finningley in 1982. (*Tim McLelland collection*)

Even if the war should end before the bombs are ready the effort would not be wasted, except in the unlikely event of complete disarmament, since no nation would care to risk being caught without a weapon of such decisive possibilities.

This type of bomb is possible because of the enormous store of energy resident in atoms and because of the special properties of the active constituent of uranium. The explosion is very different in its mechanism from the ordinary chemical explosion, for it can occur only if the quantity of U is greater than a certain critical amount. Quantities of the material less than the critical amount are quite stable. Such quantities are therefore perfectly safe and this is a point which we wish to emphasise. On the other hand, if the amount of material exceeds the critical value it is unstable and a reaction will develop and multiply itself with enormous rapidity, resulting in an explosion of unprecedented violence. Thus all that is necessary to detonate the bomb is to bring together two pieces of the active material, each less than the critical size, but which, when in contact, form a mass exceeding it.

In order to achieve the greatest efficiency in an explosion of this type, it is necessary to bring the two halves together at high velocity and it is proposed to do this by firing them together with charges of ordinary explosive in a form of double gun. The weight of this gun will of course greatly exceed the weight of the bomb itself, but should not be more than one ton, and it would certainly be within the carrying capacity of a modern bomber. It is suggested that the bomb (contained in the gun) should be dropped by parachute and the gun should be fired by means of a percussion device when it hits the ground. The time of drop can be made long enough to allow the aeroplane to escape from the danger zone and as this is very large, great accuracy of aim is not required. Although the cost per lb. of this explosive is so great, it compares very favourably with ordinary explosives when reckoned in terms of energy released and damage done. It is, in fact considerably cheaper, but the points which we regard as of overwhelming importance are the concentrated destruction which it would produce, the large moral effect, and the saving in air effort the use of this substance would allow, as compared with bombing with ordinary explosives.

One outstanding difficulty of the scheme is that the main principle cannot be tested on a small scale. Even to produce a bomb of the minimum critical size would involve a great expenditure of time and money. We are, however, convinced that the principle is correct, and while there is still some uncertainty as to the critical size it is most unlikely that the best estimate we can make is so far in error as to invalidate the general conclusions. We feel that the present evidence is sufficient to justify the scheme being strongly pressed. It will be seen from the foregoing that a stage in the work has now been reached at which it is important that a decision should be made as to whether the work is to be continued on the increasing scale which would be necessary if we are to hope for it as an effective weapon for this war. Any considerable delay now would retard by an equivalent amount the date by which the weapon could come

The three V-bomber types together, in a rarely seen formation, with a Victor B1 to starboard, a Valiant B1 to port and a Vulcan B1 in the lead position. *(Tim McLelland collection)*

into effect. We are informed that while the Americans are working on the uranium problem, the bulk of their effort has been directed to the production of energy, as discussed in our report on uranium as a source of power, rather than to the production of a bomb. We are in fact co-operating with the United States to the extent of exchanging information, and they have undertaken one or two pieces of laboratory work for us. We feel that it is important and desirable that development work should proceed on both sides of the Atlantic irrespective of where it may be finally decided to locate the plant for separating the uranium, and for this purpose it seems desirable that certain members of the committee should visit the United States. We are informed that such a visit would be welcomed by the members of the United States committees which are dealing with this matter.

His comments referring to the British working in close co-operation with the USA were certainly true at that time. British scientists were co-operating freely with their American counterparts on all aspects of the new discovery; in fact, Niels Bohr was actually sailing to New York as he made his calculations to confirm the Frisch-Meitner findings, during 1939. The Maud Committee concluded that the nuclear fission process did show great potential and if the theories could be developed into hardware, it would enable Britain to manufacture a completely new weapon

Above: HMS *Plym* pictured shortly before Penney's team detonated Britain's first atomic device on board. (*Tim McLelland collection*)

Above right: Operation Hurricane's impressive cloud of debris, just seconds after detonation. (*Tim McLelland collection*)

which might have a decisive role in the war with Germany (there was, at this time, no question of using such a weapon against any other country). Many years later Frisch said that he had:

> … often been asked why I didn't abandon the project there and then, saying nothing to anybody. Why start on a project which, if it was successful, would end with the production of a weapon of unparalleled violence, a weapon of mass destruction such as the world had never seen? The answer is very simple. We were at war, and the idea was reasonably obvious. Very probably some German scientists had had the same idea and were working on it too.

Frisch's comments held some truth, since there was plenty of evidence to suggest that Germany was indeed showing great interest in the same theory. A group of Paris-based scientists working on similar fission studies had concluded that if the rapid progress of the theoretical chain reaction was to be slowed to a controllable level, a moderating substance would be required and that 'heavy water' (deuterium oxide) would be the ideal medium. The only known source of heavy water at that time was a hydroelectric station at Vemork in Norway, and Germany had already offered to buy the entire Norwegian stock of heavy water. This was clear evidence that Germany was well aware of the potential of the fission process, and that Hitler's scientists were already putting a great deal of effort into the creation of an atomic weapon.

During the infamous summer of 1940 Britain was in the grip of a bloody war with Nazi Germany and the United States was still maintaining an absurdly neutral position,

both towards the war and the UK itself. Britain's future began to look increasingly bleak, and governmental eyes inevitably looked across the Atlantic to America's vast industrial resources. Tizard proposed what essentially became a 'trade mission' to give America access to a range of British technological developments in exchange for access to America's industrial know-how and resources. Mutual exchange certainly wasn't a new idea, although the true benefits of such exchanges had always been difficult to pinpoint and Churchill firmly believed that the idea would probably do Britain more harm than good, but Tizard (rather naively) believed that by giving technological information to the US on an unconditional basis, some vital co-operation would be given in return. It was a risky proposal that illustrated the desperate situation Britain had found itself in. A whole catalogue of scientific data was duly handed over, which included some incredibly significant developments such as Whittle's revolutionary jet engine, the cavity magnetron (which was fundamental to the development of radar) and much more besides. It was a gift that America certainly hadn't been expecting and one that it naturally accepted with surprise and glee. The Frisch-Peierls memorandum was only part of the mission's range of topics that Tizard brought to the Americans, but in retrospect it was arguably the most important, even though it probably didn't seem quite so significant at the time. The whole saga was surrounded by controversy and great debate, many officials in the UK (including Churchill himself) being set firmly against Tizard's well-meaning efforts and, as many had feared, the result was a distinctly lukewarm response from the US, which certainly gave Britain very little of value. It was probably no coincidence that Tizard found himself without a job when he returned to the UK. However, the visit did eventually have some unforeseen and far-reaching effects and ultimately laid the foundations of the 'special relationship' between the US and Britain which still survives (in various degrees of intimacy) to this day.

The British government was, of course, wholly wrapped up in its battle with Germany and its relationship with America, therefore it is hardly surprising that in September 1940 there was no reason to imagine that there was any risk of vital scientific data finding its was to the USSR. In

fact, most of the Maud Committee's findings had already made their way across Europe a whole month previously, thanks to a network of Soviet agents. Nevertheless, Britain remained ignorant of this vital development for a long time and across the Atlantic there was even less inclination to imagine that the vital secrets of atomic physics were systematically being delivered into Stalin's hands. The US government invited the Tizard delegation to visit Columbia University in order to discuss the Frisch-Peierls memorandum with Enrico Fermi, a respected Italian physicist who was also investigating aspects of the newly discovered fission process. Fermi later recalled that in January 1939 he had started working on rapidly emerging data, at the Pupin Laboratories:

In that period, Niels Bohr was on a lecture engagement at the Princeton University and I remember one afternoon Willis Lamb came back very excited and said that Bohr had leaked out great news. The great news that had leaked out was the discovery of fission and at least the outline of its interpretation. Then, somewhat later that same month, there was a meeting in Washington where the possible importance of the newly discovered phenomenon of fission was first discussed in semi-jocular earnest as a possible source of nuclear power.

At the time when Tizard's delegation met with Fermi, the Italian was still clearly looking at fission as a source of commercial power rather than as a potential weapon, even though other physicists had already reached much darker

Rare photograph of the Blue Danube bomb. The scientist pictured next to the weapon illustrates the huge size of the bomb carcass. It was this which directly led to the dimensions of the Vulcan's bomb bay and the overall size of the aircraft. (AWRE)

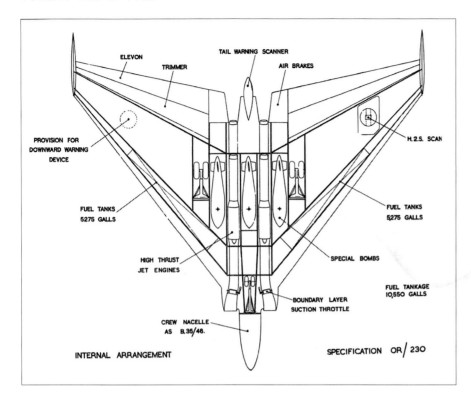

ELEVON

TAIL WARNING SCANNER

TRIMMER

AIR BRAKES

PROVISION FOR
DOWNWARD WARNING
DEVICE

H.2.S. SCAN

FUEL TANKS
5275 GALLS

FUEL TANKS
5275 GALLS

HIGH THRUST
JET ENGINES

SPECIAL BOMBS

FUEL TANKAGE
10,550 GALLS

BOUNDARY LAYER
SUCTION THROTTLE

CREW NACELLE
AS B.35/46.

INTERNAL ARRANGEMENT

SPECIFICATION OR/230

This Avro drawing illustrates how the company proposed a swept-wing design to meet the preliminary AR.230 specification (which was subsequently dropped). The same concept was carried over to the B.35/46 specification. *(BAE)*

Fermi was interested only in the peaceful potential of nuclear power (through the creation of turbine steam) and even though the military potential of nuclear fission was obvious, he remained sceptical of the Frisch-Peierls memorandum and further developments stagnated after Tizard's delegation returned to the UK. No further progress was made until Mark Oliphant (Professor of Physics at the University of Birmingham) made another trip to the United States, this time in August 1941, to try to establish why there had been such an inexplicable lack of progress, particularly in terms of developing some sort of atomic bomb. It was explained that a government committee had duly been set up to investigate fission research but (perhaps because of Fermi's influence) they appeared to have simply ignored the findings of the Maud Committee. Oliphant subsequently recalled that:

> The minutes and reports had been sent to Lyman Briggs, who was the Director of the Uranium Committee, and we were puzzled to receive virtually no comment. I called on Briggs in Washington, only to find out that this inarticulate and unimpressive man had put the reports in his safe and had not shown them to members of his committee. I was amazed and distressed.

Oliphant was disheartened, but he proceeded to meet with the government's Uranium Committee, as committee member Samuel Allison recalled:

> Oliphant came to a meeting, and said 'bomb' in no uncertain terms. He told us we must concentrate every effort on the bomb and said we had no right to work on powerplants or anything but the bomb. The bomb would cost 25 million dollars, he said, and Britain did not have the money or the manpower, so it was up to us.

conclusions. For example, in October 1939 a group of scientists had delivered a letter (signed by Albert Einstein) to President Roosevelt, warning that:

> In the course of the last four months it has been made probable, through the work of Joliot in France as well as Fermi and Szilard in America, that it may become possible to set up a nuclear chain reaction in a large mass of uranium, by which vast amounts of power and large quantities of new radium-like elements would be generated. Now it appears almost certain that this could be achieved in the immediate future. This new phenomenon would also lead to the construction of bombs, and it is conceivable, though much less certain, that extremely powerful bombs of a new type may thus be constructed. A single bomb of this type, carried by boat and exploded in a port, might very well destroy the whole port together with some of the surrounding territory. However, such bombs might very well prove to be too heavy for transportation by air.

Finally, Columbia University was awarded a grant of some $6,000 (although the money was not released until the spring of 1940 because of governmental concerns, centred on a belief that 'foreigners' would be conducting the research), but Fermi now had the means to construct the very first atomic pile at Stagg Field in Chicago, which finally went critical (i.e. a controlled uranium chain reaction was allowed to begin) on 2 December 1942.

Despite this pivotal development, American interest in the prospect of fission power was still distinctly half-hearted and the possibility of using the technology to produce a bomb seemed as unlikely as it ever had. America was not at war, even though Europe most certainly was. Interest in the concept of an atomic bomb was still very much in the hands of the scientists and it was their continued pressure that eventually led to some solid progress. Vannevar Bush (Director of the Office of Scientific Research and Development) finally convinced Roosevelt (during October 1941) to conduct a fully funded effort to build an atomic weapon. The combination of scientific pressure, the previously overlooked Maud report and the clear possibility of ultimately entering into a war was finally enough to push America into taking action. A new committee was set up to oversee the project and report to the president, meeting for the very first time just one day before Japanese forces attacked Pearl Harbor and the United States finally entered the Second World War.

Roosevelt then wrote to Churchill, suggesting that efforts to develop an atomic bomb should be 'co-ordinated or even jointly conducted' but much to Roosevelt's surprise, Churchill was less than enthusiastic. It seems absurd that after so much effort to pursue a bomb project, Britain was now evidently reluctant to co-operate with America, but this seems to have been because Churchill and his advisors grossly underestimated the cost and complexity of the project laid before them. A distinct 'go it alone' attitude prevailed, although when British scientists visited the US early in 1942 and were afforded full access to information which was then available, they were astounded by the rapid progress that was being made, especially in comparison to developments back in Britain.

Britain's position became increasingly difficult when the complexities and cost of atomic research eventually became much clearer. The British programme (code-named as the Tube Alloys Project) soon indicated to the government that full co-operation with America would be the only practical way to proceed, but by the time that Britain had reached this conclusion, America's research and development had moved far ahead of Britain's, which effectively meant that there was no longer any obvious advantage for America in sharing its knowledge. Worse still for Britain, the US

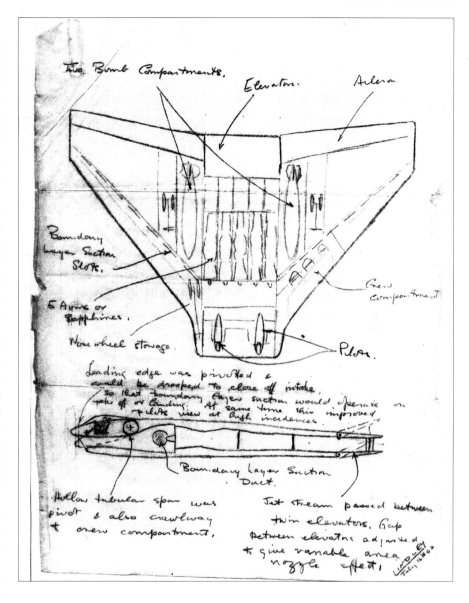

Army had now taken over control of virtually all aspects of the US programme (as the Manhattan Project) and so all sources of information quickly dried up. The situation was finally resolved through a series of diplomatic meetings that were assisted by Roosevelt's personal inclination towards a more co-operative stance. He rightly accepted that while American concerns over releases of information were largely based on potential post-war commercial use of

Bob Lindley's sketch gives a good impression of how the Vulcan's unique shape first emerged. This was Lindley's original idea, which was proposed to Roy Chadwick and subsequently developed into the Avro 698 design. *(BAE)*

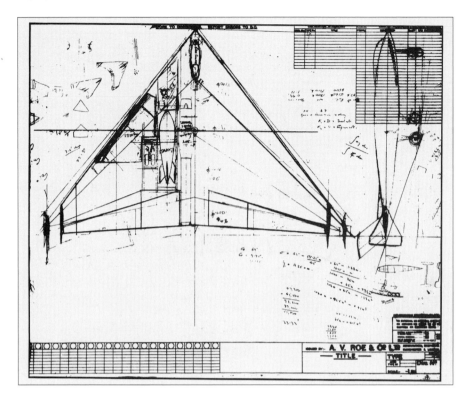

The precise origins of this drawing remain unclear, but it is assumed to have been produced by Roy Chadwick at the very beginning of the 698 project. It illustrates the original interest in a simple flying wing design. *(BAE)*

expense has fallen upon the United States; It is agreed between us. First, that we will never use this agency against each other. Secondly, that we will not use it against third parties without each other's consent. Thirdly, that we will not either of us communicate any information about Tube Alloys to third parties except by mutual consent. Fourthly, that in view of the heavy burden of production falling upon the United States as the result of a wise division of war effort, the British Government recognize that any post-war advantages of an industrial or commercial character shall be dealt with as between the United States and Great Britain on terms to be specified by the President of the United States to the Prime Minister of Great Britain. The Prime Minister expressly disclaims any interest in these industrial and commercial aspects beyond what may be considered by the President of the United States to be fair and just and in harmony with the economic welfare of the world. And Fifthly, that the following arrangements shall be made to ensure full and effective collaboration between the two countries in bringing the project to fruition.

atomic power (which America clearly identified as an asset which should remain in its hands), Britain's interest was chiefly in the creation of an atomic bomb. When Churchill assured Roosevelt that this was indeed the case (and that Britain had no direct interest in obtaining America's data on nuclear power development), the situation was soon resolved and a joint agreement between the countries was signed by Roosevelt and Churchill on 19 August 1943 (the Quebec Agreement), including the following stipulations:

Articles of Agreement Governing Collaboration Between The Authorities of the USA and the UK in the Matter of Tube Alloys. Whereas it is vital to our common safety in the present war to bring the Tube Alloys project to fruition at the earliest moments; and Whereas this maybe more speedily achieved if all available British and American brains and resources are pooled; and Whereas owing to war conditions it would be an improvident use of war resources to duplicate plants on a large scale on both sides of the Atlantic and therefore a far greater

Following the signing of the Quebec Agreement, British physicists were soon drafted into the Manhattan Project in substantial numbers, working in close co-operation with their American counterparts at the Los Alamos facility in New Mexico. Information on all aspects of the project was still only exchanged between scientists on a strictly 'need to know' basis, but this compartmentalised approach was applied as a general security measure, rather than being any direct attempt to restrict British knowledge of the wider aspects of the project (even though Britain's ignorance of some key areas was its inevitable result). In fact, Anglo-American co-operation was now better than ever and during another meeting in 1944, Roosevelt and Churchill signed another agreement, which developed the themes from the earlier Quebec Agreement. In essence, the 'Hyde Park Aide Memoire' specified that Britain and America should continue to pursue joint military and industrial atomic energy development even after the war had ended. The agreement also dismissed the idea of releasing information on Britain's nuclear programme (the Tube Alloys Project) so that an international treaty of arms control could be set up while Britain and the US still retained a monopoly of knowledge. However (and without any plausible explanation), Roosevelt failed to even show the document to any of his advisors and it quietly disappeared into his private files for several years. After meeting with the president a few days after the memoire was first signed, Vannevar Bush expressed his belief that on the basis of the agreement, Roosevelt was privately contemplating an Anglo-American agreement to maintain complete secrecy on the atom bomb's development beyond the end of the war, thereby (at least in theory) controlling the stability of the rest of the world. Bush believed that this was a flawed policy and advised the Secretary of War (Henry L. Stimpson) that it would inevitably encourage the Soviets to develop their own bomb and ultimately lead to a catastrophic conflict between the superpowers. Of course, Bush did not know that the Soviets were already well aware of the Manhattan Project. Further analysis only led to yet more confusion and, despite their misgivings, neither Bush nor Stimpson ever forwarded any viewpoints to the president. Subsequently, Stimpson commented that 'the atomic bomb might be a Frankenstein which would eat us up, or it might be the means by which the peace of the world would be helped in becoming secure'. However, although the US government had realised that the country was effectively at a proverbial crossroads in terms of policy decisions, it was still far from clear which direction the country should take, and when Roosevelt died in April 1945, the situation had still not been resolved.

By now, Britain's very significant involvement in the Manhattan Project was secure and despite the complexities of the task at hand, some rapid scientific progress was made, culminating in the detonation of the world's first atomic device at 0529hrs on 16 July 1945. This device (it was far bigger and cumbersome than anything which could be described as a 'bomb') was assembled in secret, deep in the heart of what is now the White Sands Missile Range near Alamogordo, in the New Mexico desert.

The Trinity test site device employed an implosion system that utilised plutonium (a by-product of uranium created within an atomic pile during the chain reaction process) as its key fissile component. Plutonium had by now been determined to be a more efficient fissionable

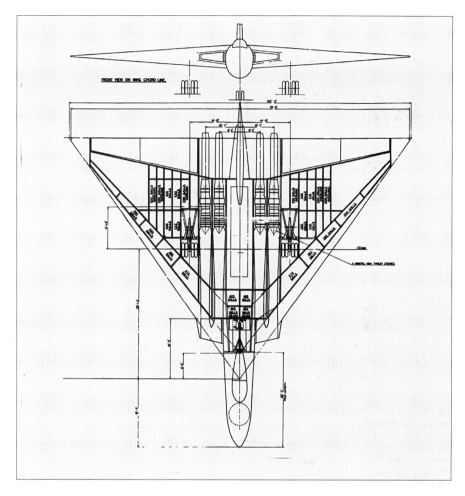

material (and could be created more easily) than uranium 235, but the reactor-produced plutonium proved to be rather less efficient than expected, which meant that a simple gun implosion detonation (effectively smashing a projectile into the core) simply wouldn't create the necessary instantaneous chain reaction. The presence of additional neutrons during the fission process meant that the plutonium would begin to pre-detonate, resulting in a bomb with a disappointingly low yield no greater than that achieved with conventional explosives. The solution was to produce an implosion device, which requires the core of plutonium to be instantly compressed from all angles by conventional explosive charges. By carefully shaping a mix of fast and slow explosives into a series of 'lenses', a shock

This Avro drawing emerged during the 698 design process. At this stage the aircraft still features a simple straight-wing delta shape, but with intakes emerging ahead of the leading edge. The crew compartment has already been relocated into a detachable section forming a short fuselage. (BAE)

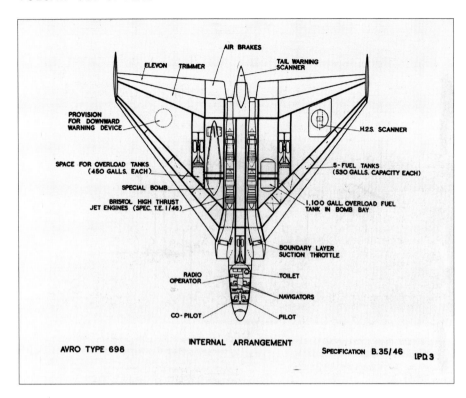

AIR BRAKES

ELEVON TRIMMER   TAIL WARNING
                         SCANNER

PROVISION
FOR DOWNWARD
WARNING DEVICE   H.2.S. SCANNER

SPACE FOR OVERLOAD TANKS   5- FUEL TANKS
(450 GALLS. EACH)   (530 GALLS. CAPACITY EACH)

SPECIAL BOMB

BRISTOL HIGH THRUST   1,100 GALL. OVERLOAD FUEL
JET ENGINES (SPEC. T.E. I/46)   TANK IN BOMB BAY

                                       BOUNDARY LAYER
                                       SUCTION THROTTLE

RADIO   TOILET
OPERATOR

                     NAVIGATORS

CO- PILOT   PILOT

AVRO TYPE 698   INTERNAL ARRANGEMENT

                     SPECIFICATION B.35/46   IPD.3

The 698 was first
designed to incorporate
two bomb bays,
placed each side of
the landing gear. The
wing tip stabilising
fins were subsequently
abandoned in favour of
a conventional centrally
placed fin (a tailplane
was unnecessary). (BAE)

wave could be accurately directed on to the plutonium core, ensuring that it would be compressed simultaneously and equally on all sides.

The result was a sufficiently efficient chain reaction fission process that required only a 10cm diameter ball of reactor-grade plutonium to produce an effective explosion. Another distinct advantage of the plutonium implosion device was that it was also much safer to handle, avoiding all the obvious risks of the crude uranium gun device, which could easily be detonated by accident. However, because the creation of explosive lenses required a great deal of research and precision manufacturing (the explosive lenses had to be manufactured with millimetre-sized tolerances), the Scientific Director of the Manhattan Project (J. Robert Oppenheimer) decided that a plutonium device would be the right choice for the first test detonation, on the basis that a uranium gun device was virtually guaranteed to function and therefore didn't even need to be tested. Informal bets were placed by the design team on the predicted outcome of the detonation, ranging from a complete failure,

through to a yield of 18 kilotons (kt, the equivalent force of TNT). Hauled by a crane on to a 100ft-high tower, the completed device was held aloft in order to maximise the destructive effect on the target area below, and to reduce the creation of radioactive fallout which would be generated by sweeping up ground debris from the desert floor. A huge and cumbersome steel canister nicknamed 'Jumbo' was manufactured to encase the device, so that the conventional explosion could be contained, should the chain reaction fail and radioactive plutonium be released. However, confidence in the successful detonation of the 'gadget' (as it was often referred to by the team) eventually convinced the scientists to dispense with Jumbo, and the 240-ton case was simply re-positioned on a tower some 800 yards from the device, so that the effect of the explosion on it could be monitored, rather than encasing the explosion in its entirety. The scheduled 4 a.m. detonation was delayed by thunderstorms, but by 5 a.m. conditions were satisfactory and the assembled scientists and military observers took up their positions in various viewing locations, mostly situated around 10 miles from the device.

As Oppenheimer had predicted, the detonation was an unqualified success. The surrounding mountain ranges were briefly illuminated by a paralysing burst of blue light, far brighter than the usual daily desert sunshine. Some mightily baffled local residents reported seeing the morning sun make a brief appearance before setting again. The light dissipated and then developed into a huge, seething ball of orange fire, which boiled and expanded into a large mushroom-shaped cloud. Forty seconds after the initial detonation a powerful shock wave thundered over the scientists who had emerged from shelter to witness the spectacle. The wall of blast and sound eventually rolled far out into the desert, rattling windows some 200 miles away. One military observer later reported:

… the lighting effects beggared description. The whole country was lighted by a searing light with the intensity many times that of the midday sun. It was golden, purple, violet, grey and blue. It lighted every peak, crevasse and ridge of the nearby mountain range with a clarity and beauty that cannot be described but must be seen to be imagined.

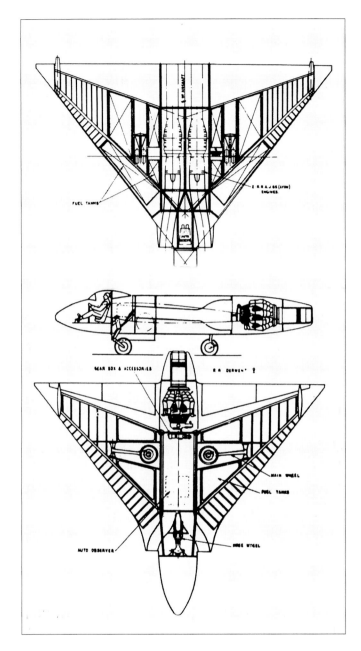

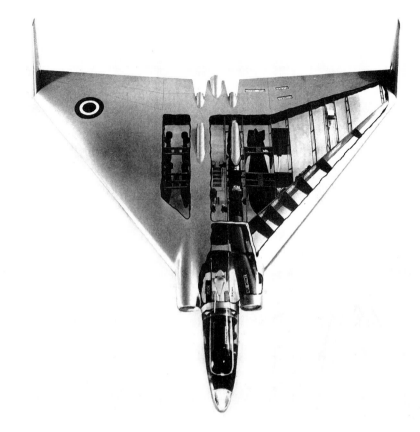

to disguise the true nature of the historic explosion, Alamogordo Air Field issued a press release stating that 'an explosion of a remotely located ammunitions dump, in which no one had been killed or injured' had been the cause of the seismic disturbance. Oppenheimer was immensely satisfied with the result of the test, but even at this stage he was only too painfully aware of what potential horrors he had unleashed. In tears, he later recalled that as he watched the fireball rise into the early morning sky, he remembered a line from Hindu scriptures, 'I am become death, the destroyer of worlds'. Test Director Kenneth Bainbridge's comments were rather more succinct. He simply said, 'Now we are all sons of bitches.'

Above: Avro display model of the 698, illustrating the unusual engine exhaust configuration, which was to have emerged above the wing centre section. Also evident are the huge circular intakes originally proposed. (BAE)

Left: The Avro 710 was to have been an intermediate test airframe between the simple, single-engined 707 and the full-scale (four-engined) 698. It was subsequently abandoned. (BAE)

The desert sand had instantly been melted into a smooth sea of green-coloured glass (subsequently nicknamed Trinitite) and although Jumbo still remained defiantly intact, its supporting tower had instantly been vaporised. The explosion had yielded an encouraging 19kt. In order

2

ATOMIC WARFARE

When Truman assumed the US presidency, he knew nothing of the development of the atomic bomb, but once he was fully informed of the Manhattan Project's progress, he set up another committee to explore the possible ways in which the atomic bomb could be used against Japan. Modern accounts of this period often suggest that the use of atomic bombs on Japan was little more than a macabre experiment, designed to record the effects of atomic bombs on both people and targets, but in reality it is clear that Truman's only concern was the continuing war, and the very obvious possibility of bringing it to a swift conclusion without any bloody invasion of the Japanese mainland. Truman did consider the situation thoroughly before reaching any decisions as to whether atomic weapons should actually be used and, even though there was a clear indication that Japan's appetite for some sort of surrender was growing, there was a firm belief that if an atomic bomb could end the war so much as one day sooner, it would be worth using it.

Oppenheimer predicted that just one bomb might well kill 20,000 people and he felt that a military installation should be chosen as a target rather than simply dropping a bomb on a city. Others felt that an isolated part of the Japanese countryside should be chosen as a pre-publicised 'showcase' in order to demonstrate the bomb's power (and hopefully persuade Japan to capitulate without the need for further attacks), but the risk of publicising the bomber's arrival would have inevitably encouraged Japan simply to shoot it down, therefore it was inevitable that a target of military significance would be chosen and destroyed without any prior notification. Of course there was also some risk that the bomb might simply fail to detonate (which would have been a huge embarrassment to the Allies if it had been publicised in advance), although the weapon was to be a relatively crude uranium device, which relied on the simple gun detonation method. The

Manhattan team's confidence in the success of this bomb's design was so high that no pre-drop tests were thought necessary and they were convinced that the weapon would function as predicted, being a far simpler device than the plutonium 'physics package' that had been demonstrated in New Mexico. Doubts had begun to grow that Japan would ever consider a complete surrender unless a devastating and direct blow was delivered on its cities, and when the Manhattan team reported that a suitable bomb could be made available by the beginning of August, there seemed to be no reason to avoid using it at the earliest opportunity.

Out in the Pacific on 6 August, a B-29 Superfortress from the specially formed 590th Composite Group lumbered into the air over Tinian island (the unit's forward base) and headed for the Japanese mainland some 1,500 miles to the west. Secured in the aircraft's bomb bay was 'Little Boy', a 9,700lb uranium bomb. Hiroshima had been chosen as the primary target, chiefly because of its significance as a military and communications centre, but also because the area had been untouched by conventional bombing, which would enable observers to examine the destructive effects of the bomb without any 'contamination' from previous attacks. Accompanied by escorting observation aircraft, *Enola Gay* (named in honour of Enola Gay Tibbets, mother of Paul, the aircraft's captain) approached the target at 31,000ft and released the weapon at 0815hrs local time.

Fitted with barometric and ground radar fusing, the bomb successfully detonated some forty-three seconds later at a height of 1,900ft above an army parade ground. A huge burst of light, heat and blast immediately engulfed the city, instantly killing 70,000 people. After turning sharply away from the target area, *Enola Gay* was hit by a violent shock wave, indicating to the bomber's crew that the bomb had detonated. Turning back towards the target once the blast wave had passed, Paul Tibbets recalled that, 'the city was hidden by that awful cloud … boiling up, mushrooming,

Far left: The huge bulk of the Shorts Sperrin gets airborne at Farnborough. Although impressive in terms of size and shape, the aircraft was conventional in design and unremarkable in performance. (*Tim McLelland collection*)

terrible and incredibly tall'. Ultimately, this single bomb was responsible for the deaths of more than 200,000 people and the complete devastation of 5 square miles of land. Truman immediately issued a statement on the bomb's devastating effects and served notice on Japan that if it did not surrender with immediate effect (as required by the Potsdam Declaration made on 26 July) then more Japanese cities would be attacked with similarly catastrophic results. Japan offered no such response and a second weapon was prepared for immediate use. On 9 August another B-29 (named *Bockscar*) departed Tinian, this time carrying an implosion device (using plutonium) nicknamed 'Fat Man'. The primary target at Kokura was obscured by cloud and so the B-29 crew opted to attack the secondary target at Nagasaki. The bomb was released at 1101hrs local time. The target point was missed by almost 2 miles, which spared a major portion of the city from the bomb's blast thanks to the masking effect created by a ridge of hills. The plutonium bomb was significantly more powerful than the uranium bomb (which had yielded approximately 13kt) and produced an impressive 21kt, but because of the topography of the local area and the inaccurate delivery, the resulting destruction was much the same (or even less) than that created by Little Boy. More bombing missions were prepared, with another bomb being assembled for use by the end of August, followed by three more for use in September, and then another three in October. However, on the same day that Nagasaki was destroyed, Emperor Hirohito announced that surrender was Japan's only option:

> The enemy has begun to employ a new and most cruel bomb, the power of which to do damage is, indeed, incalculable, taking the toll of many innocent lives. Should we continue to fight, not only would it result in an ultimate collapse and obliteration of the Japanese nation, but also it would lead to the total extinction of human civilization. Such being the case, how are we to save the millions of our subjects, or to atone ourselves before the hallowed spirits of our imperial ancestors? This is the reason why we have ordered the acceptance of the provisions of the Joint Declaration of the Powers.

The Second World War was finally over.

As Britain had been so closely involved with the development of these first atomic weapons, it was inevitable that British observers would be present to witness their use and they quickly reported back to Downing Street. Prime Minister Attlee rapidly familiarised himself with the new weapon after his party assumed power and during August 1945 he stated:

> A decision on major policy with regard to the atomic bomb is imperative. Until this is taken, civil and military departments are unable to plan. It must be recognised that the emergence of this weapon has rendered most of our post-war planning out of date. We recognised, or some of us did before this war, that bombing would only be answered by counter bombing. We were right. Berlin and Magdeburg were the answer to London and Coventry. The answer to an atomic bomb on London is an atomic bomb on another great city. Scientists in other countries are certain in time to hit upon the secret. The most we may have is a few years' start. The question is, what use are we to make of that few years' start?

Britain's military chiefs of staff were also carefully considering the impact of the new weapon's potential with respect to their future offensive and defensive policies. As a direct result of their deliberations, they advised their Technical Warfare Committee to revise the Tizard Committee report on future developments in methods of warfare, to take directly into account the development of the atomic bomb. The Tizard report had first been created in response to a request made by the chiefs of staff in November 1944 to investigate potential future developments in weaponry design. Although Tizard had (as described previously) been involved with the development of atomic research, his committee didn't have any direct access to any of the scientific or military developments as they emerged, so its report was therefore almost obsolete before it was completed, even though it described the potential for atomic bomb development together with the high-speed and high-altitude bombers that would be necessary to deliver such weapons. Most importantly, the original report touched upon the concept of nuclear deterrence, stating that '… the only answer that

Far left: The Avro 707 prototype pictured shortly after completion at Woodford. *(BAE)*

Left: One of only a few surviving photographs of the 707 prototype, this view illustrates the tall main landing gear legs and the unusual dorsal air intake for the aircraft's Derwent engine. *(BAE)*

Below: VX784 pictured during its short test career. Although revolutionary in shape, the aircraft took advantage of many existing components, such as a Meteor's nose gear and canopy, and the Athena's main landing gear. *(BAE)*

we can see to the atomic bomb is to be prepared to use it ourselves in retaliation. The knowledge that we were prepared, in the last resort, to do this, might well deter an aggressive nation.'

The revised Tizard Report established some critical points that would become fundamental to Britain's future defence policy:

Given sufficient accumulation in peace and adequate means of delivery, atomic and biological weapons might achieve decisive results with relatively small effort against the civil population of a nation, without a clash between the major military forces or the exercise of sea power. Some five or ten atomic bombs landed on the target, with the prospect of more to follow, might well cause the evacuation of cities to an extent sufficiently seriously to sap the power of waging war by conventional means of any country physically or psychologically unorganised to meet such action. Without the moral backing of adequate military power in being, with which to limit or repel invasion, or to launch an effective counteroffensive, such attack might well lead to collapse. On the other hand, some hundreds of atomic weapons might fail to cause the collapse of a country suitably organised physically and psychologically, and morally reinforced by adequate military power in being. There is no firm basis on which to assess the quantities of atomic and biological weapons required by any nation to bring about the collapse of another, and many of the factors involved are imponderable. Nevertheless, our estimate, based on such information as is at present

available, leads us to believe that some 30-120 atomic bombs accurately delivered by the USSR might cause the collapse of the United Kingdom without invasion, whereas several hundred bombs might be required by the United States or the United Kingdom to bring about the collapse of the USSR. The number of bombs required to cause a similar collapse in the United States would probably be somewhat greater than for this country, but the problem of landing them accurately in the United States at the ranges involved is much greater.

Britain's determined attempts to develop an atomic bomb were driven by the knowledge that a similar quest was probably being pursued in Hitler's Germany. This fear of Nazi know-how had been almost seamlessly replaced by an even greater fear of Soviet capability by the time that the Second World War ended. If Germany's tentative steps towards the creation of an atomic bomb had been a worrying possibility, the Soviet's interest in the same

This rare view of VX784 illustrates the dorsal engine intake, together with the splitter plate inside it. As can be seen, the airframe is surprisingly simple, despite its unusual shape. *(BAE)*

technology would undoubtedly become an even greater terror. Churchill had already expressed his fears in a telegram to President Truman sent during May 1945, in which he admitted that he was:

> … profoundly concerned about the European situation. I learn that half the American Air Force has already begun to move to the Pacific theatre. The newspapers are full of great movements of the American armies out of Europe. Our armies also are, under previous arrangements, likely to undergo a marked reduction. The Canadian Army will certainly leave. The French are weak. Anyone can see that in a very short space of time our armed power on the Continent will have vanished, expect for moderate forces to hold down Germany. Meanwhile, what is to happen about Russia? I feel deep anxiety because of their misinterpretation of the Yalta decisions, their attitude towards Poland, their overwhelming influence in the Balkans, excepting Greece, the difficulties they make about Vienna, the combination of Russian power and the territories under their control or occupied, coupled with

the Communist technique in so many other countries, and above all their power to maintain very large armies in the field for a long time. What will be the position in a year or two when the British and American armies have melted and the French have not yet been formed on any major scale, and when Russia may choose to keep two or three hundred divisions on active service? An iron curtain is drawn down upon their front. We do not know what is going on behind.

There was a pervasive belief both in British and American circles that the development of nuclear power and atomic weaponry could be placed under international control, but others feared that international agreements could not put the proverbial atomic genie back into its proverbial bottle. In a minute to the prime minister submitted during October 1945, the chiefs of staff stated that:

> We must aim for international control – it is probably the only alternative to mutual destruction. Any international agreement into which we enter should include the most

unequivocal and comprehensive rights of inspection. The whole concept of international control stands or falls on the efficacy of the arrangements for such an inspection. Russia is a country which appears to have both the natural resources and the remote areas for the secret development of atomic weapons. There is the obvious danger that we and the Americans might be led to agree not to produce atomic weapons while the Russians secretly carried out their research and production in the remote areas of the Soviet Union. The right of inspection will provide no security unless it is completely comprehensive. How this is to be achieved under the present Soviet system is the crux of the problem. It is clear that in the event of failure to secure an international agreement, possession of atomic weapons of our own would be vital to our security. The best method of defence against the new weapons is likely to be the deterrent effect that the possession of the means of retaliation would have on a potential aggressor. The Chiefs of Staff therefore consider that we should press ahead in the field of research and that it is essential that British production of atomic weapons should start as soon as possible. To delay production pending the outcome of negotiations regarding international control might well prove fatal to the security of the British Commonwealth.

It was becoming abundantly clear that no matter how atomic developments were controlled, the maturation of an atomic bomb capability laid at the very heart of Britain's future security and, with a growing political will to pursue the concept, the task of designing and manufacturing atomic weapons was finally addressed. British scientists had been an important part of the Manhattan Project and had worked in close co-operation with the American team from the very beginning of the programme, right through to its final expression in the skies above Japan. General Groves, who masterminded the project, later commented that there would probably have never been a bomb to drop on Hiroshima or Nagasaki had it not been for 'active and continuing British interest', which had pushed the project into being and had enabled it to reach its violent fruition. However, the immediate post-war political environment

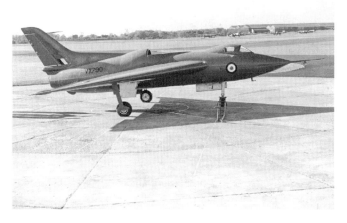

VX790 pictured at Woodford during its test-flight programme. In the far distance a variety of distinctly older Avro designs is visible. *(BAE)*

changed Britain's relationship with America, and the necessity for close wartime co-operation quickly faded as America turned its attention to peacetime commercial interests. The pivotal involvement in the Manhattan Project had undoubtedly given Britain a great deal of technical knowledge, but the compartmentalised nature of the activities at Los Alamos meant that Britain still didn't have all the necessary knowledge necessary to build her own atomic bomb without America's help. However, as Lord Chadwick (Chairman of the Weaponry Committee which reported to the Ministry of Supply) wisely pointed out, the British scientists could not be 'expected to take amnesia tablets before returning home'.

Although the emerging 'special relationship' between Britain and America had survived many crises during the war, and a very secure (if often undisclosed) military relationship continued to exist, the wider political climate was again pushing America back towards isolationism. America's increasingly cynical political opinion of Britain's new socialist government was compounded when it was revealed in April 1946 that a British nuclear physicist had been secretly passing US nuclear research information directly to Soviet agents. This was enough to convince most American politicians that sharing nuclear know-how was foolish, both commercially and militarily. Britain's hopes of nuclear co-operation with America came to an abrupt end when the McMahon Bill was passed by the

Underside view of VX790 illustrating the simple wing structure, which is broken only by the ailerons and elevators, together with their actuating mechanisms. *(BAE)*

Our continuing co-operation over raw material shall be balanced by an exchange of information which will give us, with all proper precautions with regard to security, that full information to which we believe we are entitled, both by the documents and by the history of our common efforts in the past.

Truman, presumably embarrassed by the whole saga, never even acknowledged the communication. This was probably the final sign that Britain was inevitably going to have to 'go it alone' regardless of any continuing desire to work in co-operation with America. Attlee later commented:

We had to hold up our position vis-à-vis the Americans. We couldn't allow ourselves to be totally in their hands and the position wasn't awfully clear always. There was the possibility of their withdrawing and becoming isolationist again. The manufacture of a British bomb was therefore at this stage essential to our defence.

Foreign Secretary Ernest Bevin expressed Britain's position more succinctly: 'We've got to have it and it's got to have a bloody Union Jack on it.' Britain's most immediate reaction was to secure its own supply of raw uranium from the joint Anglo-American stocks that had first been established during the Second World War. The US government believed that Britain would be able to secure good supplies of uranium thanks to favourable relations with Portugal, South Africa, Belgium and other Commonwealth countries that possessed uranium mines in various locations, but purchasing uranium was by no means easy for a country that was financially crippled – especially when it was competing with the American dollar. However, the very fact that Britain displayed an interest in securing a reliable supply of uranium, emphasised to America that Britain was certainly prepared to embark upon its own nuclear programme regardless of America's position, and there was a gradual acceptance that agreements made with Britain simply hadn't been honoured. There was also a growing realisation in America that obtaining reliable supplies of uranium was far easier for Britain, and these factors were sufficient to shift gradually the political climate back towards a more favourable one of co-operation. The troubled relationship

US Senate. Completely ignoring the earlier Hyde Park and Quebec agreements, the new Atomic Energy Act was an all-embracing piece of legislation that specifically prohibited the release of any scientific information relating to atomic power to any foreign nation. Senator McMahon subsequently stated:

The British contributed heavily to our own wartime atomic project, but due to a series of unfortunate circumstances, the nature of these agreements which made this contribution possible was not disclosed to me or my colleagues on the Senate Special Atomic Energy Committee at the time we framed the law in 1946.

This may well have been a convenient explanation for the way in which Britain's interests were ignored, but it is equally likely that McMahon's comments were true. Within America's corridors of power, Britain's fundamental importance in the development of America's nuclear capability was probably either unknown or simply overlooked. Prime Minister Attlee was disappointed, angry and genuinely surprised when the Atomic Energy Act was introduced, and he immediately sent a telegram to Truman:

At touchdown on Boscombe Down's 10,000ft runway, the high landing attitude of the 707 is very evident. Although the 707's general handling qualities were good, take-off and landing could be challenging. (BAE)

was eventually patched up during talks in January 1948, chiefly because America wanted to gain access to British stocks of uranium, even if this had to be in exchange for technical co-operation. Nonetheless, even this fresh spirit of mutual exchange didn't last for too long and by the following year the relationship had inexplicably broken down yet again, to such an extent that Truman stated: 'We have got to protect our information and we must certainly try and see that the British do not have the information to build atomic weapons – because they might be captured.' Truman's position seemed plausible to many and utterly absurd to others, but it was obvious that he was reflecting a wider view held by many American politicians that nuclear technology was far too important to give away, even to its closest allies. However, Truman's dubious concerns were,

by this stage, largely irrelevant. Britain had already decided to build its own bomb.

Those within the government who were privy to the secret developments continued to discuss Britain's position and Cabinet-level approval of plans for the new atomic weapon ultimately led to the issue of Air Staff Operational Requirement OR.1001, which finally emerged on 9 August 1946, calling for the development of a 'bomb employing the principle of nuclear fission'. Although the precise size and weight of the proposed weapon was obviously unclear at this stage, experience with the Manhattan Project enabled scientists to make a fair estimate and, from this, more precise dimensions for the bomb could be worked out. Original copies of the OR.1001 specifications no longer exist, but when it was re-issued a couple of years later, it

Underside view of WD280, illustrating the revised air intake design with 'letter box' inlets, which were more representative of the final type selected for the Avro 698. *(BAE)*

stated that the bomb should not exceed 290in in length and a diameter of 60in. Weight limit was set at 10,000lb and it was specified that the weapon should be capable of release from heights between 20,000ft and 50,000ft, and speeds between 150kt and 500kt. It was envisaged that flip-out fins would be used so that the overall dimensions of the bomb bay of the carrier aircraft would not need to be even larger than those dictated by the specified bomb size. However, back in 1946 it was still impossible to fix the precise dimensions of the physics device, the bomb into which it would be encased, the weapons bay required to accommodate it or even the overall dimensions of the bomber aircraft that would deliver the whole package with any confidence. Despite the issue of OR.1001, official governmental approval for the development of atomic weapons wasn't forthcoming until early in 1947. Lord Portal, Controller of Production of Atomic Energy, finally set the project into motion through a memo presented at 10 Downing Street on 8 January 1947, which stated:

I submit that a decision is required about the development of atomic weapons in this country. The Service Departments are beginning to move in the matter and certain sections of the press are showing interest in it. My organisation is charged solely with the production of fissile material, i.e. the filling that would go into any bomb that it was decided to develop. Apart from producing the filling, development of the bomb mechanism is a complex problem of nuclear physics and precision engineering on which some years of research and development will be necessary. I suggest that there are broadly three courses of action to choose from: a) Not to develop the atomic weapon at all, b) To develop the weapon by means of ordinary agencies in the Ministry of Supply and Service Departments, or c) To develop the weapon under special arrangements conducive to the utmost secrecy. I imagine that course a) above would not be favoured by HM Government in the absence of an international agreement on the subject. If course b) is adopted it will be impossible to conceal for long the fact that this development is taking place. Many interests are involved and the need for constant consultation with my organisation (which is the sole depository of atomic energy and atomic weapons derived from our wartime collaboration with the United States) would result in very many people, including scientists, knowing what was going on. Moreover, it would certainly not be long before the American authorities heard that we were developing the weapon 'through the normal channels' and this might well seem to them another reason for reticence over technical matters, not only in the field of military uses of atomic energy, but also in the general 'know-how' of the production of fissile material … I therefore ask for direction on two points; first, whether research and development is to be undertaken and, if so, whether the arrangements outlined are to be adopted.

The support of government ministers was unanimous, and it was agreed that research and development work should be undertaken immediately. At long last, Britain's bomb project was under way, but just one day earlier, a slightly distressed Air Vice-Marshal (AVM) Boothman's minute to Air Marshal Dickson had illustrated that even though the development of an atomic bomb was now finally progressing, the Air Staff still knew very little about the weapon they were to acquire:

I am very worried about the lack of information which exists, or is indeed given to us about our own progress in the atomic field. As you know, we stated a requirement to the Ministry of Supply last September for an atomic bomb. CS(A) immediately got in touch with the Department of Atomic Energy and discussed the whole matter with them. It now transpires that there is no organisation in Great Britain to develop the military side of atomic energy and in the opinion of individuals in the Dept. of Atomic Energy, there is not likely to be such an organisation for some time to come. The Air side of MoS have also been told that they will be ill advised to finalise the dimensions of the bomb bays of our future bombers until they obtain officially the probable dimensions of the bomb. In view of the fact that there is no organisation to do development on the bomb, things have now reached a complete impasse. I also understand that Professor Penney, who is the only technical authority in this country on the design of atomic bombs (which he gleaned during his work in America) is in honour bound not to give this information away to anybody. We have therefore arrived at the Gilbertian situation in which we have asked for long-range bombers and atomic bombs to go inside them, but the one individual who is able to satisfy the major part of our demand is unable to start things going because there is no government organisation which can produce the necessary items, and also because of some wartime promise. In view of the fact that all our appreciations on future strategy hinge on the atomic bomb and on the dates when they will be available in quantity to ourselves and other powers, I would therefore ask your guidance as to the next step to take. The information which I have given above is all hearsay and I am at a loss to know what steps to take in order to get things moving.

Of course there was now (finally) some progress being made even though the Air Staff had not been made aware of any of it. An Official Committee on Atomic Energy had

already been established and Dr Penney had already sent Lord Portal his detailed proposals for atomic weapons development. A relatively unknown scientist during the war, William Penney had already completed a great deal of explosives research before he joined the Manhattan Project in America. As one of the most important contributors to the British aspects of the project (with extensive knowledge of blast and shock-wave effects), the Americans were only too aware of his value, and they made numerous attempts to retain Penney after the war. He politely declined their offers in favour of a return to England, where he effectively assumed control of the embryonic atomic programme. Almost all of the preliminary development work was conducted under Penney's leadership, with a key RAF team being set up at Fort Halstead in Kent. Other establishments also became heavily involved in the project, most notably the Ministry of Supply (MoS) establishment at Aldermaston (where the bombs would ultimately be assembled for the RAF), Springfield (from where uranium would be prepared) and Farnborough, where the design of the bomb carcass would be developed. Perhaps most

WZ736 pictured high above the clouds, with both elevators slightly raised in an effort to maintain a slightly nose-high attitude while formatting with the Lancaster photoship. (BAE)

Avro 707C WZ744,
illustrating the revised
canopy designed for
dual-control training.
(BAE)

importantly, Britain required plutonium and in order to build up a stockpile (refined from uranium) an ambitious (and hugely expensive) facility was hastily constructed at Windscale in Cumbria. Some might say that it was in fact assembled too hastily given the difficulties experienced by the plant in later years, but Britain's first atomic pile was eventually commissioned here, and the site remains active to this day, renamed as Sellafield, now tasked purely with commercial power production.

The timescale required to set up Windscale and to begin the creation of plutonium was the key element that set the overall timescale for the development of the British bomb. Without the plutonium there was no bomb. Meanwhile, the international political situation deteriorated and relationships with the Soviet Union grew increasingly strained. The very beginnings of the Cold War emerged in 1948 and the communist take-over of Czechoslovakia, the

deployment of USAF B-29s to the UK (with atomic bomb capability) and the restriction of Western access to Berlin all conspired to create a period of great tension. When the USSR detonated its first atomic bomb in August 1949, there was certainly no longer any doubt in British minds that the decision to proceed with an atomic bomb programme had been a very sensible – if not vital – step. A third atomic pile was assembled and the British government poured more money and resources into the atomic programme in an increasingly desperate effort to attain an atomic weapons capability at the very earliest opportunity, as illustrated by a Downing Street document issued at the time: 'I attach to this expanded programme the same high degree of importance and urgency as I attached to the original. I hope nothing will be allowed to interfere with its realisation.'

However, it wasn't until early 1952 that the first supplies of plutonium finally became available, enabling the scientists and military staff to establish when and where the first test device could be detonated. Despite Britain's uneasy relationship with America, it was still envisaged that US test facilities in Nevada would be used for the first British test, and the US freely invited Britain to submit a formal request on this basis, but delays in responding, combined with many seemingly unnecessary restrictions on the parameters of the test, effectively meant that the Americans would have been conducting the bomb test on Britain's behalf, rather than handling the project as a truly collaborative effort. One State Department official commented that if he had been English he 'would turn them down flat, would proceed to carry out the British test in Australia and that this would be the best possible thing for Britain, the British Empire and indirectly for the USA'.

His comments made sense, in that Britain could not hope to build its own atomic arsenal under the stifling control of America, and in a wider sense the British programme represented a valuable opportunity to drag America out of a dangerously isolationist attitude. Australia was ultimately selected as the preferred test site, although consideration was first given to a Canadian site in Manitoba, where Penney believed he could test the weapon in shallow water. His team had concluded that this would provide useful data on the possible effects of an enemy attack being conducted through the covert transportation of a weapon inside a sea vessel, and given Britain's reliance on ports and sea power, it was an idea with some merit, especially as the Americans hadn't attempted any similar tests. Unfortunately the Canadian site was found to be too shallow to enable the project ships to reach the shore, and although a potential test area much closer to home (in north-east Scotland near Wick) was also briefly considered (but thankfully rejected), it was the Monte Bello Islands, some 50 miles from the coast of Australia, where the test programme was finally set up. With a channel some 6 fathoms deep just off the shoreline, and with only sporadic human inhabitation (pearl fishermen using them seasonally), the islands were a near-perfect solution. They certainly represented a much better option than a badly compromised deal with the US, as the British Joint Services Mission in Washington explained: 'When the British team arrived over here they would be subjected to so many petty restrictions and there

WD280 was eventually fitted with modified wing leading edges, representative of the Vulcan B1. It is pictured here during flight trials in Australia. *(Denis O'Brien)*

would be so much red tape, that in effect the Americans would explode our weapon for us and let us have only those results which they felt they could safely divulge.'

It was during 1950 that a date was fixed for the first test detonation and this was set for October 1952, under the code name Operation Hurricane. HMS *Plym*, a retired Royal Navy vessel, was selected as host for the plutonium device, and the various subassemblies were loaded on to the ship at Shoeburyness in June 1952 before departing for Australia. The all-important plutonium was finally delivered from Windscale to Aldermaston, where it was fabricated and transported to RAF Lyneham, carefully disguised inside a furniture van. The plutonium core (produced in two sections) was then flown in a Hastings to RAF Seletar in Singapore, from where an RAF Sunderland seaplane completed the delivery to the Monte Bello Islands. The various components were then assembled on board HMS *Plym* while scientists set up a variety of test and recording equipment at various key positions around the site. In addition to cameras, there were suitably positioned pieces of Lancaster and Spitfire fuselages and wings, some 200 petrol cans, toothpaste tubes, paint samples, clothing and thermometers, all designed to record every aspect of blast and heat effects. The Radiation Hazard Division constructed a variety of rather crude (but surprisingly effective) air sample filters, most of which were fashioned from household vacuum cleaners.

Finally, at 0930hrs on 3 October 1952, the device was detonated by cable from the safety of Trimouille, a small island situated nearby. Ten seconds after the detonation the

VX790 high above the
clouds during a test
flight from Woodford.
The aircraft remained
assigned to test duties
until September 1956,
when it was damaged
landing at Farnborough.
(BAE)

ground observers emerged to take a look at the results of their efforts. Expecting to see the familiar mushroom cloud (something which had already become an iconic image in the world's newspapers), they were somewhat surprised to see a rather odd cauliflower-shaped cloud that (thanks to the bomb's position at sea level inside the ship) had sucked up huge amounts of mud and ground debris, which was billowing upwards and sideways. Many uninformed observers assumed that this was a result of some bizarre and unspecified design modification made by Penney, and some members of the assembled team were surprised that the device had exploded at all, having become increasingly pessimistic during two months of frantic preparation.

HMS *Plym* had, of course, been vaporised and after just four minutes the burning cloud of debris had reached 10,000ft. One observer recalled:

> There was a blinding electric-blue light of such intensity I had not seen before or since. I pressed my hands hard to my eyes, then realised my hands were covering my eyes and this terrific light was actually passing through the tarpaulin, through the towel and through my head and body.

Winston Churchill (who had by now returned to power as prime minister) immediately sent a telegram to Penney, which began with 'Well done Sir William' and a simultaneous announcement was made by 10 Downing Street that Penney had indeed been appointed Knight Commander of the Order of the British Empire. Inside the House of Commons, Churchill announced that, 'the weapon was exploded in the morning of 3 October. Thousands of tons of water and mud and rock from the sea bottom were thrown many thousands of feet into the air and a high tidal wave was caused.' Despite the almost crippling cost, years of political turmoil and a scientific effort of huge complexity (all performed in great secrecy), the concept of creating an arsenal of fission weapons had finally been translated into practicality. Through extreme effort and at an almost devastating expense, Britain had finally entered the atomic age.

The creation of atomic weaponry was undoubtedly a pivotal step in Britain's post-war history. However,

Pictured at Farnborough during the SBAC show, VX790 illustrates the large Avro/Hawker Siddeley emblem applied to its nose. *(BAE)*

possession of a 'super bomb' was only part of the story. The bombs would give Britain no security if they were destined to languish in storage bunkers, incapable of being delivered to their targets. In order to build an effective deterrent against the growing Soviet threat, Britain would have to demonstrate that it not only had atomic bombs, but that it also had the ability to ensure that each of these bombs could be dropped – on Soviet territory. It may seem logical to imagine that this delivery capability might have been rather easier to achieve when compared to the complexities of creating the actual atomic weaponry – the RAF had of course been in the strategic-bombing business for many years. However, there was no possibility of simply loading an atomic bomb into a Lancaster or even the more capable Lincoln. The wartime-era bombers were undoubtedly ideally suited to their roles, but reaching Germany with a load of conventional high explosives is a starkly different proposition to the notion of reaching the heart of the Soviet Union with an atomic bomb. The Lincoln could have successfully lifted the atomic bomb's weight into the air, but it would not have been able to carry it very far (and probably couldn't have accommodated its bulky proportions in its already-capacious bomb bay). It stood no chance of taking a bomb to the Soviets. The aged wartime bombers lacked range, speed and altitude capability, assets which would be needed to get a bomber to Moscow and stand a good chance of getting there without being intercepted by the USSR's fighters. As the atomic bomb programme developed, it became clear that a completely new aircraft would be required with which to deliver the bomb to its target and that this would require a development programme as complex and expensive as the bomb project itself.

Magnificent image of VX770 illustrating the simplicity of the airframe design and the clean lines of the prototype. *(BAE)*

3

BUILDING THE BOMBER

In retrospect, it seems obvious that a new aircraft tasked with the delivery of atomic bombs would be powered by jet engines. However, when Britain first considered the prospect of building a new bomber, there was no such obvious conclusion. Indeed, Britain's initial thought process didn't even include aircraft at all. The size, weight and complexity of the atomic weapon seemed to be totally at odds with the concept of aerial bombardment and it seemed far more likely that the bomb would have to be delivered to its target by far less ambitious modes of transport. Sir Arthur Harris (the legendary head of Bomber Command) speculated that 'an atomic exploder' could be brought into an enemy country piece by piece to be assembled and detonated in almost any location where suitable cover could be found. Other commentators believed that the use of ships would be the ideal means of getting the bomb to its target, and it was this thinking that had influenced the first test firing of a British atomic device as part of Operation Hurricane. Some considered the possibility of incorporating the new bomb into a German V-2 rocket and although (at least with hindsight) this would seem to have been the most practical solution, it would in fact have been impossible. The estimated weight of the atomic bomb was expected to be as much as 10,000lb, which was far beyond the meagre 2,150lb that the V-2 could barely haul across the English Channel. However, it would be foolish to imagine that British thinking on this matter had been naive. German scientists had considered the very same proposition during the latter stages of the Second World War and had their development work continued, it is quite likely that they would have eventually produced what would have been the world's first nuclear missile. Nevertheless, as the development of the atomic bomb progressed, it suggested that a weapon would ultimately be produced which could be successfully delivered by air, albeit in a more orthodox winged aircraft rather than a missile. It would certainly be heavy and

cumbersome, but the bomb would be capable of being housed in a suitable 'package' within an aerodynamic bomb carcass. This meant that it could be carried by a bomber.

It was in the early post-war days of 1946 that the very first steps were taken towards the manufacture of an all-new atomic bomber. Britain's Air Staff accepted that a completely new design would be needed to replace the outdated Lincoln. Aware of rapid progress in jet engine design and technology, it was finally accepted that the bomber would inevitably have to be jet powered and would represent a more advanced payload and range capability than that which was to be achieved by the Canberra, Britain's first jet bomber, which was being developed at the time. With the atomic bomb programme very much in mind, the Air Staff assumed that the new bomber would carry this weapon, but in 1946 there was no guarantee that atomic weaponry would ultimately prove to be either practical or affordable as a means of conducting strategic warfare. The Japanese experience demonstrated that atomic bombs worked, but it didn't demonstrate that the same weaponry could penetrate a heavily defended USSR. Consequently the initial plan was to create a bomber that would maintain a conventional HE (High Explosive) bomb-carrying capacity,

The Avro 707C was to have formed the basis of a simple dual-control trainer system for Vulcan students. However, the Vulcan's docile handling qualities made a lead-in trainer unnecessary. (BAE)

but which would be able to carry the bulk and weight of an atomic bomb, on the assumption that this would be the bomber's ultimate payload.

This Operational Requirement (OR.230) called for a landplane capable of carrying one 10,000lb bomb (i.e. an atomic bomb) to a target 2,000nm from a base situated anywhere in the world. As it would undoubtedly have to encounter enemy radar and defences, it would need to be capable of flying at high altitude (between 35,000ft and 50,000ft) and also be able to fly at high speed (some 500kt). Although it would be expected to carry warning devices and defensive equipment, it would not (unlike the bombers which had previously been in RAF service) be armed with any self-defence guns, as this would add greatly to the all-up weight of the aircraft and therefore inhibit its speed and altitude performance. It was thought that the ability to fly high and fast would be enough to evade enemy defences and, although this assumption ultimately proved to be incorrect, at the time that this specification was issued, the decision to opt for an unarmed aircraft was made on current military appraisals of Soviet capabilities. It was thought that if the RAF's new bomber flew high enough and fast enough, it would remain invulnerable to any attempts to intercept it. However, even without defensive armament the aircraft was expected to be heavy and cumbersome, and with an all-up weight not exceeding 200,000lb it was unlikely to be capable of operating from existing RAF runways, many of which were only 6,000ft in length or even shorter (likewise, the bomber would probably have been incapable of fitting inside the RAF's wartime-era hangars, which could barely accommodate the Lancaster). The draft requirement was eventually dropped by December of the same year, when it was concluded that a bomber with such ambitious capabilities could neither be successfully constructed nor successfully operated from existing facilities. However, although the prospect of creating something so ambitious had been placed in abeyance, the basic concept of a fast and high-flying jet bomber had at least been established and any notion of developing another antiquated piston-engined bomber had finally gone forever.

The Air Staff immediately addressed the issues surrounding OR.230 and accepted that its specifications had been unrealistic from the outset. Even if an aircraft could somehow have been developed to meet the criteria, its cost would have been so high that the RAF would have been obliged to accept only a handful of operational machines, with little practical value. However, it was quickly established that some of OR.230's basic performance specifications had been unnecessarily ambitious and more than was actually required for a bomber which essentially needed only to reach Moscow. A new Operational Requirement (229) eventually emerged and, with it, Specification B.35/46. The Air Staff's new criteria still specified that the bomber would have to be capable of carrying the same bomb load (the 10,000lb 'special weapon'), but range would now be set at a more modest 1,500nm with an unchanged operational ceiling and an all-up weight now not exceeding 100,000lb. As with the original requirement, the bomber would be capable of carrying conventional weapons if necessary, but fundamentally it would now be designed in order to carry just one atomic bomb, the dimensions of which were still unclear but estimated to be roughly equivalent to the wartime Grand Slam high-explosive weapon, which had been carried by Lancasters. As with OR.230, the aircraft would not carry defensive armament and (unlike earlier operational bombers) the crew of five would not be spread throughout the aircraft, but housed together in a pressurised compartment that should be jettisonable in an emergency and fitted with parachutes for retardation during descent, although as an alternative it was specified that jettisonable seats could be fitted. Chief Ministry of Supply representative Stuart Scott-Hall commented:

> The conclusion had been reached that the long-range bomber, the all-up weight of which would be in the region of 200,000lb, represented too great an advance in design to be entertained at the present juncture. Considerable research and development would be necessary – including, in all probability, the construction of half-scale flying models.

He therefore recommended that 'consideration should be given to the medium-range aircraft, holding the long-range requirements in abeyance for a time'. He went on to propose a three-phase development. Firstly, there

An unusual image of VX770 performing at Farnborough. The outlines of the bomb bay and the landing gear bays are clearly visible. The relatively cluttered appearance of the prototype's underside contrasts with the clean lines of the aircraft's upper surfaces. (Rolls-Royce)

This rare photograph of VX770 illustrates the aircraft shortly after its first flight and the loss of its main landing gear doors. Also visible are the extended lower airbrakes. (*Tim McLelland collection*)

This rare photograph of VX770 illustrates the aircraft shortly after its first flight and the loss of its main landing gear doors. Also visible are the extended lower airbrakes. (*Tim McLelland collection*)

would be an 'insurance design' that would be a relatively simple aircraft created purely as a direct replacement for the Lincoln and could be developed easily without risk. Secondly, there would be the medium-range jet bomber and, thirdly, the original long-range jet bomber, which would still be regarded as a long-term project.

The terms of OR.229 were now agreed and it was therefore formally issued on 7 January 1947. The next day (which, by coincidence, was the day on which the decision to authorise development of atomic weapons was also finally made) Scott-Hall began sending letters to Britain's aerospace manufacturers, setting out the terms of the requirement and inviting them to submit tenders. The first letter went to Handley Page, with another going to Armstrong Whitworth, and further letters to Avro, Bristol and Shorts the next day, and, finally, English Electric was notified some days later. On 24 January, invitations were given to Avro, Armstrong Whitworth, English Electric and Handley Page to submit formal design tenders meeting the new Specification B.35/46, although Shorts and Vickers-Armstrong also submitted designs.

A tender design conference was held on 28 July and it was decided that an order should be placed for the Avro design, together with a smaller flying model, which could investigate the design inexpensively. Additionally, it was agreed that either the Handley Page or Armstrong Whitworth design should also be ordered (together with flying models), but only after further research had been completed on

the designs by the Royal Aircraft Establishment (in its high-speed wind tunnel) at Farnborough. Although all of the B.35/46 designs were ambitious and unusual, confidence seemed to rest primarily with Avro's submission, even though Sir Fredrick Handley Page (with typical flair for business) had tried to persuade Scott-Hall to accept his design even before the conference, having sent a letter to him a few days previously explaining why he had already turned down a delta design in favour of a crescent wing. However, Handley Page's design was even more bizarre than Avro's and the Royal Aircraft Establishment (RAE) felt it prudent to research the concept of a crescent wing before committing to an aircraft design programme. Ultimately, after having given financial cover to Avro's design in November 1947, similar cover was given to the Handley Page design late in the following month. As for the fate of the other submissions, it seems that there was insufficient confidence that Armstrong Whitworth would have the necessary design and manufacturing capabilities to complete its design successfully, and both this submission together with that supplied by Shorts, which was dismissed for similar reasons, were judged (rather unfairly it would seem) to be best suited to an unmanned and expendable design. Given the huge cost of production, however, their fates were consequently sealed. While little evidence has emerged to explain the lack of interest in the Bristol design (which showed as much potential as the others), the submissions from both Vickers-Armstrong and English Electric were deemed to be unimaginative and English Electric was already heavily committed to production of the Canberra, which suggested that taking on another major project would simply be unsustainable for the company. Of course it is also quite likely that since both Avro and Handley Page were unquestionably the 'big players' within the industry, they had the distinct advantages of good design and production track records with which to back up their proposals. In reality, all of the designs were unusual and radical, and there was very little reason to favour one design above another at this early stage.

When the terms of the fledgling B.35/46 programme were clarified, the consideration of Scott-Hall's 'insurance type' aircraft eventually resulted in a separate specification (B.14/46), issued on 11 August 1947. Although this design would be rather more conventional, with straight (instead of swept) wings and a significantly poorer performance (and therefore not much of an improvement over the existing Lincoln and Washington (B-29) fleets), there simply wasn't sufficient confidence in any of the B.35/46 proposals to be able to afford the luxury of pinning all of the RAF's requirements on just one hugely ambitious design. The worsening political situation created an increasing urgency for an aircraft capable of successfully and reliably delivering an atomic bomb, and although both the Avro and Handley Page designs looked promising, there was a very real fear that either (or indeed both) of the designs might prove to be fundamentally flawed, or require a long period of design and developmental work during which Britain might ultimately be found in possession of an atomic bomb, but no aircraft capable of carrying it. In the prevailing political climate this was a position that Britain couldn't comfortably contemplate. Consequently, the 'insurance bomber' made good sense since it was almost guaranteed to provide the RAF with a functional bomber, even if it was one that was much less able than those proposed by Avro and Handley Page. It wouldn't be ideal and it would certainly have no guaranteed capability of striking at the heart of the Soviet Union, but it would undoubtedly be better than nothing.

The specification was based on the original requirements set out during the previous January and stated that 'The Air Staff require an additional aircraft built as nearly as possible to Requirement No. OR.229, but constructed on more or less conventional lines, so that it could go into service in the event of the more exacting requirement being held up or delayed an undue length of time'. With less demanding requirements on both speed and altitude, but with weight kept down to 140,000lb or even 120,000lb if possible, so that existing airfields could be used, the Advanced Bomber Project Group chose Belfast-based Shorts to build a suitable aircraft. However, even from the outset there was serious doubt as to whether the Shorts design would even be capable of meeting the modest performance figures as set out in B.14/46. The Director of Military Aircraft Research and Development stated:

It has been apparent for some months now that the Short B.14/46 design will not quite meet the performance

requirements written by DOR in OR.239 and incorporated by us as the Appendix B in Specification B.14/46. The advisory design conference on this aeroplane was held on 10 July and we are now fairly clear on the probable extent of the deficiency. I consider that Shorts have made the best job as they can of this design and it is no discredit to them that they have fallen a little short on performance.

VX770 touching down after completing a display at the SBAC Farnborough show. Clearly visible are the extended airbrakes, particularly the lower pairs, which were later redesigned as one-piece items. (Rolls-Royce)

In essence, the Shorts design was based on the fuselage originally drawn up to meet the B.35/46 submission (albeit with the addition of a conventional tail), but with simple straight wings each containing a pair of engines, in effect a relatively basic Second World War-era bomber, but with jet engines.

The three designs (two B.35/46 projects and one B.14/46 proposal) were given official ITP (Intention to Proceed) in December 1947, even though preliminary work had been taking place before then. However, although the complicated procurement process already seemed to be encompassing an almost absurdly diverse number of projects, the situation was to become even more complicated following a visit made by Scott-Hall and colleagues to the Vickers-Armstrong headquarters at Weybridge.

The growing acceptance that no less than three individual aircraft designs were being pursued in order to meet just one requirement was enough to disturb almost everyone involved in the procurement exercise, but these worries were only exacerbated by the fear that even the uncomplicated 'insurance bomber' might prove to be no insurance at all, if it was no more capable than the Lincoln it would replace. The visit to Weybridge suggested the possibility of acquiring yet another (fourth) design, in effect an 'interim-interim' project that fitted somewhere between the Shorts B.14/46 and the Avro and Handley Page B.35/46 aircraft. Vickers-Armstrong's chief designer (George Edwards) had been appraised of the situation and was asked to look at the possibility of creating an aircraft that would incorporate an all-up weight of 115,000lb, a tandem wheel arrangement which would enable the aircraft to operate from existing runways, a total bomb load of 10,000lb and the removal of the jettisonable cabin requirement. It was agreed that English Electric should also be asked to look at revising its B.35/46 submission based on these new requirements. Consequently, the development of Britain's new atomic bomber looked even more uncertain than ever, as expressed by VCAS (Vice Chairman of Air Staff) Air Marshal Sir William Dickson:

We have set the Ministry of Supply two main tasks in the production of replacements for the Lincoln. The first is a long term replacement, a bomber which will have an approximate performance of 3,350nm range at 45,000ft at 500kt. In our specification we have said that it is desirable that the all-up weight of this type should not exceed 100,000lb and we have stressed that this aircraft should be able to operate from existing heavy bomber airfields. To meet these requirements it is inevitable that we must venture into revolutionary changes in aerodynamics. In other words the delta wing. At the current rate of research and development it is unlikely that an aircraft of this performance will be ready for production inside eight years. As an insurance against the possibility that the firms in question will not be able to solve the aerodynamical problems involved in the production of this new type of bomber, we have asked the Ministry of Supply to build a bomber of conventional design with a reduced performance of not less than 3,350nm at a height of 40,000ft and a speed of 435kt.

While this reduced requirement is less than we think to be essential, we cannot afford to have a replacement for the Lincoln which is already obsolescent if not obsolete. To meet our requirements for this 'insurance' bomber, the Ministry of Supply have already placed an order with Shorts. We are not at all happy about this because from what we know, the Short design is very unimaginative and its estimated performance is already dropping below the Air Staff figures I have quoted above. From our knowledge of the work of this firm it is probable that the performance will drop still further, which is very serious bearing in mind that we do not expect to get even this 'insurance' type into production inside 6–7 years. We also know that since the Ministry of Supply have placed this order, two further designs have been submitted for this 'insurance' specification, one from English Electric and the other from Vickers. From what the Air Staff know these designs are superior to that of Shorts. On the other hand these two alternative designs are based on a new jet engine, which is still on the drawing board, whereas the Short design employs an engine which is much further advanced in design.

The situation seemed to have developed into a saga of absurd proportions. The two advanced bomber designs were still hoped for but by no means guaranteed. The 'insurance' design was guaranteed, but it seemed incapable of offering the RAF a bomber with any credible capability. The Vickers bomber looked far more suitable and it seemed to be far more achievable too when compared to the exotic proposals being pursued by Avro and Handley Page. Four bomber designs seemed ludicrous, but if the atomic bomb was to be a credible weapon, the RAF had to assure its delivery. The rising tension between East and West simply didn't give Britain the luxury of 'taking a chance' on any one design. The growing complexity and cost of the entire bomber programme was reviewed towards the end of 1947 and a few months later the introduction of the fourth design within the programme seemed to have been accepted, as indicated by an Air Staff report which said:

A complete review of the Bomber Programme has been made in view of its great importance. It has been decided

that another type of bomber should be built to bridge the gap between the conventional medium-range bomber – the Shorts B.14/46 – and the two more advanced types which have been ordered from Handley Page and Avro – the B.35/46. Design studies were received from a number of firms and that of Vickers has been judged to be the most promising and a contract is about to be placed for prototypes of this aircraft. The Vickers medium-range bomber will have a still air range of 3,350nm carrying a bomb load of 10,000lb at a speed of about 465kt and height of about 45,000ft. It will weigh approximately 110,000lb and this will be distributed on a multi-wheeled undercarriage. The aircraft will be powered by four Rolls-Royce Avon engines and will start with an initial sweep back of 20 degrees on the outer plane with the possibility of increasing this in future development to 30 degrees and later 42 degrees. The inner section of the wing is swept back to 42 degrees initially.

Wintry scene at Woodford as VX770 returns from a test flight over northern England. (BAE)

Second prototype Avro 698 VX777 taking off from Farnborough during a display at the SBAC show. The landing gear is partially retracted, with the main-wheel bogies almost vertical. *(Rolls-Royce)*

The Ministry of Supply gave Vickers an ITP notice in April 1948 and this was followed by a contract for two prototypes of its Type 660 in February 1949, to be delivered to the RAF as early as possible.

Meanwhile over in Belfast, work on the Shorts S.A.4 was already progressing. Oddly, Shorts based much of its original design work on the results of hydraulic analogy tests performed in the company's seaplane tank at Rochester, since it didn't have the luxury of its own wind tunnel (Shorts normally relied on access to RAE and National Physics Laboratory facilities, but by the mid-1940s the waiting times for access had become excessive). In contrast to the company's original B.35/46 submission, the S.A.4 was extremely conventional in layout, having a uniformly tapered wing featuring a constant dihedral from root to tip. Likewise, the fuselage was of fairly straightforward construction and included a large Sunderland-style tail unit. The engine layout was rather less orthodox, with a pair of Rolls-Royce Avon turbojets mounted above and below each wing in huge, one-piece nacelles that, despite their bulky appearance, created surprisingly little drag. The advantage of this arrangement was that servicing

could be completed easily and the wing construction could remain simple, keeping the all-up weight of the aircraft commendably low.

At Shorts Belfast factory, three production jigs were set up, one for each prototype and a third for a static structural test specimen, and the first aircraft (VX158) was completed early in 1951. However, by this time the S.A.4 (which was by now named Sperrin) was already facing an uncertain future. The Air Staff continued to compare the predicted performance of the Shorts and Vickers designs, and as more knowledge of swept-wing performance was established, it gradually became obvious that the Vickers design would meet the RAF's initial requirements, thereby making the Sperrin redundant, as AVM Pelly commented:

At a meeting held at the Ministry of Supply on 11 October, I said that we could do without the B.14 for the following reasons: If the long term planning dates to which the whole of our programme is aimed are still valid, there is every reason to hope that one of the B.35 designs will be available in time. We still need one earlier type with which to re-equip Bomber Command in order to practice the techniques involved in long-range operations at such high altitudes and to be ready at the same time as the special bomb. Nevertheless, only one type of aircraft would be required and I feel sure that the B.9, in view of its better performance, offers a far better solution to our problem, the only disadvantage being that it is six months behind the B.14. Although the B.9 is of more advanced design than the B.14, the increased knowledge gained lately on swept-back wings and other high-speed complications leads to the belief that no major troubles need to be expected with the B.9 and therefore, production of that aircraft could start early in 1953 if need be and would, I understand, match up with the production of the special bomb.

It was eventually agreed that the Sperrin should not go into production, but it was also accepted that the two prototypes were worth completing and that they should be used for research and development work for the expanding bomber programme. Sperrin VX158 made its maiden flight on 10 August 1951, some three months after the Vickers design had also taken to the air for the first time. It appeared at the 1951 SBAC (Society of British Aircraft Constructors) show at Farnborough (resplendent in a striking black, grey and red paint scheme) and then returned to Belfast to embark upon a series of trials from Sydenham before moving to Farnborough, where it was employed on navigation and bombing development. The second Sperrin (VX161) flew during 1952 and became more directly involved in the B.35/46 programme as a host aircraft for the vital bomb-loading and drop trials performed by the Armament and Instrument Experimental Unit (AIEU) at Martlesham Heath. For this task it was based at nearby Woodbridge, in company with the resident USAF Republic F-84G Thunderjets, and from here the aircraft regularly operated to and from the Orfordness ranges, carrying a variety of dummy bomb carcasses which eventually led towards a definitive design for the Blue Danube bomb casing carried by Valiants, Victors and Vulcans in RAF service. Likewise, the Sperrin was also involved in development of the Blue Boar guided bomb, which was also intended for the B.35/46 bombers, though it was eventually abandoned (and replaced by the Blue Steel missile).

Although they were undoubtedly an aerodynamic dead end, the Sperrins had been a necessary development at the time that they were first proposed. They enjoyed a relatively short but varied flying career, providing valuable contributions towards the development of the Blue Danube bomb, Blue Boar missile and Gyron engine, as well as the design of landing gear eventually fitted to the Britannia airliner. The Sperrin would never have matched the performance figures attained by the rather more advanced Vickers design, but despite the rapid development of engine technology and the eventual reductions in the predicted performance of the Vickers aircraft, there wasn't much to separate them in terms of performance. However, it was accepted that any advantages in performance would be worth achieving, no matter how small. The Sperrins were never intended to be high-performance aircraft. By definition they were designed to be simple, predictable and, most importantly, achievable designs on which the Air Staff could rely.

Perhaps the only irony in the Sperrin story is that the original design submitted by Shorts in response to OR.229

VX777 at low level, illustrating the second prototype's longer nose section and the extended four-panel airbrakes. (Rolls-Royce)

was possibly the most advanced design of all, based on the development of an unusual swept wing layout which avoided the natural tendency of swept wings to twist under aerodynamic load, by moving the wing's torsion box further aft. This 'isoclinic' wing was judged too imaginative and unpredictable for the MoS' conservative tastes, but despite being dropped from the original OR.229 selection process, Shorts eventually embarked upon production of a one-third-scale glider employing the proposed wing layout. The completed glider was a great success and it encouraged Shorts to construct a powered version, fitted with small Turbomeca Palais jet engines. This aircraft (the S.B.4 Sherpa) also served to prove that despite the unusual nature of the Shorts wing design, it worked very well, avoiding many of the unusual aerodynamic difficulties created by the swept wing. With the movement of the wing's torsion box further aft along the fuselage datum, the wings were less inclined to flex and pull upwards towards the tips, thereby avoiding the usual problems with unpredictable (and unwanted) changes in the wing's lift properties in various configurations. It was a great shame that the MoS hadn't shown more faith in the original Shorts design, especially when so much interest was shown in the little Sherpa when it appeared at the 1954 SBAC display, where it was estimated that a full-scale version of the aircraft would probably have been more than capable of exceeding the requirements set out by OR.229. However, by then the future path of the B.35/46 programme was effectively fixed. Nevertheless, the question of aeroelastic flexing on a swept-wing design was an issue that Avro had also been considering, and its interest in a 'flying wing' bomber also encouraged it to address this potential problem, the layout of a 'delta' wing being ideal for the creation of torsional strength across much of the wing's surface. Perhaps Shorts had been ahead of its time.

The swept-wing Vickers design was finally ordered for the RAF as the true 'interim' bomber that would give Britain an atomic bomb capability at the earliest opportunity. Although the original Vickers B.35/46 submission was initially regarded as possibly too simple (and therefore unlikely to perform as well as might be hoped), its relative simplicity was a distinct advantage when the Air Staff found itself relying on the success of two very radical designs. Vickers already had an excellent history of aircraft production, having created types such as the Wellesley and Wellington bombers and, more recently, the Viking and Viscount airliners, and chief designer George Edwards could clearly be trusted to produce an aircraft that would meet the performance figures specified for it. Edwards argued that the relative simplicity of his revised B.35/46 design was its main virtue and it would enable the RAF to be equipped with an adequate (if less than ideal) aircraft in good time for the arrival of the first atomic bombs, far in advance of the anticipated completion of the advanced Avro and Handley Page designs. The Vickers design was modern but fairly conventional. It didn't require a long research and development programme, and wouldn't require the expensive and time-consuming creation of flying scale models. Such was his confidence that Edwards even went so far as to guarantee a production timescale for the Type 660 (eventually named Valiant after a company competition to select a suitable name chose it in preference to Vimy), promising that a flying prototype would be ready in 1951, followed by a production version in 1953 and quantity deliveries in 1955.

Once the 'interim' Specification B.9/48 had been issued and an ITP given to Vickers, development of the Valiant began, effectively ordered 'off the drawing board' in order to save time (indeed the airframe design was well established even before wind-tunnel tests had been conducted). The first prototype made its initial flight from the (then) grass airfield at Wisley on 18 May 1951, piloted by Joseph 'Mutt' Summers, a respected and capable test pilot who had previously conducted the first flight of the legendary Spitfire. The impressively generous proportions of the Valiant were dictated by the size of its bomb bay (which, in turn, was proportioned to accommodate the Blue Danube bomb), with a huge 'backbone' member supporting the fuselage and bomb bay structures, on to which two right-angled branches formed the main wing spars. Although the basic structure was conventional in design, the Valiant did introduce some innovations, not least all-electrical systems, the only exceptions being hydraulic brakes and steering. The overall design of the aircraft proved very successful and test flying continued without difficulties, leading to first deliveries to the RAF early in 1955, just as Edwards had promised. With the introduction of the 'insurance bomber' now under way, attention turned to the two advanced designs, which were still being developed and represented the ultimate requirements of the Air Staff.

At Avro's headquarters in Manchester, the B.35/46 project began to consume more and more of the company's resources. Initial studies had begun during 1946, but the project didn't get under way in any substantial form until January 1947. The legendary Roy Chadwick commanded a team of highly skilled engineers and with his distinguished background (he was responsible for the immortal Lancaster as well as many other significant aircraft), the Avro workforce were confident that they could produce a design that would meet the Air Staff's needs. However, their confidence was tempered by the knowledge that such an ambitious requirement would need an equally sophisticated aircraft, which would rely upon a great deal of radical design and expertise. Even so, Avro had always enjoyed a reputation for simplicity and, even with the demanding requirements set out by the Air Staff, Chadwick's team worked hard to find a solution that would provide a fast, agile and rugged aircraft capable of matching the specification without any undue reliance upon untried technology.

Probably as a result of its passion for simplicity, the Avro team looked at a variety of general design configurations, but almost inevitably came back to a basic flying wing design with no discernable fuselage, wing tip stabilisers instead of a conventional rudder and a simple delta-shaped wing planform. It wasn't surprising that the idea was considered so seriously, since the basic concept had been the subject of much discussion for some time, following the discovery of the many design developments that had been taking place in secret within Nazi Germany. A great deal of information had come from Germany since the end of the war and there was a significant amount of aerodynamic data on the potential of tailless designs, which had been pursued by Walter and Reimar Horten, ultimately leading to the creation of their H-1 glider and the Go 229 fighter-bomber, which was about to go into production as the war ended. Although many of the Horten brothers' design drawings had been systematically destroyed in anticipation of the Allies' advance, a great deal had still survived and examination of documentation and hardware estimated that the Go 229 would have been capable of achieving almost 600mph at sea level and an initial climb rate of 4,000ft/min, with a bomb load of 4,400lb and four 30mm cannon. It was impressive by any standards and the designs captured the interest of many British designers, not least the Avro boffins in Manchester.

Dr Alexander Lippisch was another leading German designer, famous as the creator of the Messerschmitt Me 163 Komet rocket fighter. He was particularly interested in the potential of all-wing designs and many of his early experimental designs included triangular delta-wing configurations, which he succeeded in testing in a supersonic wind tunnel – a facility that only Nazi Germany possessed at the time. As the war ended, Lippisch was working on a revolutionary delta-winged glider, known as the DM-1, and when Allied forces captured his factory at Weiner Wald in 1945, the DM-1 was transferred to the USA, together with its talented designer. Lippisch continued his work in the United States and ultimately developed the XF-92A, the world's first delta-winged jet aircraft to fly (it appeared in 1948). It eventually led to the design and

Left: Rare photograph of the two Vulcan prototypes together outside the flight sheds at Woodford. (*Tim McLelland collection*)

Below: The spectacular sight of both 698 prototypes in formation with the Avro 707 test aircraft over the SBAC show at Farnborough. (*Tim McLelland collection*)

manufacture of iconic aircraft such as the F-102 Delta Dagger and the magnificent B-58 Hustler.

Back in Britain it was Armstrong Whitworth that pioneered research in this field, with the construction of an all-wing research glider, the A.W.52G, which first flew in March 1945. Two larger designs were subsequently built and Armstrong Whitworth maintained an interest in the concept for many years, even though its work never resulted in an operational aircraft, at least not in a direct sense.

American pre-war interest in flying wing designs also continued and Northrop became particularly keen to develop the concept into an operational bomber, eventually creating the huge XB-35 which, although successful, was ultimately abandoned in a quagmire of technical and

political issues. However, Northrop's confidence in the flying wing design never diminished and after the passage of many years (and many advances in aerodynamic knowledge, as well as the introduction of computerised flight control systems), it re-emerged as the B-2 Spirit, which currently spearheads the USAF's offensive capabilities. Although revolutionary by nature, the flying wing was undoubtedly a sound principle.

For Britain, however, the end of the war had not been particularly fruitful in terms of recovered scientific data. Most of the theoretical aerodynamic data available in Germany had been secured by the Americans, largely as a serendipitous result of the route taken by American forces as they advanced across central and southern Germany, where most of the research facilities had been located. Despite this unfortunate situation, a considerable amount of data had nevertheless managed to fall into British hands, together with some hardware, all of which was gathered by the RAE at Farnborough, eventually culminating in a series of reports that were issued to British aerospace manufacturers. The information caused a great deal of interest and it inevitably influenced the thinking of every designer, not least Avro's Bob Lindley, since he had already been to Germany during 1945 to study a great deal of the recovered data in person. He recalled:

The Operational Requirement for the aircraft was put into the Project Office in early 1947. Before we had managed to get very far the great fuel shortage hit us and the plant was closed down except for a few of us who huddled together in the offices along the front of the main building. If I remember correctly another upheaval was taking place at the time, and Chadwick was at home suffering from shingles. The performance requirements of the OR were rather startling to people nurtured on Lancasters and Tudors, and the only jet investigations we had made up to that time were for the Tudor 8 and the Brabazon 3 projects, and the latter was designed for a Mach number around 0.7. The original conception of the delta was not a result of spontaneous inspiration, but was arrived at by what seemed at the time to be an honest design study encompassing a whole series of aircraft, some with tails, some tailless, each type checked

for a range of aspect ratios and weights. In retrospect I shudder to think just how much reliance was placed on the wing weight formula used, but the end product seems to justify the means. The first preliminary study was made for aircraft of aspect ratios not less than four and the result clearly showed that the aircraft required would be tailless and would give a much lower aspect ratio – probably about two. A second investigation covering the lower aspect ratios gave a solution of 2.4, which was inevitably a delta wing. I knew that Lippisch had been working on a delta fighter – I had managed to see some reports on his coal-burning ram jet delta in Frankfurt during my trip to Germany in 1945 – and the possibility of making use of this configuration for a bomber was most intriguing. More elaborate checks were made, but only served to confirm the delta configuration.

Lindley continued:

The original arrangement of the aircraft was, of course, somewhat more advanced than that which was finally proposed in the original brochure, in fact I think it would still look advanced today. It had boundary layer suction combined with a movable cockpit so that the pilot could have good vision even when the aircraft was at 30 degrees incidence, and it had a very elaborate arrangement of combined elevator, airbrakes and variable area jet pipe nozzle. Just about the time these first drawings were finished, Chadwick recovered from his illness. I must say that he was considerably shaken to see the proposal – he had left the project as a sort of jet propelled Lincoln and returned to find something apparently from a *Buck Rogers* comic strip in its place. He expressed his doubts very forcibly. I remember going home and sulking all weekend. I was very much in love with my project and couldn't stand the criticism. However, by Monday he had decided that it had its good points, and from there on he waded in with great enthusiasm and did much to make it a practical aeroplane. During this period of early development the aircraft underwent a number of changes. My original proposal had five Avons or Sapphires. In the interests of simplicity we decided to go for a twin-engined version,

Far left: Pictured over Hampshire (RAF Thorney Island is in the background) en route to their memorable flypast over the 1953 SBAC show, the two Vulcan prototypes and a quartet of Avro 707s. *(BAE)*

49

and for this we required an engine of around 20,000lb static thrust. Chadwick wrote around the engine industry for proposals for such an engine and the replies were very interesting, ranging from supreme optimism from Armstrong-Siddeley, to complete pessimism from Metro-Vickers. I can recall Chadwick taking a 1/48th scale model of this twin engined version up to London. The model was left with Air Marshall Boothman – Chadwick described how Boothman had 'flown' it round the office, presumably making appropriate noises. At this stage we heard of the Olympus, and the four-engined version was investigated and adopted for the brochure. The other feature that was kicked around considerably was the crew accommodation. The first proposal had the crew compartment inside the wing, with the pilots under two fighter type hoods. Then the requirement for a jettisonable crew compartment was emphasised, and we devoted much effort to getting the crew into the minimum nacelle, demountable just aft of the pressure bulkhead, and with a multiple parachute packed into the fairing aft of the canopy. This design was put forward in the brochure. In those days the radar scanner was installed inside the wing. The first issue of the brochure was finished, I think, in April 1947. After completing this we produced the drawings for the very beautiful 1/24th scale plastic model. We did some work on a civil version of the aircraft, employing a slightly higher wing loading and operating at a lower height than the bomber project. I remember it made a very attractive transatlantic aircraft. Headwinds didn't seem to worry it too much.

It is difficult to establish precisely who was responsible for first identifying the advantages of the all-wing design. Roy Chadwick is inevitably credited with the idea, although it would be wrong to portray Chadwick as a lone genius. Indeed, he presided over a large and talented team that included Stuart Davies, who had worked with Chadwick to produce the legendary Lancaster. Davies recalled that Chadwick was 'obsessed with the idea of the all-wing aeroplane, so when he came back and found that his lads had finished up with an all-wing aeroplane by accident, this delighted him more than somewhat'. This observation contrasts with Lindley's assertion that Chadwick was in fact

reluctant to consider the idea when it was first presented to him and (contrary to the comments made by Davies) it seems clear that Chadwick had first been confronted with the idea before he took time off due to illness. It seems likely, therefore, that if the bomber's unique shape could ever be credited to any one person in particular, it was probably Bob Lindley, who later left Avro and became Vice-President of McDonnell Douglas, overseeing the Mercury space capsule programme and eventually working on the Space Shuttle Project.

Chadwick's initial scepticism was soon replaced by enthusiasm and he concluded that an all-wing design would prove to be the best solution to the Air Staff's demanding requirement, both in terms of aerodynamic efficiency (and therefore performance) and also structural integrity. However, he was also aware that the radical design required a figurative leap of imagination and in its present form it would probably be a little too exotic for the tastes of the Air Staff to be considered as a serious contender. Chadwick feared that when they looked at the proposal, the Air Staff would dismiss it as pure fantasy. However, it was clear that on the basis of the German research and data, a triangular delta wing was probably the right option and it is also fair to say that the early Avro delta drawings bore more than a passing resemblance to an earlier design submitted by Bristol ahead of OR.229, which suggested that Avro's thinking wasn't quite so radical as might be imagined. Likewise, Blackburn also submitted an early proposal that may well have been the very first long-range jet bomber design to have ever been drawn up and it too featured a similar delta design. Nonetheless, even if the Air Staff could be convinced of the design's merits, the aircraft looked likely to exceed the required maximum all-up weight figure by a considerable margin.

Avro looked at ways in which the wing could be made thinner, but every revision simply pushed the projected weight still higher. With a specified cruising speed effectively fixing the basic design configuration, it was clear that the structure's weight would always be too high unless the payload was gradually reduced until such an extent where it no longer met the terms of OR.229. It was at this stage that the design team had again looked more seriously at the possibility of using the wing tips to provide

longitudinal control, creating vertical surfaces and rudders which could be attached to each wing tip, effectively making any fuselage-mounted assembly redundant and thereby saving a great deal of weight and aerodynamic drag. This re-emphasised the original concept of a flying wing and Avro's studies suggested that despite its unorthodox appearance, it would offer the most logical solution to the Air Staff's requirements. With a 45-degree wing sweep, combined elevators and rudders (ruddervators), and small fins and rudders placed at the wing tips, the gross weight dropped to 137,000lb and both Stuart Davies and Robert

Lindley believed that they had finally identified the best design configuration, after having considered an endless variety of potential solutions over a period of more than a month. Continued examination of German data and some knowledge of Armstrong Whitworth's growing experience in tailless design were combined with the knowledge of Northrop's continuing development of the XB-35 (which was in the process of being converted into the jet-powered YB-49), indicating that Avro's thinking made good sense. However, the team also determined that despite the all-wing design seeming almost ideal, it would still be rather

After their daily appearances at the SBAC show, the two Vulcan prototypes were placed in a high-security compound overnight at Farnborough, sharing space with the competing Handley Page design. (*Tim McLelland collection*)

Final assembly of Vulcan
B1 airframes at Avro's
Woodford factory. *(BAE)*

heavier than they would have liked it to be. The obvious way to reduce weight would be to make the wing section deeper, but in order to achieve high subsonic speed, the thickness/chord ratio had to be kept as low as possible, and so the root chord was increased to compensate. Further attempts to reduce wing span while maintaining the same wing sweep, thickness and overall area, meant that the 'missing' wing space had to be effectively relocated in the space between the wing's trailing edge and the fuselage. By March 1947 the design team had followed this process to its logical conclusion and concluded that the relatively simple delta-shaped, all-wing design was indeed the logical choice, but even more weeks of research were devoted to consideration of how the air intakes, radar, crew compartment, fuel tanks, engines, undercarriage and weapon load could be incorporated into the configuration.

Thanks to the relatively deep wing section (which was still sufficiently reduced to meet performance figures), all of the necessary equipment could be fitted neatly into an all-wing design, including the crew compartment (which resulted in a pair of fighter-type blister canopies for captain and co-pilot). However, the Air Staff's subsequent specification for a jettisonable crew compartment required a fairly radical redesign of the bomber, with the crew being relocated in a pressurised nacelle positioned ahead of the wing leading edge so that it could be separated by means of a bulkhead. This effectively destroyed the clean lines of the flying wing configuration and formed the basis of the design that eventually went into production, but it was with some irony that the plan to provide a jettisonable crew compartment was later abandoned, after it was established by Avro, Handley Page and Vickers that the complexity, time delays and overall cost of such a feature would seriously hinder any progress on the overall design. The Air Staff could not afford to run the risk of any significant delays, nor could it risk any unnecessary additional cost, and so the capsule proposal had to be dropped in favour of more conventional ejection seats for the two pilots, leaving the rear crew with only a ventral escape hatch through which they could (if they were lucky) bale out. Consequently, the extended nose section that became so characteristic of the Avro design was never actually needed, and had the escape capsule proposal been abandoned earlier, the design team could have continued to develop a true flying wing layout.

Once the position of the crew compartment had been fixed, the air intakes emerged ahead of the wing leading edge and were positioned each side of the short fuselage section. Each intake was routed through the wing and bifurcated into a pair of vertically stacked trunks, each feeding an engine, with the upper engine exhaust emerging through the wing trailing edge a few feet ahead of the lower exhaust. The huge bomb bay for the 10,000lb bomb was positioned within the inner section of the wing, but (unusually) was not positioned on the centreline, as had always been the case with previous bomber designs. Avro's radical proposal was to create two identical bomb bays each side of the aircraft's centreline, although there must have been some debate as to the aircraft's predicted handling and trim qualities if a 10,000lb weapon was dropped asymmetrically. However, when further research was conducted in Farnborough's wind tunnels, it was determined that the wing section was still too thick and after much discussion, the Avro team accepted that the thickness/chord ratio would have to be reduced still further. This meant that the engines and intakes could no longer be stacked vertically within the available space and they were consequently re-positioned in a horizontal side-by-side configuration. There was now insufficient space to accommodate the twin bomb bays and so a more conventional single bomb bay was located on the aircraft's centreline. The undercarriage was initially envisaged as being similar to that employed by Boeing on its B-47 Stratojet, with centreline-mounted main gear and smaller outrigger wheels at the wing tips, but once the bomb bay had been fixed in a more conventional position, a traditional tricycle undercarriage could be comfortably

incorporated into the design, which met with Avro's liking for simplicity and ruggedness.

Much consideration was also given to the idea of using moveable wing tips in place of traditional ailerons, moving the wing tip fins slightly inboard in order to accommodate power and drive units. By September 1947, however, this concept had been abandoned after the conclusion that individual elevators could be fitted to the wing's inboard trailing edge, with ailerons on the outboard sections, simplicity again being a key aim. This effectively meant that a larger, one-piece fin on the centreline could usefully replace the wing tip fins, especially after concerns were raised that the latter might provide insufficient control. It meant that the design weight would again increase, but it was agreed that a more traditional fin section would provide a convenient mount for an equally traditional tailplane unit, should further aerodynamic research indicate that one was needed, and nobody wanted to run the risk of pursuing a complicated design that – once fixed – required huge effort and expense to change. It's interesting to note that if a conventional tailplane had ultimately been needed (which of course it wasn't), the bomber would have looked like a scaled-up version of Gloster's distinctive Javelin fighter, although the similarity was superficial and only temporary, as the Avro team opted to remove the large, circular intakes of its design and replace them with horizontal 'letter box' intakes fitted within the extended wing leading edge, a move which seemed to make aerodynamic sense, even though little was known about the performance of intakes designed to this configuration. In fact, the horizontal intakes did create some headaches as the design entered the test phase.

XA890 about to touch
down at Farnborough.
The airbrakes are fully
extended, illustrating the
twin-panel arrangement
under the wings, which
was later modified to a
single unit. The overall
silver finish is disrupted
only by the grey and black
dielectric radome panel
under the nose. *(BAE)*

4

DELTA WINGS

During the summer of 1947, Chadwick had a series of meetings with Ministry of Supply and Air Staff officials, in order to convince them that the revolutionary Avro design was practical and that it was being developed without undue difficulty. It was probably the fact that Chadwick had a well-deserved reputation within the aircraft industry that enabled him to maintain official confidence in the Avro design when it may well have been abandoned in other circumstances, in favour of something rather more conventional. Chadwick's assurances did a great deal to convince the Air Staff that they were not pursuing a pipe dream and without his enthusiasm the bomber would almost certainly have never proceeded. Sadly, Roy Chadwick was killed when the Tudor 2 prototype crashed on take-off from Avro's airfield at Woodford on 23 August 1947 (it was later established that the aircraft's aileron control cables had been fitted the wrong way round). The shock of Chadwick's sudden death reverberated around the Woodford facility and the Chadderton factory, and there was a natural fear that the bomber programme would now be abandoned without his leadership to keep it alive. Predictably, the Air Staff's interest in the design did indeed begin to wane, because there was a widespread belief that the design and development of the aircraft would inevitably suffer from Chadwick's absence, resulting in delays that would be unacceptable. However, William Farren was appointed as Avro's new Technical Director and as a former director of RAE Farnborough he had an equally formidable reputation, which he immediately used to restore faith in the Avro project. The proposed bomber was undoubtedly a bold design, fraught with potential for failure, but promising to deliver an outstanding aircraft for the RAF. J.R. Ewans (who later became Avro's chief aerodynamicist) wrote a detailed account of the aerodynamic theories behind the choice of the delta wing early in 1951, which explains clearly the basic thinking behind what became the Avro Type 698:

So far as can be ascertained, the idea of using a triangular plan form for aircraft wings, now known as the delta wing, was first put forward in 1943 by Professor Lippisch, who will be remembered for his association with the Messerschmitt company. His studies led him to think that this form was most suited for flight at speeds in the region of the speed of sound where conventional designs were already known to be in trouble. By the end of the war, he had a number of delta wing projects in hand, including an un-powered wooden glider intended to explore the low speed properties of the wing. This was by then party built and was later completed under United States orders. The idea of the delta wing was studied by many other aeronautical experts and a strong recommendation for its use was give, for instance, by Professor Von Karman at the 1947 Anglo American Aeronautical Conference. At the time of writing, three British delta aircraft and two American are known to have flown, and it is pretty certain that others are on the way. In the date order of their first flight these are: Consolidated-Vultee XF-92,

XA890 performing at Farnborough, landing gear extended, illustrating the huge main gear link struts and the main wheel bogies, below their capacious wing bays. (*Tim McLelland collection*)

Avro proudly applied its
historic logo to the fin of
XA890 in preparation for
its public appearances at
the SBAC show. *(BAE)*

Avro 707, Boulton Paul PIII, Douglas XF-3D and Fairey
FD-1. With the exception of the last named, which is
fitted with a small fixed tail plane for the first flights, all
the above aircraft are tailless.

The following notes are intended to give a logical
explanation of why there is this considerable interest in
the delta wing, and just what advantages it promises the
aircraft designer. But consideration must first be given
to the type of aircraft the designer is trying to produce.
The delta wing is of value only for very high-speed
aircraft and at the present stage of engine development
this implies the use of jet engines. When projecting
his high-speed aircraft, the designer will attempt to
produce something carrying the greatest payload over
the greatest distance at the highest speed, and for the
least expenditure of power (i.e. using the least amount of
fuel). This applies to all types of aircraft whether they be
bombers in which the payload is bombs, or civil aircraft
in which it is passengers or cargo, or fighters in which it
is guns and ammunition. The most fundamental factor
determining the ultimate achievement is the height at
which the aircraft flies. As height increases the density
of air is reduced so that drag is less; it is possible to fly
at a given speed at, say 40,000ft, for an expenditure
of only one quarter of the power required at sea level.
The advent of the jet engine has enabled the aircraft
designer to get his aircraft up to considerable altitudes
and take advantage of the reduced drag, but a new factor
is coming in to limit the speed of the aircraft. This is the
speed of sound.

The speed of sound occupies a fundamental position in
the speed range of aircraft. It is roughly 760mph at heights
above 36,000ft. Because the speed of sound is of such
importance, aircraft speeds are commonly related to the
speed of sound using the term Mach number (the ratio of
the speed of an aircraft to the speed of sound at the same
height). As an aircraft approaches the speed of sound,
in fact for conventional aircraft when a speed of around
70 per cent of the speed of sound (Mach 0.7) is reached,
the effects of compressibility become important, for the
characteristics of airflow change fundamentally. There is
a very large increase in the air resistance, or drag, and
an excessive expenditure becomes necessary to increase
the speed any further. For transport and bomber aircraft
the speed at which the drag starts to increase (known
as the 'drag rise' Mach number) becomes the maximum
cruising speed, because if the aircraft is flown at higher
speeds the disproportionately higher thrust required
from the engine means excessive fuel consumption and
loss of range. At a rather higher Mach number there
will be changes in the stability of the aircraft and in its
response to the pilot's control, leading possibly even to
the loss of control. In order to progress to higher speeds
it is therefore necessary to design aircraft so as to
postpone and/or overcome these effects.

We have noted that with an old fashioned type of
aircraft, i.e. that of jet propelled aircraft current in 1945,
the limiting speed in steady cruising flight is likely to
be a Mach number of 0.7 (higher speeds have of course
already been achieved and a number of aircraft have
exceeded the speed of sound, but only for short periods
by either diving or by use of rocket power). However,
from the knowledge now available, it appears possible,
by careful aerodynamic design, to postpone the rise in
drag until a Mach number in the region of 0.9 is reached
and this figure is likely to be the practical limit of cruising
speed for transport aircraft of all types for many years
to come. The designer of a civil aircraft, a bomber or a
long range fighter will, therefore, bend all his energies
to achieving a Mach number of this order without any
change in drag rise. In addition, he must pay attention
to the changes in stability or lack of control which might
occur in this region, and this will occupy his attention

to the same extent as the purely performance aspect of the drag rise. It is quite easy to design a fuselage shape which is relatively immune from Mach number effects. It is the design of wings which is difficult, particularly since a wing that is suitable for high speed must also give satisfactory flying properties at low speeds for take off and landing. As air flows past a wing its speed is increased over the upper surface to a considerable extent and over the lower surface to a lesser extent, so that there is greater suction on the upper surface than on the lower surface. Thus, at whatever speed an aircraft is flying, the speed of the air around the wing will in fact, be higher. In the case of an aircraft flying at a Mach number of 0.8 the speed of the air around its upper surface may be equal to the speed of sound or may easily exceed it. At this stage the airflow pattern round the wing will be considerably changed and it is in fact this change which gives rise to the drag and stability effects mentioned above. It is essential therefore, to keep the velocity above the wing as little in excess of the speed of the aircraft as possible. There are four ways of improving the behaviour of a wing. They are all different methods of keeping down the air velocities and can all be applied simultaneously: 1) sweep back 2) thinness 3) low wing loading 4) low aspect ratio.

1) Sweep back – The amount of sweep back is measured by the angle at which the tip of the wing lies behind the centre line. The extent of the gains possible from sweep back is very considerable, and sweeping back a wing may easily lead to a postponement of the compressibility effects by a Mach number of 0.1.

2) Thinness – Keeping a wing thin leads to a reduction in the amount of air that must be pushed out of the way by the wing, and this helps the passage of the wing through the air. The thickness of a wing is measured by the thickness/chord ratio, which is the maximum depth of the wing divided by its length in the line of flight. In the past the thickness/chord ratios of aircraft wings have ranged from 21 per cent down to perhaps 12 per cent. Now values of 10 per cent down to 7 per cent are becoming common.

Roly Falk's spirited displays at Farnborough also included some very impressive landings, with the Vulcan's huge brake parachute being deployed well before touchdown. (BAE)

3) Low wing loading – The wing loading is the weight of aircraft carried by a unit area of wing, measured in pounds per square foot. Mach number effects are postponed by keeping the wing loading as low as possible, i.e. by supporting the weight of the aircraft with a large wing area. This is particularly important for flight at high altitudes where the low air density puts a premium on keeping the wing loading low. In fact, flight at high altitudes becomes virtually impossible unless this is done.

4) Low aspect ratio – Aspect ratio is the ratio of the span of a wing to the average chord. For moderate speeds, a high aspect ratio, i.e. a large span relative to the chord, gives greatest efficiency. At high Mach numbers this consideration is no longer important, in fact some alleviation of compressibility effects is given by reducing aspect ratio.

There is another reason for choosing a low aspect ratio. One of the disadvantages of sweeping a wing back is that the flying characteristics at low speed become poor. A typical symptom is that the wing tip of a swept wing stalls, giving violent behaviour if the speed is allowed to fall too low. Research has, however, shown that this bad characteristic of swept wings may be overcome relatively easily. Although almost any aspect ratio can be accepted with an un-swept wing, for wings of 45 degrees sweep back, an aspect ratio of a little over 3 is the most satisfactory. There is yet a third reason for choosing a

XA891 pictured over the
Mersey during a post-test
flight photographic
rendezvous. *(BAE)*

low aspect ratio – the behaviour (as regards stability, etc) in the high Mach number region. Compressibility effects are minimised and a transition from speeds below that of sound to the speed of sound and above is much more readily accomplished if the aspect ratio is low, say in the order of 2 to 4. Put the above requirements together, and the result is an aircraft highly swept back, with a thin wing, a moderately large wing area and a low aspect ratio. A little consideration of the geometrical properties and possible plan form of wings leads to the conclusion that the delta wing is the only form which satisfies these requirements. It possesses high sweep back and low aspect ratio. The wing area will, of necessity, be generous for the size of aircraft and, for reasons which will be detailed later, it is easy to build it with a low thickness-chord ratio.

Next, how does the delta plan form, indicated from considerations of aerodynamic performance, line up with practical design requirements and, in particular, the over-riding necessity for keeping weight and drag low in order to obtain maximum performance? A preliminary question is whether a tail plane is necessary. From the earliest days of flying, the question has been raised as to whether aircraft can be flown satisfactorily without a tail plane. Confining attention only to the case of the high-speed jet aircraft, each of the functions of a tail plane will be examined in turn, in relation to the delta wing aircraft. The functions are:

a) To trim out changes of centre of gravity position according to the load carried and the consumption of fuel. Investigation shows that a control surface at the trailing edge of the wing, provided that the latter has a large root chord (as has the delta) can cater for all but extreme centre of gravity movements.

b) To deal with trim changes due to landing flaps, etc. With the low wing loading associated with the delta wing, take off and landing speeds are moderate without the use of flaps, and this question does not therefore arise.

c) To deal with loss of stability or control power, consequent on distortion of the wing structure at high

Airframe technician at work under a Vulcan B1. Although the Vulcan was not designed with modern ease of maintenance in mind, the engine compartments were readily accessed from the ground thanks to a series of large, hinged doors. (*Rolls-Royce*)

High above the clouds, the first production Vulcan B.Mk 1, XA889, poses for Avro's photographer. *(BAE)*

XA891 completed a significant number of test flights before being destroyed in a crash during July 1959, after suffering electrical failure. *(BAE)*

a delta wing would not be powerful enough to ensure recovery from a fully developed spin. A tail plane appears to be the only way of dealing with the problem. This restriction is of small significance for transport or bomber type aircraft. It can therefore be concluded that for a delta wing aircraft of the transport type, a tail plane is unnecessary. Its deletion leads immediately to a considerable saving of weight and drag, and to a major gain in performance.

We have now shown that, compared with a conventional aircraft, the delta wing aircraft will be simpler by the omission of the following items: the tail plane, the rear fuselage necessary in order to carry the tail plane, wing flaps and other high lift devices, such as the drooped wing leading edge. There is a saving of weight, of design and manufacturing effort, and of maintenance when the aircraft is in service. These economies will have a considerable bearing on the initial cost and the manpower necessary to produce and maintain a number of aircraft. Because of its shape and the large root chord, the delta wing provides a large internal volume in relation to its surface area, even when using the thin sections which, as noted above, are essential for high speed aircraft. Simple calculations show that for the same wing area, the delta wing has 33 per cent more internal volume than an un-tapered wing, while if the inboard half of the wing only is considered (as this represents a more practical case from the point of view of the aircraft designer) the internal volume of the delta wing is more than twice that of the corresponding tapered wing. It is found that without exceeding a wing thickness of as little as 8 to 10 per cent, it is possible on a moderate sized delta wing aircraft to bury completely the engines, the undercarriage and sufficient fuel tanks for long range. The fuselage also has a tendency to disappear into the wing at the root. The result is the attainment of an aircraft consisting only of a wing, a fin and a rudimentary fuselage, representing a degree of aerodynamic cleanliness which has never before been reached. In fairness, it must be pointed out that this is achieved at the expense of a rather larger wing area than usual, but investigation shows that the drag of this area

speed (aeroelastic distortion). At very high speeds, all aircraft structures distort to a greater or lesser extent under the high loads imposed, and this distortion alters the aerodynamic form. In extreme cases this leads to loss of stability or control power, making the aircraft dangerous or impossible to fly at high speeds. An aircraft with a high aspect ratio, swept-back wing would need a tail plane to deal with this, but the shape of the delta wing makes it extremely stiff both in bending and in torsion and a tail plane does not appear necessary.

d) To provide for spin recovery. Although this point has not been proved, it is expected that the controls on

is less than that due to a conglomeration of items such as engine nacelles, tail plane, etc.

From the design point of view, the shape of the delta wing leads to an extremely stiff structure without the use of thick wing skins, and strength becomes the determining feature rather than structural stiffness. This avoids the inefficiency of conventional swept back wings where the wing has to be made stronger than necessary in order that it shall be stiff enough. Summing up, it can be said that in order to meet the requirements of large

loads for a long range at high speed, the high performance transport or military aircraft of the future will cruise at a considerable altitude, at a speed not much below that of sound. The delta wing provides the only satisfactory solution to these requirements for the following reasons:

1) It meets the four features necessary for avoiding the drag rise near the speed of sound, i.e. it is highly swept back, it can be made very thin, the wing loading is low, and the aspect ratio is low.

Part of a cinefilm showing the tragic loss of VX770 at Syerston. The wing structure has already collapsed in this image. *(Tim McLelland collection)*

The second 698 prototype, VX777, at altitude, displaying the redesigned wing layout that was later adopted for the B2 fleet. *(BAE)*

2) Extensive wind tunnel and flight tests have shown that the low aspect ratio delta wing gives minimum changes in stability and control characteristics at speeds near the speed of sound.

3) In spite of the wing being thin, its internal volume is large, so that the engines, undercarriage, fuel and all the necessary equipment can be contained within the wing and a rudimentary fuselage.

4) Adequate control can be obtained by control surfaces on the wing, thus eliminating the need for a conventional tail plane. Together with item No. 3, this leads to a considerable reduction in the drag of the aircraft and, therefore, to high performance.

5) Auxiliary devices such as flaps, nose flaps or slots, and the all-moving tail plane are unnecessary, thereby saving weight and design effort, and simplifying manufacture and maintenance.

6) The delta wing is very stiff and free from distortion troubles.

The much-anticipated ITP, which covered the construction of two Avro 698 prototypes, was issued in January 1948 and although this obviously didn't represent a full-scale contract for production aircraft, it was sufficient to allow the programme to continue, encouraging Avro to assume that a production contract would soon follow. At last, the revolutionary concept of a delta-winged bomber would be translated into hardware.

Even at the very start of the B.35/46 project there had been a great deal of doubt as to whether a design could be produced which would fully meet the requirements that were set out by the specification. The Air Staff's dreams of a long-range bomber had already been put on hold (in fact they'd effectively been abandoned) and the decision to build what was often described as a 'Medium Bomber' was based more on semantics than practicality. Even though the B.35.46 specification called for an aircraft less ambitious than the machine first proposed, it was still in effect a strategic bomber that would have to be capable of reaching the USSR to deliver a heavy bomb. It was also essential that the aircraft had sufficient speed and altitude capability to out-fly any of the Soviet defences that would inevitably be encountered.

It was clear that meeting the necessary requirements couldn't be achieved by relying on traditional or conventional designs, but Britain also couldn't afford simply to hope that the ambitious designs proposed by Avro and Handley Page would succeed. If they failed, Britain would have an atomic bomb but no practical means of delivering it which, in terms of a credible deterrent, meant that the bomb would be useless. The decision to build the Sperrin had provided a means of ensuring that if the new bomber designs did prove impossible to build, there would at least be some means of carrying the atomic bomb to the USSR, even if it was unlikely that many Sperrins would have successfully avoided interception. However, when the Avro and Handley Page projects began to look viable, the Sperrin was obviously worthless. The Valiant, by contrast, presented a different type of 'insurance bomber', in that it offered a reasonable performance and could be manufactured quickly, and would therefore be available when the first atomic bombs were completed. If there were any unforeseen delays in the production of the Vulcan and

Victor, the RAF would at least have a credible bomber that stood a fair chance of putting an atomic bomb on to its target. The Valiant wouldn't be an ideal solution, but in the absence of the two advanced aircraft, it would undoubtedly be better than nothing at all.

As the Valiant project developed almost without any concerns, the future of the Vulcan and Victor was far less certain. As had been proposed from the outset, the Ministry of Supply eventually decided that much more research was necessary and in order to gain some practical knowledge of the seemingly bizarre crescent- and delta-wing designs being proposed, a plan was made to create flying scale models for each type, which could be manufactured quickly and cheaply, in order to gain some flight-test data.

To explore Handley Page's crescent wing, a single research aircraft was ordered, in the shape of the H.P.88. This comprised a Supermarine Attacker fuselage, fitted with a scaled-down representation of the new crescent wing. It flew for the first time during June 1951, but after only a brief period of testing it crashed two months later, killing its pilot. The full-scale bomber was already well advanced by this stage and so it was deemed pointless to produce another scale model. Meanwhile, Avro was instructed to produce no less than three test aircraft. The first would be a basic scale model incorporating the delta-wing design. The second would be a larger version powered by two engines and the third would be a full-scale representation of the final bomber design, produced in simplified form as an aerodynamic test vehicle. Not surprisingly, Avro was reluctant to devote time and resources to three concurrent projects when it was already heavily committed to the actual bomber design itself. The concept seemed unnecessary to Avro, which had envisaged building only a glider test model to investigate the delta wing. Eventually it was agreed that the twin-engined model and the full-sized test specimen would not be pursued, but that a series of small one-third scale models (each powered by a single Derwent jet engine) would be built, leading to the construction of two full-scale prototype bombers. The MoS thus ordered three Avro Type 707 aircraft; two allocated to low-speed flight research and one assigned to high-speed testing.

The decision to construct the 707s made good sense – at least in principle. They would be extremely simple in design (using many components from existing aircraft) and therefore relatively inexpensive. Likewise, they wouldn't require an undue level of resources or attention from the Avro design team. They would provide useful research data, which could secure confidence in the ongoing design of the full-sized prototypes, and perhaps even speed up their development. However, in order to realise the value of these research aircraft it was fundamentally important that they were (as much as physically possible) true scaled-down versions of the full-sized bomber and that they would be available at the right time to allow the gathered data to be used in making any necessary changes to the machine tooling being set up for the Type 698. Unfortunately, in many respects the diminutive 707s failed to meet these criteria and they effectively became a separate development programme that continued in parallel to the main bomber programme, often diverting attention and resources away from the very project for which they'd been designed to assist. They did contribute valuable data, but Avro regarded them as more of a nuisance rather than a valued asset.

The MoS issued Specification E.15/48 for the Type 707 on 3 November 1948, calling for a simple research aircraft with a top speed of 400kt. Initially, the Avro team proposed building the 707's wing from wood, but eventually it was decided that simple pressed sheet metal around two supporting spars would give the aircraft sufficient strength for the job, while providing space for internally housed fuel and test-monitoring equipment. The canopy and nose wheel assembly for the first aircraft were taken from a Gloster Meteor fighter and the main landing gear assemblies were existing items designed for the Avro Athena. The no-nonsense design was created at Avro's Chadderton factory and work on manufacturing the aircraft commenced towards the end of 1948, with the new (scaled-down) delta wing inside its construction jig early the following year. The sole purpose of the 707 was to test the all-important wing design; therefore the rest of the aircraft was created as simply as possible, with a short nose section manufactured from welded steel tubing covered with light metal-alloy skin, and removable panels surrounding the single Rolls-Royce Derwent turbojet engine, which was positioned below the swept fin and rudder. The engine intake was faired into the upper fuselage with a bifurcated duct feeding down above the wing spars. There were no powered flying controls and there was (surprisingly) no ejection seat, but as a concession towards flight safety an anti-spin parachute was fitted in a fairing at the base of the fin assembly.

Finished in silver with a prototype 'P' marking applied to its nose section (plus national insignia and serials), the little 707, VX784, was assembled at Avro's Woodford airfield and subjected to a series of engine trials and short taxi tests before being dismantled and transported to Boscombe Down in Wiltshire on 26 August 1949 for re-assembly. The first flight was scheduled for 3 September, but a steady 20kt crosswind prevented the aircraft from flying until the next day. Having already completed some short 'hops' at Boscombe Down, test pilot Flight Lieutenant Eric Esler (chief test pilot at the Aeroplane & Armament Experimental Establishment) taxied VX784 on to Boscombe's huge 10,000ft runway at 1930hrs on 4 September. He proceeded to conduct a very satisfactory twenty-minute test flight in the local area. Esler was satisfied with the 707's handling and Avro immediately issued a press release announcing the aircraft's first flight, claiming that the new delta would 'permit controlled flight at and above the speed of sound' and that it would be 'necessary to conduct a vast amount of aerodynamic research over a large range of speeds before application of the new configuration can be made to either civil or military operational aircraft'. At the time of the 707's first flight, the new delta shape was perceived as something exciting and experimental, and Avro often used the innovation as a promotional tool, even though by this stage it didn't regard the delta wing as unusual. A great deal of work had already taken place on various delta designs in the United States and by this stage the Avro 698 was making considerable progress, as was Gloster's Javelin fighter, and so Avro actually regarded the 707 as no more than a useful tool with which to explore the low-speed aspects of the design in advance of the full-scale prototype's completion.

The following two test flights (totalling two and a half hours) completed what was, in effect, the 707's 'shake down' process and test pilot Esler then flew the aircraft directly to Farnborough, where it was proudly placed on static display for the 1949 SBAC air show. After a few days at Farnborough,

Esler flew the aircraft back to Boscombe Down and Avro's flight-test team installed test and data-recording equipment before beginning the aircraft's research programme. It continued to handle remarkably well and Esler reported that the general handling characteristics were much the same as those found in more conventional aircraft, with the possible exception of the take-off run, which required a considerable distance before the aircraft got airborne (not least because of the Derwent engine's relatively poor thrust). The test flying proceeded smoothly until 30 September, when tragedy struck and VX784 crashed near Blackbushe, killing Esler. The cause of the disaster was never fully explained and at the time many cynical observers used the accident to cast doubt upon the delta design itself and the wisdom of proceeding with the Avro 698 programme. However, investigations suggested that the cause of the crash was not attributable to the delta wing and was probably the failure of a control circuit which may have locked the airbrakes in their extended (open) position, causing a low-speed stall from which Esler (without an ejection seat) had no means of escape. Work was suspended on the second 707 until more details of the accident were obtained, but despite the tragic loss of Esler, there was great relief that the cause was determined to be something other than the design of the aircraft's wing, which would have thrown the whole project into doubt. The Avro design team quickly concluded that the second 707 should have an ejection seat and, as the first Avro 707A (destined for high-speed research) was already under construction, it was decided that the most speedy and effective way forward would be to take the nose from the 'high-speed' 707A and fit it to the new 707, VX790, effectively lengthening the fuselage by some 12ft. In response to Esler's findings concerning the lengthy take-off run, a new (longer) nose-gear assembly (from the Hawker P.1052) was installed, in hopes of lowering the 707's 'unstick' speed and allowing the elevators to become effective at an earlier stage on the take-off run. This relatively simple act was in fact one of the most important contributions that the 707s made to the 698's development, as the full-size bomber's nose gear was lengthened as a direct result of Esler's findings, while the design was still at the drawing-board stage. Wing sweep was increased slightly and the cockpit canopy design was revised. The wing airbrakes were revised (although, rather

Far right: VX777, complete with its redesigned wing, shares the tarmac at Woodford with XA893, an aircraft that performed many electrical systems trials in support of the Vulcan B2 fleet. Also present is a Shackleton – another Avro aircraft manufactured and assembled at Woodford. (Avro)

Vulcan B.Mk 2
production and final
assembly at Avro's
Woodford factory. (BAE)

oddly, not to the same design which had by now been approved for use on the 698) and the fuselage airbrakes were deleted, but the revisions to the 707's design delayed its completion and it wasn't until September 1950 that the aircraft was ready to fly.

Emerging from the flight sheds at Avro's Woodford facility, the new 707B, VX790, (painted in a bright blue colour scheme) was prepared for a first flight on the 5th. The pilot was to be Wing Commander R.J. 'Roly' Falk, Avro's recently appointed chief test pilot, who had previously worked for Vickers-Armstrong and had also been RAE Farnborough's chief test pilot. After a series of pre-flight checks, darkness was beginning to fall over Greater Manchester and Falk elected to confine the day's activities to a series of hops along the runway, before making a successful first flight of some fifteen minutes' duration the next day. Following completion of the flight, Falk telephoned Avro's Managing Director (Roy Dobson) and Air Marshal Boothman (Controller of Supplies-Air) in order to obtain permission to fly the aircraft to Farnborough immediately, so that it could join the static line-up at the 1950 SBAC show. Arriving at the end of the day's flying, it was a testament to Falk's and Avro's faith in the design that VX790 made its public debut just a few hours after its very first flight.

Following the SBAC show the 707B returned to Woodford and began test flying, eventually reaching a maximum speed of 350kt. It was found that the air intake was suffering from a degree of air starvation because of the cockpit canopy immediately ahead of it, and modifications had to be made (following tests in the Rolls-Royce wind tunnel at Hucknall) before the flight envelope could be extended further. Ultimately, the intake area was replaced with a completely new NACA (National Advisory Committee for Aeronautics) venturi design, which proved to be much more efficient. Minor oscillations in the pitching plane were also reported, but after investigation the cause was found to be out-of-phase movement of the elevators, and as the 698 would have powered flying controls, the problem was ignored. Although these minor problems were peculiar to the 707 (and therefore only served to distract attention from the 698 programme) the 707B did make a significant contribution to the 698's development when

a series of flights aimed at investigating trim settings at different engine outputs led to the 698's engine exhausts being positioned downwards and outwards (in relation to the fuselage) to minimise trim changes. Perhaps most importantly, the 707B served to confirm that there were no fundamental flaws in the wing design, and there was no reason to doubt in the 698's continuing development. It was probably just as well, because the 698 had by now established its own pace, and was making good progress, independent of the concurrent 707 programme.

The sprightly 707B impressed Falk, who reported that the aircraft was very stable and didn't show any tendency to depart from normal flight characteristics. It was indeed very manoeuvrable (rolls and loops being performed effortlessly) and stable; Falk repeatedly took the aircraft down to speeds below 100kt, and up to angles of attack around 30 degrees, and it was clear that the aircraft showed no inclination to stall at angles that would have been well beyond those at which many other aircraft would have simply tumbled out of the sky.

Without cockpit pressurisation, Falk was obliged simply to cope with conditions at altitude. One particularly florid Avro press release stated that Falk was 'in the habit of taking a surfeit of oxygen for an hour or so before high altitude flights, and then putting-up with discomfort for short periods at upwards of 40,000ft'. Part of VX790's test programme was conducted from Dunsfold, where the aircraft thrilled all of the pilots lucky enough to fly it. The aircraft's rate of roll could exceed 200 degrees per second, and one pilot even managed to execute a complete inverted loop, which – by any standards – was very impressive for a 1950 design. When Air Marshal Boothman had an opportunity to fly the aircraft in September 1951 he was also greatly impressed and immediately issued an instruction that 'twenty-five selected pilots must fly it at once'. After completing around a hundred hours of test flying from Woodford and Dunsfold, the 707B suffered a landing accident and was withdrawn for repair, after which it was transferred to Boscombe Down to continue work on other research programmes which had no direct relevance to the Vulcan.

After suffering another landing accident at the hands of an ETPS (Empire Test Pilot's School) student in September

The short-lived XA897 shortly before its tragic loss at Heathrow after returning from its hugely successful overseas tour. (BAE)

Vulcan B1 XA895 spent most of its service life at Waddington and Finningley with the RAF's Bomber Command Development Unit. (BAE)

1956, the aircraft was judged to be beyond economical repair and its flying career was brought to a premature end. The airframe was used as a spares source for other 707s and eventually the aircraft was moved to RAE Bedford, where it was dumped in 1960. However, following the manufacture of the 707B, work had continued on the 707A. There was some doubt within the Avro team as to whether there was actually any point in allocating more resources and time to this (the third) 707 when the 698 programme was so well advanced. With the concept of the delta wing proven, there clearly wasn't much that the third aircraft could contribute other than simply continuing to verify the design of the full-scale aircraft as it progressed.

After having discovered the deficiencies of VX790's air intake (and undertaken the time-consuming modifications necessary to correct it) it was finally agreed that the 707A (WD280) should be fitted with 'letter box' intakes similar (but not identical) to those which had now been fixed into the design of the 698, although it was accepted that even if the 707's new intakes highlighted any necessary changes to their design, it would be too late to influence the construction of the 698 prototype. It was precisely the sort of situation Avro had wanted to avoid from the outset, but the MoS expected its order to be fulfilled and construction of the 707A continued, WD280 duly emerging with new wing-mounted air intakes, new true-to-scale elevators and ailerons, and servo tabs and balances to assist the manual flying controls. Painted in a very unusual 'salmon pink', the new 707A finally took to the air on 14 July 1951, by which time metal was already being cut on the 698 prototype. As predicted by Avro, despite some ninety-two hours of test flying, WD280 had no direct influence on the design of the 698. Indeed, when Roy Ewans (who became Avro's chief designer) was asked just how much the design team had learned from the 707s he replied, 'not a great deal, apart from the reassurance that the thing would fly'.

The 707s did yield useful information at a later stage, however, when a series of flights was conducted to explore buffet boundaries, which required the pilot to apply a high amount of g-force at the greatest possible speed and height. It was quickly found that the airframe 'buzzed' (a high-frequency vibration) at speeds and heights that would easily be achieved by the 698. After a great deal of investigation, it was finally established that the 707's wing leading edge needed to be modified, reducing the angle of wing sweep inboard before increasing it outboard, producing a 'kinked' effect which would give the outer wing a greater chord and a mild leading edge droop. WD280 was modified accordingly, but it was too late to make any changes to either the prototypes or the initial production 698s, since the unusual 'reverse envelope' jigs (in effect a sort of female mould) for the bomber's wing leading edge had already been constructed. Consequently, the wing modification had to be retrofitted and sixteen sets of wing leading edges for subsequent 698s, which had already been built, had to be destroyed. It was this kind of absurd situation that plagued the 707 programme, which persistently lagged behind the 698's development instead of being ahead of it.

At some stages the Avro team was obliged to spend time making changes to the 707s in response to developments on the 698, a situation that clearly should never have been permitted to occur, the sad loss of the first 707 having led to a mismatch of programme co-ordination from which Avro never fully recovered. With the benefit of hindsight, it could be said that the 707s were an unnecessary and expensive waste of resources, but at the time that they were first ordered, the Ministry of Supply firmly believed that they would save time and money. In retrospect, perhaps Avro's original view should have prevailed and the whole 707 programme could have been avoided.

Despite the controversial nature of the 707 project, a second 707A was ordered in 1952 (under Issue 2 of Specification E.10/49) but this was not as part of the 698's development programme. WZ736 (painted in a bright orange-yellow scheme) was constructed for the Royal Aircraft Establishment to conduct various trials not directly related to Avro's 707 programme. Flying for the first time from RAF Waddington on 20 February 1953, the aircraft spent most of its life at Farnborough and Bedford, engaged on general test duties, most of which centred on auto-throttle development, before being withdrawn in 1964. After spending some considerable time in storage at RAF Finningley, the aircraft now resides at the Manchester Museum of Science and Industry, appropriately positioned next to the mighty Shackleton – another famous Avro creation.

Finally another 707 was built in the shape of WZ744, an Avro 707C fitted with side-by-side seating under an enlarged fighter-type canopy. No less than four 707Cs were originally envisaged (two being part of the second issue of E.10/49) to form the basis of a trainer aircraft on which RAF pilots could familiarise themselves with the handling qualities of the delta wing before progressing to the full-scale 698 bomber. However, as the 707 programme continued, it became clear that the bomber wouldn't suffer from any unusual handling vices and it would be perfectly acceptable and safe to

RAF Waddington in 1957 and the first Vulcan B1s delivered to the newly formed 83 Squadron. (Tim McLelland collection)

conduct the RAF's conversion training on the actual aircraft rather than a scaled-down version that would require its own manpower and technical back up. Consequently, three of the 707C aircraft that had yet to be constructed were subsequently cancelled, but WZ744 was completed at Avro's Bracebridge Heath factory and, upon completion, the silver aircraft (carrying national insignia and serials) was towed the same half-mile stretch of A15 that WZ736 had followed, to Waddington's northern perimeter gate, and prepared for flight to Woodford on 1 July 1953 in the hands of Squadron Leader J.B. Wales. Like the second 707A, WZ744 had no direct effect upon the 698 programme, but the aircraft enjoyed a useful career conducting a variety of test flights (mostly connected with the development of fly-by-wire electrically signalled hydraulic flying controls) before being retired to storage at RAF Finningley in 1967, from where it made an annual appearance at the station's open day, alongside its operational counterpart. The aircraft now resides within the RAF Museum at Cosford, and although it contributed virtually nothing to the 698's development, it serves to illustrate yet another aspect of the ambitious bomber programme.

This close-up look at the Vulcan B1 illustrates the position of the ventral bomb-aiming blister, the open crew-access door and the sextant position just under the canopy fairing. *(Rolls-Royce)*

BRISTOL OLYMPUS ENGINES

5

AIRBORNE

While the 707 programme continued, work on the Type 698 made good progress and actual construction of the first full-sized airframe began in 1951. The process was delayed by some three months because of a variety of 'last-minute' changes reflecting the findings of research data as it emerged. Most significantly, RAE Farnborough had been conducting a series of wind-tunnel tests, and these had predicted a degradation of performance, caused by poor distribution of air pressure over the wing surfaces and air intakes. The data suggested that the onset of compressibility drag rise (which effectively capped the 698's maximum speed) would take place at a lower altitude and lower speed than had previously been expected. The RAE's view contradicted Avro's conclusions and the slow pace of the 707 programme meant that no data had emerged from these test flights to support the RAE's findings. However, from December 1949 until May 1950, the Avro team worked long and hard to revise the 698's wing shape, moving the thickest section forward to the leading edge, instead of being close to the root chord centre as had been envisaged. The result was a wing root that was almost as deep as the short fuselage to which it was attached (this being some 9ft in diameter) and in many respects it shifted the design back to more of a blended 'flying wing' layout from which the basic design had first emerged. In addition to the aerodynamic improvements this created, it also enabled Avro to improve the shape, size and efficiency of the air intakes and create internal space for bigger engines, which were likely to become available in subsequent years. In fact, it was the projected need for more powerful engines that ultimately convinced Avro to revise the wing shape, rather than the theoretical advice from the RAE, which the designers were often tempted to dismiss. A total of 190 draughtsmen were assigned to the 698, together with thousands of engineers with Avro and various subcontractors around the country. Companies such as Dowty, which produced the multi-wheel bogie undercarriage, and Boulton Paul, which designed the power controls, produced detailed component designs for the 698 in response to Avro's often vague and constantly changing requirements, long before a proper contract was issued by the MoS.

Construction of the 698 began at Avro's Chadderton factory, where the huge centre section and forward fuselage were manufactured. The equally massive wings were built at the Woodford factory, the plan being to bring the Chadderton sections to Woodford by road, for final assembly prior to flight. Notification of a production contract for an initial batch of twenty-five aircraft was received in June 1952. Avro's delight at this news was tempered by the fact that an equivalent order was also issued to Handley Page for a similar batch of H.P.80 bombers. It was assumed that a decision would eventually be made between the Avro and Handley Page designs, but with the MoS and Air Staff still unconvinced that either aircraft promised any significant advantages or potential deficiencies when compared to the other, there was no enthusiasm to make a final choice between the two, especially when both Chadwick and Handley Page were making such strenuous efforts to convince the Air Staff that their aircraft was the better option. With a typical twist of British compromise, it seemed that the way forward would be to adopt both aircraft and spilt the first order for fifty aircraft between the two companies, but nobody could be sure that this even-handedness would extend beyond the initial orders. The Avro design team was also somewhat disheartened to learn that Handley Page appeared to be taking the lead, having announced that its H.P.80 prototype had been transported to Boscombe Down by road (carefully disguised, for some inexplicable reason, as a ship) ready for re-assembly and a first flight. This encouraged Avro to make even greater efforts to ensure the 698 was ready for

XA900 (pictured at Finningley) was the last surviving Vulcan B1. It was retained by the RAF Museum at Cosford until 1986, when it was scrapped. (*Robin Walker*)

a public appearance at the all-important 1952 SBAC show, where – if all went to plan – Avro could proudly show the new bomber to the public and media, and thereby convince the Air Staff that the 698 was the right aircraft to purchase in larger quantities.

When the prototype's centre section was completed at Chadderton it was loaded in one piece on to a flatbed trailer, ready for transportation through the streets of Greater Manchester. The 17-mile road journey was a particularly challenging task for Avro, since the massive inner wing and fuselage section was almost too big to be successfully transported through some disturbingly narrow Manchester streets. As it was, the route had to be carefully planned and measured, with various signs and posts repositioned, and even some street lamps were redesigned so that they could be hinged downwards to enable the huge structure to pass by. The ponderous journey through Manchester was conducted overnight and as the local residents slept in their beds, few people were aware of the carcass of Britain's new strategic bomber passing by outside their windows. Those who caught a glimpse of the road convoy during daylight hours were under no illusions as to what they were seeing, which adds even more mystery to the attempts that Handley Page made to disguise its aircraft. With everything gathered together at Woodford, final assembly of the prototype was completed during August and the aircraft was towed across the airfield to Woodford's flight sheds, from where engine-running trials began.

On 30 August, test pilot Roly Falk taxied the fully functional prototype (VX770) on to Woodford's runway

in anticipation of the first flight. Handley Page had been obliged to transport its H.P.80 to Boscombe Down in order to get it into the air, the runway at the company's Radlett airfield being judged too short for such a potentially perilous procedure. In contrast, no such concerns were raised over the 698's first flight and Avro enjoyed the relative luxury of retaining its aircraft and flight-test team on its own airfield. Falk back-tracked the 698 to the turning circle at the eastern end of the runway and opened up the four Avon engines, releasing the brakes to allow the aircraft to lurch forwards. This first run along the runway provided Falk with an indication of the speed at which the nose wheel would unstick and, once satisfied that the aircraft would be capable of safely getting airborne from Woodford's relatively short runway, he concluded that further test runs would be unnecessary and, rather than risk overheating the wheel brakes, he announced that he was ready to get airborne. He taxied VX770 back to the runway threshold to position for take-off. After a brief interlude while a flock of potentially hazardous seagulls was cleared from the area, the four Rolls-Royce Avon RA.3s were opened up to full power again and, with a deafening roar, the gloss white-painted bomber leapt forwards, jumping upwards slightly on its nose wheel as the pressure came off the brakes. With a relatively modest combined power of 26,000lb, the 698 might have been expected to require the full length of Woodford's runway to get airborne, but with no operational equipment or huge fuel load on board, the aircraft was in fact remarkably light. As it thundered towards the centre of the airfield, Falk gently raised the nose and VX770 lifted cleanly into the air and settled into a steady climb. Much to the delight of the observers scattered around Woodford, the awe-inspiring white delta was airborne.

As the 698 roared skywards, Falk raised the undercarriage and the aircraft began a steady climb to 10,000ft, where he proceeded to make a series of gentle manoeuvres to establish a feel for the controls and check that everything handled as predicted. Once satisfied that the aircraft wasn't hiding any unpleasant characteristics, Falk completed his preliminary handling evaluation and commenced a long, gentle descent back to Woodford. Just thirty minutes later, the prototype was back in Woodford's airfield circuit, and immediately caused a great deal

of excitement in the neighbourhood, where countless spectators had emerged to see the magnificent spectacle. The noisy departure had only added to the fuss and the residents of nearby Woodford and Poynton stopped in their tracks to marvel at a sight and sound that seemed to be of fantastic proportions. Nobody had seen or heard anything like it before. Falk brought the aircraft back to a respectable approach speed and lowered the undercarriage.

It was at this stage that the control tower staff at Woodford noticed something falling from the aircraft's underside. Falk was notified and reported that everything appeared

normal from inside the cockpit and that the undercarriage warning lights were indicating that the landing gear had safely locked in the extended position, but rather than risk a catastrophe, he decided to hold the aircraft in the airfield circuit while two other test pilots frantically got airborne in a Vampire and Avro 707 to make an airborne rendezvous with VX770, in order to examine the aircraft for signs of damage. It didn't take much scrutiny to notice that the objects that had fallen from the aircraft were the rear doors attached to the main undercarriage, which had simply broken clean off as they emerged face on into the

A trio of Vulcan B1s, led by XA907, pictured during a photo call prior to an overseas goodwill tour. (*Tim McLelland collection*)

Vulcan B1 XA900 served with 101 Squadron and 230 OCU, based at Waddington and Finningley, prior to being withdrawn for instructional use during 1966. *(BAE)*

airflow. Having established that the incident was a minor one, the chase planes cleared the area while Falk brought the 698 back on to final approach and gently settled the aircraft back on to Woodford's runway, before popping the huge brake parachute. Despite the minor problem with the gear doors, the first flight had been a great success and everyone was delighted, not least Falk, who commented that the aircraft had been easier to handle than the stately Avro Anson that he'd flown many times before.

Over the following days, two more test flights were made from Woodford, before the aircraft was flown south to Boscombe Down, for another three hours of initial handling trials. Flying from Boscombe, VX770 was able to make the short hop to Farnborough for daily appearances at the SBAC show, just as Avro had hoped. It was decided that for both security and technical reasons it would be unwise to allow the bomber to land at Farnborough and so the gleaming all-white aircraft was flown from Boscombe Down each day to make a series of fly-bys, flanked by the red 707A (flown by Jimmy Nelson) and the blue 707B (flown by Jimmy Orrell). This patriotic sight of the huge bomber in company with the diminutive 707s was magnificent and stirred the emotions of countless spectators and brought great satisfaction to the many industry and service chiefs who were present, all of whom were eager to see some tangible results from the protracted and hugely expensive bomber programme. The stirring sight of Avro's formation was proof positive that Britain's atomic bomb programme was on course.

A total of five displays was completed during the Farnborough week and because there had been no time to re-attach the prototype's main undercarriage doors, Avro's personnel at Boscombe Down made daily checks on the various micro switches and other components in the exposed undercarriage bays, and made strengthening modifications to equipment where necessary in response to Falk's lively flying display, which got a little faster and more flamboyant each day. After the SBAC show, media interest in the 698 was widespread and everyone with an interest in aviation wanted to know more about the unusual and futuristic bomber prototype. Speculation began to mount as to what name would be applied to the aircraft, and following the appearance of the Vickers Valiant, a variety of suitably alliterative names were put forward, including 'Albion' and (probably Avro's most popular choice) 'Avenger'. However, the matter was finally resolved when the Chief of the Air Staff announced his preference for a class of 'V-bombers', which prompted Handley Page to give the name 'Victor' to its design and, of course, Avro's 698 had the hugely appropriate name 'Vulcan' bestowed upon it by the Air Council.

Once the SBAC show appearances had been completed, the undercarriage doors were replaced (more securely this time), some instrument positioning was revised and the second pilot's seat was installed in the cockpit. Roly Falk had been heavily involved in the design of the cockpit from the outset (particularly the instrument layout) and it was he who had suggested the installation of a fighter-type control stick rather than the more traditional 'spectacle' wheel, which would normally be found in the cockpit of a four-engined bomber. Although there was certainly a case for using more conventional controls, Falk was keen to create an environment where the pilot would immediately appreciate the light, fighter-style handling qualities of the Vulcan, and the control joystick certainly gave the impression that the Vulcan wasn't just another cumbersome heavy bomber and actually possessed a performance capability that out-classed many contemporary fighters. When the second pilot's seat was finally fitted there was some media speculation (which is sometimes perpetuated even to this day) that it was literally crammed under the small canopy hood into what was essentially designed as a single-seat cockpit. In reality this wasn't the case, as the 698 had always been designed to have seating for two pilots, but for the purposes of the initial test flights time simply didn't allow the second seat to be installed. The Vulcan was never visualised as a one-man bomber, but its astonishing handling qualities were certainly very different from those which had traditionally been associated with aircraft of such size and weight.

Progress after the Farnborough show was encouraging, and by the end of January 1953 VX770 had completed thirty-two hours of test flying and was returned to the factory for modifications, including the installation of fuel cells in the wings; so far a temporary fuel system had been used, fitted inside the bomb bay. The cockpit pressurisation system was made operational and the Avon engines were replaced by Armstrong Siddeley Sapphire ASSa.6 turbojets, each rated at 7,500lb thrust. This gave the Vulcan the same engine power as Handley Page's Victor prototype and immediately enabled the aircraft to reach higher speeds and altitudes. It had been the design team's intention to fit Bristol BE.10 engines (each rated at 11,000lb) right from the start of the flight-test programme, but in the early 1950s, jet-engine development was a relatively new science and progress with new engines continually lagged behind development of the aircraft which required them. The Sapphires made a suitable interim replacement for the Avons and VX770's test programme was resumed in July 1953. By this stage the second prototype (VX777) was nearing completion and, although some initial ground trials of this aircraft were completed with Olympus Mk 99 engines fitted, they had been replaced with 9,750lb Olympus 100 engines in time for the second prototype's first flight on 3 September 1953.

In response to emerging data from the 707 programme, VX770's nose wheel leg was extended by a few inches during construction in order to give the aircraft a 3.5-degree angle of incidence in relation to the ground, thereby allowing it to unstick at a lower speed and use less runway length. This design modification was built into VX777 from the start and, rather than relying on a telescoping mechanism to allow the gear to fit into the wheel bay (as had been the case with VX770), a one-piece leg was fitted to VX777 together with a correspondingly larger nose wheel bay to accommodate it. As a result, the entire nose section of VX777 was slightly

longer and also included a bomb aimer's blister under the nose, complete with a clear forward panel. Less than a week after its first flight, the second prototype appeared over Farnborough at the 1953 SBAC show. It was at this event that the aircraft participated in what has become one of the most iconic events in British aviation history, when VX777 led an enormous 'delta of deltas' formation over Farnborough, the two Vulcan prototypes being flanked by four Avro 707s, creating a sight which will never be forgotten by those who were lucky enough to witness it. It was a brilliant demonstration of Britain's emerging military and technological prowess, which inevitably made the world's media sit up and take notice.

After Farnborough week, VX777 was delivered to Boscombe Down in preparation for high-speed and high-altitude trials, but before they could begin, a series of modifications were made to the Olympus engines and their control and fuel systems, and almost six months were to pass before flight trials commenced. VX777's troubled beginnings were exacerbated when the aircraft suffered a heavy landing while conducting flight trials at Farnborough, and this caused significant damage to the airframe, which had to be stripped and partially rebuilt. This created yet another delay in the flight-test programme (particularly in terms of engine development) and another six months went by before flying could resume, much to the growing frustration of the Avro design team. During the time in which VX777 was laid up, new Olympus 101 engines were installed, each rated at 10,000lb, and the whole airframe was structurally reworked, using data from a static test specimen that had also been constructed. While VX777 remained grounded, the first prototype remained active on flight trials, achieving as much as possible within the limits of its design.

When VX777 eventually resumed flying duties in 1955, the exploration of the high-speed and high-altitude characteristics of the aircraft quickly confirmed the predicted mild buffeting that was expected to occur when pulling g at speeds of Mach 0.8. This problem had been highlighted during the 707 test programme, but only at a fairly late stage, and with 9,000lb thrust engines it wasn't a significant difficulty. However, with projected improvements in engine thrust likely to result

Classic publicity
photograph of a Vulcan
crew in front of a B1
from 230 OCU. The open
crew door illustrates
how emergency inflight
evacuation from the
hatch was only possible
if the landing gear
was retracted. *(Tim
McLelland collection)*

in significantly more powerful engines, the high-altitude buffet would probably be reached with only the slightest application of engine power. This would inevitably lead to problems with bomb-aiming accuracy for operational crews and also create a significant risk that the outer-wing sections could ultimately fail through fatigue stress. This potential problem prompted Avro to develop what became known as the Phase 2 wing, which eventually emerged with a 'kinked' leading edge that neatly solved the problem. However, because the modification was made at such a late stage in the development programme, the first production Vulcan (XA889) was rapidly nearing completion and it was too late to incorporate the new wing modification. Consequently, while VX777 re-emerged with a revised wing leading edge, the first production Vulcan made its first flight on 4 February 1955 with the original straight wing leading edge still installed. Painted silver, complete with national insignia and a striking dark-coloured radome made from glass fibre/Hycar sandwich, XA889 successfully got airborne a whole twelve months ahead of Handley Page's first production Victor, much to the glee of the Avro team, which was still very keen to be visibly ahead of Handley Page in terms of development progress. There was still a great deal of doubt as to whether a choice would ultimately be made between the Vulcan and Victor, and nobody could predict which design would finally receive the most orders. The second production Vulcan (XA890) joined the flight-test programme later in 1955 and although it too was not fitted with the Phase 2 wing, both it and the first production aircraft were eventually retrofitted with the new wing design, complete with vortex generators along the upper surface, which re-energised boundary layer airflow across the wing. Roly Falk took XA890 to the 1955 SBAC event and once again he stole the show, this time by executing a neat barrel roll at a surprisingly low altitude in front of an assembled mass of truly astonished spectators, who had never imagined that they would see a strategic bomber perform such a hair-raising manoeuvre. The SBAC president (Sir Arnold Hall) was just as surprised as every other observer and immediately forbade Falk from repeating the performance on subsequent show days. Falk confidently explained that the manoeuvre was well within the aircraft's capabilities, providing that it was kept

within a steady 1g throughout the roll, but Hall remained unconvinced. Although he accepted that Falk was right, his main motivation for stopping what would have easily been the daily highlight of the show was that the manoeuvre would ultimately set a bad example to service pilots, and in some respects his comments did indeed prove to have some prophetic value, as other pilots did eventually try to repeat the manoeuvre (some without the same degree of success), until it was ultimately forbidden by senior industry and RAF chiefs. On 7 September, Prime Minister Anthony Eden arrived at Farnborough in a Central Flying School (CFS) Dragonfly helicopter and, after watching Falk's Vulcan display (without the barrel roll), he was invited on board and treated to a short flight during which he occupied the co-pilot's seat and briefly took control of the aircraft before Falk brought it back to nearby Blackbushe. After the flight, Falk received a handwritten note from Eden, thanking him for the experience.

In March 1956 the first production Vulcan (XA889) was delivered to Boscombe Down to begin acceptance trials with the RAF. The initial CA (Controller of Aircraft) release was subsequently issued on 28 May, as follows:

Tests have been made on the first production Vulcan B.Mk.1 to assess the type for use by the Royal Air Force, in the medium bomber role. The trials programme was completed in 26 sorties, totalling 48 hours 15 minutes flying time. During these tests the aircraft was flown over the full centre of gravity range, and at take off weights up to a maximum of 165,220lb. The first production Vulcan, XA889, was representative of service aircraft in all respects save those of operational equipment, automatic pilot, the rear crew stations and certain items of cockpit layout. The aircraft incorporated the drooped leading edge outer wing with vortex generators, the longitudinal auto-Mach trimmer, the pitch damper and revised airbrake configuration. These modifications have successfully overcome the unacceptable flying characteristics exhibited by the second prototype in the preliminary assessment carried out by this establishment, and when all stability aids are functioning, the Vulcan has safe and adequate flying qualities for its primary role as a medium bomber.

The CA release comments certainly contrasted with those made after the A&AEE trials with the second prototype, VX777:

A preliminary flight assessment has been made on the second prototype Vulcan in 17 sorties totalling 27 flying hours. During these tests the aircraft was flown at a mid centre of gravity and take-off weights of 119,000lb and 130,000lb. The expected operational take-off weight of production aircraft is about 165,000lb. The expected cruising Mach number is 0.87M (500kt) and the design Mach number is 0.95M. Above 0.86M a nose-down change of trim occurred which became pronounced with increase of Mach number towards the limit, making the aircraft difficult to fly accurately and requiring great care on the part of the pilot to avoid exceeding the maximum permitted Mach number. This characteristic is unacceptable; the Firm propose to eliminate it in production aircraft by the introduction of an artificial stability device (a Mach trimmer).

With increase of Mach number above 0.89 the damping in pitch decreased to an unacceptably low level, particularly near the maximum permitted Mach number, and the aircraft was difficult to fly steadily. The Firm propose installing a pitch damper in production aircraft. As tested the Mach number/buffet characteristics were unacceptable for a high altitude bomber, but considerable improvement is hoped for with the drooped leading edge and vortex generators. Associated with the buffet were oscillating aileron hinge movements which in these tests imposed severe manoeuvre limitations from considerations of structural safety. Making allowances for the differences in engine thrust and aircraft weight between the aircraft tested and the production version, the performance, in terms of attainable altitude, was not outstanding. The likely target height with a 10,000lb bomb will only be about 43,000ft with 11,000lb thrust engines, and the high altitude performance will be poor. The level of performance is considered to be inadequate for an unarmed subsonic bomber, even under cover of darkness. In summary, although the aircraft has certain outstanding features, serious deficiencies are present, particularly in and above the cruising Mach number range, and until these are rectified the Vulcan cannot be considered satisfactory for service use.

Although the report was primarily concerned with the highlighting of deficiencies by its very nature, it's clear that the prototype (with an unmodified wing) was never going to match the performance required by the RAF. Despite being extremely manoeuvrable and easy to handle, the early Vulcan in its prototypical form was simply not suited to the role for which it was designed. However, with further works and the all-important modification to the wing's leading edge, Avro demonstrated to the A&AEE that the Vulcan now possessed excellent handling qualities and would give the RAF the very aircraft that it wanted – and needed.

The Vulcan's design development required huge effort and seemingly endless resources. The work force at Chadderton, Woodford and other facilities shifted more and more attention to the project until it became Avro's priority programme. Countless workers contributed to the 698's ongoing development and among them was Peter Rivers, who had joined Avro after working for Handley Page, the Hertfordshire company directly competing with Avro on the B.35/46 programme. Peter's recollections provide a fascinating insight into life at Woodford as the Vulcan programme took shape:

The design of the H.P.80, which later became the Victor, had been progressing for just over a year when I arrived at Handley Page and the aircraft's shape had not yet settled into the final configuration, the tail in particular being much smaller and with the tailplane wandering up and down the fin as the design continually changed. The department that I joined was small but expanding and was responsible for the theoretical design calculations for all mechanical systems such as hydraulics, cabin systems, de-icing and anti-icing, fuel supply, etc. We shared a small area in the open-plan design office with the electrical engineers with whom we worked closely, but we had little contact with other technical departments or the general drawing office, which was in another part of the building. Maybe this was because we were not really involved with design detail at this stage, but there was a general practise at Handley Page of channelling

our results to the Chief Designers and the heads of the other departments, via the head of our own department. This was a system which contrasted dramatically with my experience at Avro. Compared to the stress and aerodynamic departments at Handley Page, our calculations did not involve any higher mathematics. Even differential equations were very rare, but the range of environmental conditions which we had to investigate was vast, especially for the anti-icing systems. Endless computations of complex arithmetical relationships had to be carried out, and the discovery of a simple mistake could mean the scrapping of work which might have taken a month or two to complete. We didn't have the luxury of computers as they didn't arrive in the industry

until the late 1950s, but the more favoured departments had electronic calculators, each one being about the size of a typewriter. We had hand-wound mechanical versions, rather like old-fashioned cash registers, and they always jammed if one tried to work too quickly.

Thanks to Handley Page's economical ways, even pencils were rationed to one per month, so if one had a heavy spell of writing, one had to go begging to other people who hadn't used up their rations! Our main difficulty was that there was virtually no relevant input data to feed into our calculations, and whereas work was being done at the RAE and elsewhere into the radically new aerodynamic and structural aspects of the design, nothing was being fed into our side of things, or at least

The damaged **XH498** pictured after making an emergency landing at Ohakea. *(Tim McLelland collection)*

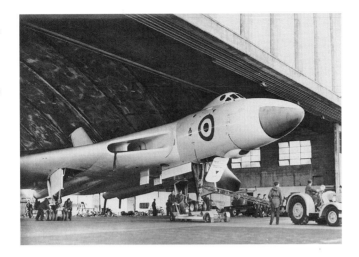

XH498 was repaired at Ohakea prior to making a successful flight back to the UK. As can be seen, its fin cap was removed and the nose gear jacked up in order to fit the huge bomber inside Ohakea's hangar. (*Tim McLelland collection*)

some work was being done, but tended to appear only after we had finished! This was especially true of icing work, which depended crucially on the proportion of water droplets in an icing cloud which would be caught on the wing or deflected around it. That required detailed mapping of the streamlines around the nose of the aerofoil sections, and the only highly theoretical plots which had been made in the US were for aerofoils that were most unlike the Victor's wing. All we could do was modify the results by factors which we hoped would be realistic. At least we knew that nobody else knew any better. The figures for the actual icing conditions were a little more reliable but still subject to annual changes. They came from NACA (the predecessor to NASA), who had an ageing C-46 which spent each icing season plodding around, flying into freezing clouds, with a variety of weird instruments sticking out of the windows to measure things like the total water content in each cubic metre of air. When we had spent a year doing our complicated step-by-step 'catch and heat' calculations, NACA would issue the next annual report, saying that last year's was wrong, so we had to start all over again! Another area which caused us headaches was the design of jet pumps to mix high-pressure air, bled from the engine compressors (which was too hot to pass directly through the light alloy wing structure) with cold ram air, in order to achieve the maximum usable air temperature while still delivering a high enough pressure to force the air through the heat

exchange passages in the wing and tail leading edges, although railway engine designers had been using the same principle for the better part of a century.

There was no reliable theory for the mixing of air streams in the kind of proportions necessary to achieve the pressure performance that we needed. We adapted the few theoretical analyses that we could find, and pounced upon the odd wartime German paper that came through from the post-war translators, but the results, which had to be turned into some massive pieces of hardware, were based upon guesswork to an even greater extent than our usual work. Ironically, just after all this work was complete and the detailed design finalised, a classic paper on the subject was published, and although I was working for Avro by that time, I was able to check that our answers had been pretty accurate. I've described this work in some detail because the same things were going on at Avro at the same time, and when I joined them I found that very similar conclusions and guesses had been made there. It was interesting to have worked on the Victor during the paper stage and then the Vulcan, when the theory was being put into practice. One question did arise concerning the Victor which didn't affect the Vulcan, and that was heat loss from the fuel during long flights at high altitude, which might cause the fuel to freeze or at least turn waxy. The Vulcan's tanks were separate items within the deep wing structure, whereas the Victor's were integral, with the inner metal skin separated from the outer one only by stringers and heavy spar booms at the corners of each span-wise bay. The latter feature meant that as well as encountering heat flow directly from one skin to the other, some would flow along the inner skin to the conductive boom. A rather unusual adaptation of some standard school physics was needed to solve the problem, and a further surprising extension of my calculations was used years later, when we were trying to establish the fuel temperature variations through day and night, for the Avro 730 supersonic reconnaissance bomber, for which the skin temperature was expected to be around 225°C. In this design the fuel was to be the heat sink for all cooling purposes. The same system was later used in the Concorde.

Towards the end of 1951 I was getting tired of Handley Page, and I needed some practical experience away from a desk, so I joined the test section of Fairey's missile division at Heston. They were developing the beam-riding Blue Sky missile at the time, and I quickly determined that missile work, especially trials, would not be much fun, so after a few months I was looking for a way out. In September of the same year I saw the Avro 698 prototype performing at Farnborough, never imagining that within three months I would be part of the Vulcan design team. I attended a lecture at the RAeS [Royal Aeronautical Society] in London, presented by Dr Still, the Technical Director of Teddington Controls, who were to supply much of the control equipment for the V-bomber hot air systems. At the lecture I met a former colleague from Handley Page, who had joined Avro a couple of years previously. He was about to leave for Canada, and after introducing me to Avro's Chief Designer and the head of his own department, he virtually left me his job to step into.

It's probably worth describing the design organisation at Avro as it was somewhat unusual for a British company. They had adopted a more American practise, with an individual Project Designer for each type of aircraft, all reporting to the Chief Designer, as did the heads of the separate technical departments, these being Stress, Aerodynamics, which included New Projects, Weight Control, and the Drawing Office. The job of each Project Designer was to push through his machine, regardless of the efforts of the other Project Designers, and this form of organisation ensured that one man at least would be committed to the success of each project, ensuring that maximum effort was provided by every department that worked for him. Compared to Handley Page, the Drawing Office was enormous, as was the whole Avro organisation, especially the production side. There was an old saying that when it was foggy outside, and it often was around Manchester, the far end of the Drawing Office was pretty hazy too! Each project was allocated a numbered Drawing Office section to carry out all the detail design, and only the Project Designer could issue instructions to them, and he had six Project Engineers to do the necessary work.

The group which I joined at Avro had grown up during the post-war period and expanded with the Vulcan design requirements, but unlike my department at Handley Page, it had remained as a group of individual specialists, each reporting to the Chief Designer, in parallel with the Project Designers and heads of the major technical departments. We were called Specialists, but we were much less so than the people in the Stress and Aerodynamic offices. Our position was rather odd in that we had direct access to the top, but we couldn't actually instruct any department to do anything without the authority of the Project Designers. Because the final assembly, test flying and work on the aircraft was done at Woodford, we travelled between there and the main offices at Chadderton, roughly 15 minutes away, several times each week. Because we were involved with the cabin and control system, we dealt directly with the test pilots and flight crews. The only person we didn't talk to was Sir Roy Dobson himself, although we did sit in on post-flight inquests which he chaired. With all of the other directors we were on first-name terms; with the people who had produced thousands of Lancasters. During 1954 the head of my department left for Woodford to take charge of a new department that would produce our own control equipment, replacing the items previously supplied by companies such as Normalair and Teddington, as their supplies were often underdeveloped and delivered late. I then took charge of the Systems group, essentially a bunch of individuals, as we didn't actually call ourselves a department as such. Throughout the time I spent with Avro, from December 1952 to December 1960, the Vulcan was only one of several projects that we were working on simultaneously and we were involved in every stage of development from initial project studies to sorting out problems in service, as nobody else within the company had a detailed knowledge of our systems. Before my arrival, the company had started a practise of writing simple descriptions of each system, describing the design and operation for the benefit of our Senior Designers, inspection staff, pilots, flight test crews and anyone else who needed to understand. We called them Children's Guides but they also helped us to understand better what we were doing and they were sufficiently well written to be used by the Technical Publications Department as the basis for Operating Manuals for the type.

Apart from the very open form of organisation and the direct personal friendship at all levels, there were other noticeable differences between Avro and Handley Page. At the latter company, design had the upper hand over production, and no matter how complex or difficult the structural or detail design might be, the production side had to find a way of making it. At Avro, however, production was dominant and if some feature was judged to be too difficult to produce economically or easily, it was simply redesigned. This resulted in more simple and therefore more reliable and easily maintained machines, and whenever we found ourselves thinking in too complicated a way, we'd say that it was 'becoming a Handley Page design' and then reconsider the subject in an effort to simplify it. At the same time as trying to keep the design simple and aiming to use established production methods, the Avro production 'machine' was capable of thinking big in a way that Handley Page never was. If a major alteration was found to be necessary, such as the Vulcan's extended and kinked leading edges, a modified production facility would be set up without delay, and massive jigs would often appear in the shops every few weeks.

When I joined Avro, the Vulcan prototype VX770 had been flying for about three months. It was without most of the systems with which I was concerned. There was a hydraulics system for the undercarriage and bomb doors, electrical power for the airframe and the electro-hydraulic powered flying controls, but the cabin was unpressurised and had only a rudimentary ventilation system. The aircraft was a long way from being fitted with production-standard engines, but even then the engine bays were large enough to accommodate the ultimate Olympus variants. Handley Page, of course, had to redesign and enlarge the entire Victor centre section when they changed to Conway engines. Also, when I joined Avro, they were working on the 720 rocket-propelled fighter, early schemes for the Atlantic, which was an airliner derivative of the Vulcan, some Shackleton developments leading to the Mark Three,

and the clearing of the last of six Ashton high-altitude research machines for delivery. The main activities in 1953 were the testing of hot air systems on ground rigs, analysing flight results on the first prototype's flying controls and preparing for the fitting and operation of the fully equipped and pressurised second prototype, which flew in time for the Farnborough show in September, but wasn't pressurised until the following year. The contracts for the V-bombers called for all mechanical systems to be tested on realistic ground rigs before they were operated in flight. Before the first flight, the hydraulic system had to be tested with all components and pipework in their correct dimensional positions. A separate powerplant and engine intake rig was set up in a building behind the flight sheds. This had the wing root intake set at the correct height and angle above the ground. The rig which simulated the hot air system, which would feed the cabin and icing systems, caused large problems. A source of air at a temperature and pressure corresponding to that of a jet engine compressor was not available and a supply had been devised from standard ground-type compressors and storage vessels, with heat from combustion heaters. These were specified to burn with a clean flame so that their output, when mixed with the main airflow, would not contaminate the aircraft equipment. The ducting was supported on a steel framework in the exact configuration of the aircraft system, with a used boiler of the correct volume to represent the cabin. When the rig was started up, control of the flow and heat inputs seemed to be excessively tricky and required the entire test department staff, standing at different valves and regulators around the system, frantically twiddling them in an attempt to get stable operation. After a few hours of this, without any useful results, the electro-pneumatic controllers started to misbehave and they were found to be clogged with soot and corrosion from the supposedly clean burners. The whole concept of the rig was seen to be a disaster, but the difficulty was solved by a quick and forceful decision made by the Chief Designer, who ordered a complete ducting system to be removed from the powerplant test house. It was laid beneath the engine intake, and connected to the engine compressor. With this realistic supply we began to get usable results for temperate conditions, although we were unable to simulate the maximum engine output temperatures. The engine test crew controlled the powerplant from inside their specially designed soundproof control room, but the mechanical test people had to stand in the open, below the engine bay, wearing what were obviously rather inadequate ear protectors to protect them from the terrific noise.

The pressure cabins were built at Chadderton and in their boiler-like form, with a blanking plate over the pilot's canopy, they were pressure tested to 1.5 times their maximum operating differential of 8psi and leak tested to a schedule of pressure against time. Following the problems with the de Havilland Comet, which occurred at the same time, structural testing to the point of failure was carried out in water tanks, in order to avoid the explosive effects of the rupture of an air-filled cabin, but obviously this could not be done with usable cabins and in any case we hardly expected a failure at what was a normal proof pressure by industrial standards. All the same, the area at Chadderton where the tests were done was roped off to keep bystanders away, and the inspector making the test had a heavy armoured screen to stand behind. The cabin of the first prototype had been completed and had flown before I arrived, and I doubt if it was ever pressure tested. The second prototype's cabin was tested, and the next one, destined for the first production aircraft, surprised us all by blowing up. This is how it happened. The front bulkhead of the cabin was domed, the usual way to carry pressure economically on the end of a cylinder. However, the rear bulkhead was flat because it could not take up space in the nose wheel bay, which was full of equipment. It was strengthened by massive vertical beams, which carried the nose wheel leg and operating jacks. When the cabin was pressure tested the support was missing, as the cabin couldn't be tested once it was mated to the fuselage. So a dummy structural bay was bolted to the rear bulkhead to give it the necessary strength. When the prototype cabin was tested, the holes in the two pieces of structure didn't line up very well and they were opened up and aligned to take the temporary connecting bolts. With the next cabin the holes were again out of line, the bolts were consequently

a little slack, and the stiffening effect was inadequate, so the bulkhead blew out. The effect was like a sizeable bomb going off and impressed all concerned, especially the inspector, who had only just retreated behind his screen after checking the manometers attached to the bulkhead, which were fundamentally more accurate than the gauges. So in total, one more cabin was completed than the actual number of airframes.

With the first flights of the second prototype with full pressurisation scheduled for early 1954, it was decided that I should go on all of the early flights to take charge of the pressure and air conditioning controls, which were on the panel of the port side rear crewmember. It was evidently thought that if the system misbehaved, I would understand and know what to do. In case such a failure resulted in cabin pressure being lost at more than 40,000ft, I had to wear a pressure suit. It was an American-designed, close-fitting, nylon partial pressure suit, which pulled tight when required through laces and pneumatic tubes along the arms and legs. Unlike the original American version, which had a helmet with opening visor, the British version had a cloth headpiece with a hard leather inner shield and a fixed visor. Each one

A 230 OCU Vulcan B1 from Waddington basks in the Lincolnshire sunshine. The national insignia on the white-painted Vulcans was subsequently replaced by washed-out 'anti-flash' insignia in pastel colours, to reduce the aircrafts' radiation absorption qualities. (Tim McLelland collection)

but I couldn't do anything about it as I was held firmly on my chair by my suit.

After all the preliminary testing, the actual flying seemed quite tame, but it was interesting to be among the first people in Britain to fly regularly at 50,000ft and near to Mach one. Most of the flights I participated in were around February–March 1954 and after five or six flights it was clear that the system was not going to fail or do anything untoward, so I stopped flying. The usual routine for each flight was to take off from Woodford, climb through what seemed to be a permanent overcast heading south and fly straight ahead for about 30 minutes. That would place us over the Isle of Wight. I could see the ground through the small porthole window above the rear crew's bench when we were well banked over. We would then turn north, flying for an hour until we were over the central Highlands of Scotland, before turning south again. Heading back to Lancashire, we would finally home in on the voice transmissions from controllers at Woodford and sometimes with the help of the radar controllers at Manchester airport. The last flight I flew on included the Minister of Supply, the infamous Duncan Sandys, who was permitted to fly the Vulcan himself for a few minutes, making the customary flattering remarks afterwards. The flight was reported in many newspapers and I was listed as part of that crew. One particular feature of each flight was the buffeting which occurred when flying at altitudes in the high 40,000s at high Mach numbers. It seemed quite gentle to me, just a low frequency shaking like driving along a bumpy road, but of course it led to the extended and drooped wing leading edges that were retrofitted to early Vulcans.

From early 1954 onwards we were concerned with production machines, of which the first few were used for trials, and I remember XA894 and XA897 in particular as they were used for cabin systems and anti-icing development. Perhaps it would be helpful if I described the arrangement of the hot air systems on the Vulcan. These were fed by a tapping at the high-pressure end of each main engine compressor and were designed for a maximum pressure of around 200psi and a maximum temperature of 400°C – figures which

Trio of Vulcan B1s during a goodwill visit to Ohakea, New Zealand. *(Tim McLelland collection)*

was custom fitted and all our test crews were provided with one, but the Chief Test Pilot, Roly Falk, refused to wear one as he felt it would hamper his movements and create a potential danger. To take account of possible decompression, our Bomber Command liaison pilot, Wing Commander C.C. Calders, rode in the second pilot's seat, wearing a pressure suit, and really did little other than wait for an emergency. If a failure had occurred, his suit and my suit would have inflated, and we would have brought the aircraft down to a level where the remaining three crew would hopefully have regained consciousness. Late in 1953 therefore, I was fitted with my suit at the appropriately named Frankenstein's works in Manchester and had a trial inflation while seated on the edge of a table. It was shaped to a seated position, and when pressurised it took all the weight off one's arms and legs and you felt like you were going to float up to the ceiling. I then went to the Institute of Aviation Medicine at Farnborough to experience a proper inflation of the suit in their decompression chamber, where pressure was explosively changed from 8,000ft to 70,000ft. I shared the chamber with a representative from an equipment company, who passed out and flopped over, were unprecedented at that time. The ducting was all stainless steel, 0.28in thick, which led to some tricky welding problems. Simple things like joints, clamps and sealing rings took on a great deal of our attention and the long runs of ducting, typically 4in in diameter, had to be supported from the aircraft structure with flexible steel bellows at the anchor points, to allow for differential expansion of the ducts and structure, with the wide temperature ranges which went through. This is an area which troubles the designers of ground-based pipe systems even today, but we must have got things pretty well right, as I never heard of any major failures in RAF service. The ducts in each pair of engine bays ran forward, joined up into one from each side, and met on the rear wall of the nose wheel bay (in each wing root a branch went off to supply the anti-icing jet pump and, as described for the Victor, each one was a hefty device about 8in diameter and 6ft long). From the junction, a single duct ran forward along the port side of the nose wheel bay, to the air conditioning pack (consisting of a cold-air expansion turbine, usually called the CAU), heat exchangers (supplied with cooling air from that unobtrusive intake inboard of the engine intake fence) and control valves. From the pack, the air entered the cabin through a non-return valve on the rear bulkhead (so that the cabin would hold pressure if the ducting or supply failed). Cabin pressure was controlled, as always, by an outlet valve on the front bulkhead (so that leakage from the cabin structure did not affect the control), ventilated the radar in the nose, and finally left through the small grilles low down on the nose. The flow of air to the cabin was far greater than necessary to keep the crew comfortable because the requirement for cooling the radar and navigational sets was overpowering. These sets were in sealed drums about the same size as a typical dustbin, and what was inside was so secret that we were not allowed to discuss the cooling load, only supply what the Ministry specification called for. Years later when we did find out what was inside, it confirmed our suspicions – the designers may have known plenty about electronics, but they hadn't a clue about heat and all our efforts were being devoted to the cooling of a few hot spots, such as sensitive valves placed right above

heat-generating components. This was the pre-transistor era, and the valves in this case were of the electronic kind, unlike those mentioned previously! The pressure control side of things, manufactured by Normalair, didn't give us any undue trouble, but the flow control side, made by Teddington, turned out to be a major headache, both on technical grounds and unreliability. At the time they were the only suppliers of high-temperature valves with sliding carbon gapes, which were used for shutting off airflows from the engines and initially for regulating the flows to the different parts of the system. The valves were moved by electric motors and it was therefore logical for Teddington to develop electrical flow sensing control units, to operate the valves. Unfortunately the controllers were underdeveloped when they were installed in production Vulcans and I personally felt that they were designed to unrealistic specifications, typical of the time, especially in the case of equipment with which the Ministry was concerned. For example, a requirement for airflow to be controlled at 40lb/min with a tolerance of plus/minus 11lb/min led to complicated and unreliable gadgetry. To my way of thinking it didn't matter if the flow was forty or forty-five, as long as it was steady, and I later changed the systems to this standard.

Our early tests, starting with the rig, showed that the flow controllers were not stable and could not cope with various aspects of the special requirements that we considered unrealistic, but which the Ministry insisted upon. Teddington kept adding more fiddle units to back up the ones that were misbehaving, without doing much good. At one stage they turned up with yet another gadget, saying that it had got Handley Page out of trouble and it would do the same for us. Of course, Handley Page was regarded as a major competitor and during the war it was often said in Avro circles that the company had three enemies: Handley Page, the Ministry and the Germans, in that order! However, having previously worked for Handley Page, I telephoned my old colleagues to enquire how they were getting on with Teddington's new panacea. They said that Teddington had told them that the gadget had worked for Avro, so it would work for them too, just as they had told us. At one stage I visited Teddington's factory, and found that the inspection department, to save themselves undue effort, were leaving ready-signed clearance forms for items that had yet to be tested. That didn't improve my opinion of them and when their deliveries turned out to be late and unreliable, Avro, in typical ruthless style, virtually took over their test and inspection department with our own people, ensuring that whatever happened to everyone else's orders, the Avro units would be completed on time and work properly. In the end I solved our flow problems by throwing out all the Teddington equipment, except for the shut-off valves, for which there were no alternatives, and putting in Normalair controllers of an extremely simple kind, based on the ones which had been used in smaller aircraft since the Second World War. One thing which we could not do with the Vulcan, was to keep the aircrew comfortable on the ground in hot conditions, although neither could any other military or civil aircraft design at that time. By the time we had reached the Vulcan Mk 2, the operational procedure had changed, making crews spend long periods on board the aircraft on standby, and the heat situation could not be tolerated. The RAF's answer was to put the crews in ventilated suits which were a light nylon overall design, with fine tubes directing conditioned air to evaporate sweat from appropriate areas of the aircrew's bodies. The additional airflow drawn from idling engines or a ground supply, and the tight temperature control needed (too hot or too cold either cooked or chilled the unfortunate crewman) meant that we had to install a separate conditioning pack, which was somehow squeezed in next to the existing one. This was again a Normalair unit, with a fighter-sized air turbine running it at over 100,000rpm, and we did not have any particular troubles with it. I should add that there was no connection between the fact that I'd worked for Normalair and the way that they took over many of the Vulcan's systems; it was just that they were slightly less unreliable than the other suppliers! I cannot recall doing any useful testing of the icing system as installed. All we could check was that the surfaces were being evenly heated, as it would have been impossible to fly in real icing conditions as the RAE's attempts to find such conditions with an instrumented Valetta had indicated how difficult it would have been,

and we couldn't have measured the complicated icing factors anyway. As the extended and drooped leading edges were introduced on the Vulcan Mk 1 and extended further on the Mk 2, our heating passages were getting hacked about and restricted by the changes in internal structure and there was nothing we could do about it. Airframe icing was becoming less of a concern and I presented a paper at a Napier icing symposium to show that with the fast-climbing and descending flight profile which the V-bombers were designed for, they would go through the icing layers in a matter of seconds, so that even with no heating system the amount of ice picked up would be unimportant. Of course, I did not anticipate that in a few years' time virtually all operations would be conducted at low level, but even so I never heard of any icing problems with the Vulcan.

I made myself pretty unpopular at one stage by pointing out that years of calculating anti-icing performance and agonising over the assumptions we had to make, simply resulted in our demanding more bleed air from the engines then we were allowed to take, so that all we were able to do was to take as much air as we could and spread it around evenly. Nevertheless, the Ministry insisted that we certify that the system would meet their requirements on paper, as we were still calculating and refining our figures when Avro installed the first computer in the industry. It was about the same size as a bungalow, and we jumped at the chance to have many more points in the icing envelope calculated. Of course, the occasional accidents which the Vulcan suffered often affected us on the design side and such events have only been briefly mentioned in other historical accounts. Aircraft accidents often have a funny side when nobody gets hurt, and the first one we had was like that. One of the prototypes, VX777, was being demonstrated to one of the RAE pilots at Farnborough in 1954, and at the time the early Vulcans were being thrown about in an almost care free way, and on this occasion the crew had made a rather snappy yawing manoeuvre, probably a sort of stall turn, as the rudder was locked hard over but stayed there. At this stage the aircraft didn't have any periscopes, so the pilots could only see the wing leading edges as far as the wingtips, and no further aft.

Periscopes were later fitted for navigation and were essential to enable the crew to see what was going on behind them, such as the undercarriage position, bomb doors position or, in this case, whether the fin was still attached. The crew flew VX777 past Farnborough's control tower and received confirmation that the fin was still there. They then landed, using asymmetric power to counter the jammed rudder, but this meant that the brakes were unable to stop them before the aircraft rolled off the end of the runway on to soft ground, where the undercarriage collapsed. As there was no great danger of a fire, there wasn't any hurry to abandon the aircraft, but the question on the crew's minds was how to actually get out, with the entry door firmly wedged into the ground. Oddly enough, the situation had been discussed in our design office a few weeks previously, and it had been concluded that the pilot would have to hold up the canopy while everyone else climbed over the side. The canopy could be jettisoned in flight and sucked away by the airflow, but there was no way of getting rid of it on the ground, other than by unlocking it and tipping it over the side. The crewmembers were unwilling to do this, feeling that they'd caused enough damage already, so Roly Falk, who was quite tall, held the canopy on his shoulders while everyone got out. After that, explosive jacks were fitted to the canopy for ground jettison. The next job was to raise the aircraft, by digging holes under the wings for lifting jacks, and it was then revealed that the ground had been used by cavalry regiments for a century or so of army occupation, and they were digging into feet-deep layers of manure! When the Vulcan was finally lifted, the undercarriage was fixed down with structural steel and VX777 was flown back to Woodford.

The cause of the rudder failure was a fine example of how deadly tiny details can be. The power controls were all Boulton Paul electro-hydraulic units, in which an electric motor drove a swashplate pump (one with an angled driving block which could be swung in either direction to give flow either way) to a jack, which moved the surface. The pilot's control moved the swashplate of each unit and for the rudder there was a standby unit, which idled while the normal unit did the work, with a spring strut arrangement to keep the standby out

Unusual publicity photograph of a portable starter unit system, illustrating the Vulcan B2's revised wing leading edge extension and the type's bulky main undercarriage legs and bogie assembly. *(BAE)*

of action until the normal unit stopped. On the wing units, four of which operated elevators, and four on the ailerons (the Mk 2 changing to elevons), the philosophy was that if one stopped, there would still be three to keep going and even two failures left half power available. In the case of the VX777 accident, the rudder had been kicked over so hard that the spring in the telescopic strut had expanded more than was intended, so that it jammed inside its tube. A simple problem really, and one which didn't take much of a modification to prevent it happening again.

The next accident which affected us was the infamous Heathrow tragedy, at the end of a very successful tour of Australia and New Zealand, with Air Marshal Harry Broadhurst as second pilot. There was no technical failure of the aircraft this time, but the fact that the pilots were able to eject and the rear crew could not, led to a media and political outcry about ejection seats for navigators and other crew, creating a great deal of design investigation for us. The basic cause of the crash was as old as flying itself: We must land at place A because the welcoming VIPs and brass bands are there, never mind the weather, even though our alternative place B is basking in sunshine. The inquiry into the affair was revealing and conducted by an electronic's pundit, and the Vulcan's final flight path was a perfect example of divergent oscillation due to the time lag between the

Vulcan B2 from 83 Squadron illustrating the distinctive leading edge extension to the original straight wing structure. (*Rolls-Royce*)

GCA [ground-controlled approach] controller and the pilot. You could have reproduced it exactly on a cathode ray tube with appropriate time resistances for the two participants. The controller hadn't handled a fast jet before, and Podge Howard, the pilot, had not used civilian GCA before. The delay in the pilot's response to the controller's instructions and the delay in the controller following the radar plot, led to the flight path swinging further and further above and below the correct one until the final low point caused the aircraft to hit the ground, pushing the undercarriage through the wing's flying controls. When we came to investigate the possible fitting of rear crew ejection seats, the problems became quickly apparent. Apart from having to remove virtually the complete top of the pressure cabin, which would have been a structural nightmare, there was no way that we could get the rear crews out safely. As they sat facing aft, the seats would come out on a forward trajectory, and probably hit the tail, which the pilots' seats would probably clear. To enable the rear seats to fire on a rearward trajectory meant a complicated drill of turning one round at a time, because of the cramped

width, and the procedure would take so long they would never get out in time at low level. At high altitude there was no problem in getting out by the normal crew entry doer as already designed. Although Martin-Baker did later offer a suitable escape system it was never adopted, probably because the huge expense was felt to be wasteful for an aircraft that wouldn't be in service all that long, never realising just how long the Vulcan's service career would be.

Once the RAF got their hands on the Vulcan, they started touring all around the world and one aircraft, XA908, suffered a major electrical failure while flying over Canada. The Vulcan B1s had DC electrical systems with batteries to supply reserve power. The machine suffered a progressive generator failure in which the load cascaded in the main distribution system so that an initial failure of one generator led to all four cutting out.

Following the accident, all B1s were modified, including our test aircraft at Woodford, but before our last aircraft (XA891) was modified it suffered the same fate soon after taking off from Woodford. Fortunately our chief test pilot, Jimmy Harrison, and his crew were able to aim for open countryside and bale out close to Hull. Jimmy later remarked that he hadn't previously realised what a beautiful machine the Vulcan was until he saw it from above, presumably after he had got rid of the ejection seat face blind and disengaged from his seat. The last Vulcan accident for which we provided a design explanation, although there was no fault with the aircraft as such, was the crash of the 698 prototype, VX770, at Syerston in 1958. Our old friend had been passed to Rolls-Royce at Hucknall for engine test work, and it was being flown at a Battle of Britain display by a Rolls-Royce crew, when it broke up during a low flypast. The visual evidence was primarily drawn from an amateur cine film, from which the famous picture featured in many books and articles was taken. We took the film to Chadderton and ran it through many times, but major changes took place between frames and the complete disintegration took place over no more than four or five frames. However, we had some solid technical evidence to work on. The accelerometer on the normal flight panel showed the maximum g-forces that had been applied and we were also able to read the airspeed at which electrical power was cut off from the artificial feel units, and we quickly concluded that the combination was outside the aircraft's safe flight envelope. Once power flying controls were introduced, pilots had to be given some sort of artificial feel, pushing against springs in effect, to stop them from breaking the aeroplanes. The Vulcan's feel units were 'q' feel, in which the leverage against the spring increased in proportion to the pitot pressure and was thus the square of the speed, which was the way manual control forces normally behaved. The actual mechanism was a lever and roller moving in a curved slot, known as the Banana Lever, shifted by an electric motor responding to a signal from a pitot pressure capsule, as in an airspeed indicator. So the position at which the levers stopped, when the aircraft disintegrated, gave us the speed at which it happened.

Power controls and the associated technology were taken out of my care early in 1956, but my group was still involved with cooling the controls and everything else too. On the Mk 1 the Boulton Paul units were inside the wing, which was relatively deep all the way along, and one unit was positioned in front of each section of control surface. Each had a small NACA-type intake in the lower wing surface ahead of it, and the outlet air spilled into the wing interior, escaping through gaps around the control surfaces. With the Mk 2 the two inboard units on each side were the same, but the new outer wing was too thin for the outboard units to fit inside, so they were mounted underneath the wing in long blister fairings. There was no fundamental difference from our point of view, and as we were busy with other work we let the drawing office get on with the new installation, without paying attention to what they were really doing. So on the Mk 2's first flight these outboard control units overheated drastically and the drawing office, backed up by the Project Designer's people, quickly descended upon us to find out what we had allowed them to do wrong! I had a look at the drawings and pointed out that the units were in sealed fairings with air intakes, which they had faithfully copied, but there was no outlet, because there had been no obvious one before, so how could they expect air to go in and around the power unit, if it could not get out? There was a great

The Vulcan has always been a show stopper wherever it appears. This image from a 1950s show at RAF Middleton St George illustrates just how flamboyant the RAF's first Vulcan displays were. (dtvmovements.co.uk)

fuss about needing to fly the next day, so I said that they simply needed a backwards-facing hole and the easiest way to get one would be to cut the back end of the fairing blisters. A quick 'guesstimation' of how forward to cut and off they went. The cooling was adequate thereafter and that is why, if you look at the Mk 2's control blisters, you'll see that they are cut off a few inches short of the trailing edge, even though the riveted flanges continue all the way. Designing with a hacksaw was one of the things that the great Roy Chadwick was noted for, so I felt like I was following a great tradition.

My last flight in a Vulcan was in the first Mk 2 as I claimed a flight every now and then just to see how things were feeling inside the aircraft, while in flight. This flight was also the only one where I rode in the second pilot's seat and was given a chance to handle the machine at altitude, not doing anything fancy, just gentle turns and speed variations. However, it was a notable flight as Jimmy Harrison did a beat-up over Woodford, culminating in a climbing roll, so I was able to experience one of the famous Vulcan manoeuvres, which had been a feature of many displays up until that time. It was just as well that I did have a good forward view as if I'd been in the back I wouldn't have known that we were doing anything more than a gentle turn. The trick of doing these rolls was to keep the manoeuvre barrelled just enough to keep a little over $1g$ all the way around. I called in at Woodford during 1984 in connection with some work I was doing at the time and in the reception hall I met a member of the flight shed staff from the late 1950s and without introduction he immediately recognised me and recalled the day when Jimmy Harrison had rolled me in the Mk 2. Eventually the RAF asked Avro to stop rolling the Vulcan as some service pilots were trying it, but hadn't quite got the knack, so the airframes were in danger of being overstressed. One funny incident was when Jimmy visited Finningley for some reason, departed with the usual beat-up and roll, only to return to Woodford to find a letter from Bomber Command asking him not to do it anymore – but the letter had arrived after he'd left!

Navigation on these test flights had some amusing moments too. Having described the typical flight plan of the early tests, I recall that the later flights tended to amble around the coastline, as even with extensive weather systems and low-level cloud there was normally some recognisable part of the coastline visible. If we could only see a small area of the ground, the first thing we checked was the colour of the soil, which tended to establish the region we were flying over pretty well, with red soil in Devon, chalky soil in Sussex, black in the Fenlands, and so on. If an aerodrome was visible the type of aircraft on it gave us a second clue, the RAF having a huge variety of aircraft in those days. One day though, the crew had been flying on a steady course for some time while taking performance measurements that required steady conditions. We were below 40,000ft when a flight of Meteors shot past, and one of the pilots commented that he'd never seen Meteors carrying red, yellow and black roundels before. It turned out that we were over Belgium! After that, the first visual check we made was to see which side of the road the cars were driving on!

In the summer of 1958 I attended a meeting at White Waltham where we discussed the whole question of escape from the Vulcan's cabin. To start with, there was a move to co-ordinate the various connections that the crews, pilots in particular, had to make on getting into their seats, and therefore had to break on leaving to bale out, such as intercom, oxygen, suit air and so on. Each item had been developed by small departments in the Ministry and a crewmember had many separate pipes and plugs to undo every time he got out of the aircraft.

Eventually two companies were given contracts to do what the Ministry apparently could not, to bring all the systems to a common point and develop a multi-way connector, so the crewmember had only one fitting to connect. M. L. Aviation did the job for bomber aircraft and they also had a contract to improve escape systems generally, so they built a full-size mock-up of the cabin, with no skin so that one could see what was going on inside. In theory, every piece of equipment, or bracket on which one could get snagged, was in place. We gave them all the drawings and they gathered equipment from various sources, but I doubt if every item could have been fitted. However, a meeting was set up at White Waltham, with myself and a deputy from Avro, representatives from the Ministry, the Air Staff, Institute of Aviation Medicine and so on, plus an RAF crew from Waddington to act as guinea pigs in the cabin. The mock-up cabin was in a large room, with everyone seated on benches either side. It was an incredibly hot day, and we sweated away until M.L. Aviation brought in an air conditioning van they had built, and poked a large hose through the room's window to provide cooling air. It made so much noise that nobody could hear what was being said, so we opted to go back to the heat. The crew of course, played up and pretended to be as clumsy and awkward as possible, so it was a lengthy performance. When it came to looking at belly landings, the pilots climbed over the side, having disposed of the canopy, but the rear crew pointed out that the narrow gap between the ejection seats would delay their escape. They suggested that they should have a switch to blow the pilots' seats out, but the pilots were obviously not very enthusiastic about the rear crew having the power to shoot them out, if they had a disagreement or, more seriously, triggered the switch by mistake. This was the tone of the meeting and it continued throughout the day, finally ending at about seven with no real conclusions having been reached.

I left Avro at the end of 1960 to try my luck in general industry and it was the only company that I was ever really sorry to leave. The last year or so had been darkened by the shadows of missiles. Avro set up their missile division at Woodford and introduced a bunch of rather high-toned individuals from Farnborough and places like that. Their

attitude was that their work was far beyond anything that we had being doing and our old-fashioned ideas about sound engineering didn't really apply to missiles. However unprecedented the performance we were designing for, we always had been very careful to stick to sound principles of reliable engineering. The missile work was regarded as being so advanced and secret that the service requirements couldn't be discussed with us, and we just had to provide the airflows or whatever else was called for, and not ask any questions. It reminded me of the radar cans mentioned earlier and no matter what, we always thought of the Vulcan as 'our' aeroplane.

XA904 lost its power controls on approach to Waddington in March 1961. It veered off the runway on landing, smashing the undercarriage. The aircraft was written off. (*Tim McLelland collection*)

Vulcan B1A XH479
illustrating the B1A's
larger tailcone (housing
ECM equipment) and
the nose-high attitude
of the aircraft, thanks
to the B1's relatively
long-stroke nose gear
leg. (*Tim McLelland
collection*)

6

SETBACKS

Although the Vulcan was undoubtedly a very advanced design at the time of its creation, the aircraft had an airframe built along remarkably traditional lines, which reflected Avro's well-known preference for the adoption of simple and reliable engineering solutions. Apart from the most highly stressed parts of the airframe, the whole structure was manufactured from standard grades of light alloy and there was virtually no integral stiffening or machined and tapered skinning to be encountered anywhere within the structure. Even brazed or bonded metal honeycombs, upon which very extensive research was conducted at Chadderton, were confined to localised areas in the control surfaces and in the access doors on the underside of the aircraft. Almost all the remaining parts of the airframe were built up from standard sheet and sections with a small number of machined forgings, castings and extrusions where necessary. With only a few exceptions, the entire airframe was manufactured within the Hawker Siddeley Group (of which Avro was part), and it was, in fact, quite difficult to find any parts of the structure that were not actually a product of A.V. Roe (the company's full name, inevitably abbreviated to 'Avro').

At the time of the Vulcan's creation, Avro maintained four principal facilities for airframe production. The main factory was at Chadderton, situated between Manchester and Oldham. Smaller facilities were located at Bracebridge Heath, just half a mile from RAF Waddington's runway, and Langar in Nottinghamshire (a former Royal Canadian Air Force base), where airframe parts such as fins and rudders were manufactured. The main assembly shops were, of course, situated at the company's aerodrome at Woodford in Cheshire. In addition, some sheet-metal parts were made at the Empire Works in Manchester and Armstrong Whitworth Aircraft manufactured some Vulcan components, such as the elevators and ailerons, at its Baginton factory, in Coventry.

The entire airframe was broken down into a number of major assemblies. These were connected at bolted transport joints and, in conformity with the Ministry of Supply's requirements, complete interchangeability was achieved right from the start of production, so that one airframe was in effect identical to any other (this certainly wasn't the case with Handley Page's Victor). Most of the airframe construction started in the detail shops at Chadderton and the smaller components were then brought together in major component jigs, which were nearly all welded from standard girder sections. Among these portions was the complete centre section (in effect the heart of the whole aircraft and a particularly capacious component in the form of a rectangular box approximately 65ft x 28ft x 9ft 7in); the wing leading edges; the intakes and forward fuselage (aft of this portion there was scarcely any fuselage at all, as this area merged into the wings); the front fuselage, incorporating the pressure cabin; the nose, largely filled with radar bombing equipment; and the inner trailing edge and tail section of the fuselage.

At its root the wing had a thickness/chord ratio of the order of 12 per cent. This may seem unlikely for an aircraft with almost sonic performance, but it is not a truly indicative figure, as the wing's interior was largely occupied by the engines and associated ducting, so the equivalent thickness of a conventional wing would be very much less. Root chord was of the order of 58ft and the depth was in excess of 6ft for a considerable axial distance. The wing had two principal spars, each of which was conventionally built up from a plate web and strong upper and lower booms. Across the centre section both spars were straight and truly transverse. The front spar web was built to the shape of an ellipse with widely spaced foci, being made in one large sheet with continuous machined boom members along the upper and lower edges. There were circular holes for the four engines, and the central portion formed the front face

XH503 served with 44 and 83 Squadrons at Waddington. The early application of disruptive camouflage also resulted in slightly repositioned tail insignia and serials on some aircraft. (*Tim McLelland collection*)

starboard portions correctly located relative to each other. Staging was provided at frequent intervals, which enabled the manufacturing personnel to work on all parts of the structure with relative ease. At this point the circular-section fuselage began to merge, with the lower part housing the nose undercarriage and the upper section being occupied by fuel tanks. At the forward end of this portion was a transverse plate frame, which formed the rear pressure bulkhead of the crew compartment. To the lower part of this bulkhead was attached the nose undercarriage which, like the main gear, was manufactured by Dowty. The loads from the main pivots were taken out through massive vertical beams running the full depth of the fuselage. As a consequence, the rear pressure bulkhead was constructed flat. The crew compartment itself was of circular section and was, in most respects, an entirely conventional structure, terminating at a slightly concave front pressure bulkhead featuring eight radial stiffeners. Forward of this point the fuselage consisted solely of a cantilevered upper portion carrying the inflight refuelling probe and from this same structure the radar bombing gear and numerous other components were hung. All the rest of the nose was formed from the immense Avro-manufactured radome, which was one of the largest glass-fibre mouldings to have been put into production anywhere. The wing leading edges were manufactured with envelope tooling, of the type pioneered by Fairey. This gave the requisite degree of manufacturing accuracy and resulted in an admirably well-finished part, notwithstanding its irregular profile, with a kinked planform and a varying camber. A double skin was fitted inside the leading edge proper, providing chordwise passages roughly 0.125in deep for de-icing air.

of the bomb bay and was covered with electrical circuitry, bomb-door jacks and other necessary equipment. Each Olympus engine was enclosed in a separate fireproof box so that the complete centre section included six vertical plate members, arranged in the axial direction in the form of ribs. The innermost pair of these corresponded roughly with the width of the fuselage, which was a secondary structure forming a relatively unstressed circular cross-section.

Major loads were transmitted by strong arches between the innermost axial rib-like members, and these arches also supported the weight of whatever bomb loads were hung beneath. During assembly this portion was mounted horizontally on spherically located supports, with various temporary ties being inserted to join the lower edges of the innermost ribs. The circular peripheral members around the engine holes in the spar transmitted the major wing-bending loads, and so these were machined from high-tensile steel. At the extremities of the front spar were large High Duty Alloys forgings, to which the corresponding member of the outer wing was attached. The latter was swept back and the forging accordingly had a fairly complex shape, with large tongues projecting along the axes of the front spar, outer-wing spar and engine rib. The rear part of the inner wing was built up on the rear spar, which was similarly a single sheet across the centre section, with strong peripheral circles around the low-slung jet pipes.

Due to their considerable size and unusual form, the intakes were assembled in vertical jigs, with the port and

This description outlines the manufacturing work completed at the Chadderton factory. Once these large portions of the airframe reached completion, they were transported by road to the assembly plant at Woodford, located some 10 miles south of Manchester. By far the largest portion was the centre section and it was this monstrous piece of engineering that gave rise to the bizarre sight of numerous hinged lamp posts appearing on the ring road network, so that the structure could be safely transported through the streets of Manchester and Stockport. In order to ease these very difficult transport

problems, the production process was subsequently changed so that the airframe could be split down the vertical centreline into port and starboard halves, effectively halving the size of each main section, but all of the early aircraft were manufactured as continuous structures between the root ribs of the wings.

When the centre sections arrived at Woodford they were lifted by a travelling crane and placed on one of four large concrete jigs fixed rigidly to the factory floor and provided with numerous locating points to ensure that complete airframe interchangeability was maintained. These jigs could hold the centre section at the correct angle and height above the floor so that the considerable amount of additional manufacturing and installation work could take place. At the same time the main triangular inter-spar portion of each wing was assembled in one of a quartet of horizontal jigs. These inter-spar areas were built up principally from a great number of sheet ribs spaced as closely as 1ft apart. The ribs were not notched, and spanwise stringers were mounted on the ribs by small angle attachments , leaving a peripheral space between the rib and the skin. Riveted angles were also used to attach the ribs to the webs of the spars. When the whole box was finally put together, it was skinned with strips roughly 15in wide and extending from root to tip parallel to the front spar. Each strip featured several stringers, assembly being assisted by men working on the structure from inside the wing. When the component was completed, the travelling crane picked up the centre section and placed it on a large trolley, which, although not mounted on rails, could roll in the direction in which the aircraft was facing.

The wings were brought up on separate trolleys and located correctly on the root ribs by means of hand jack-screws. Finally the big and bulky Dowty main legs and eight-wheel bogies were hung from their pivots and the nose gear was attached, permitting the aircraft to be moved forward on its own wheels. Installation of the powerplant, control surfaces, operational gear and equipment then proceeded normally, after which the aircraft was subjected to extensive systems testing and pre-flight checking. It

Previous page, this page and opposite: XH478 spent a considerable amount of time assigned to test flight duties. As part of a series of inflight refuelling trials the aircraft appeared (as illustrated) with fluorescent orange strips applied to the nose, tail and wing tips. Trials were also performed in conjunction with the A&AEE's Canberra, WV787. After withdrawal from use in 1969, XH478 was flown to Akrotiri, where it was used as a ground instructional airframe for fire and rescue training. During its time on the airfield's dump it acquired a variety of 'zaps' from visiting RAF units, most notably 56 Squadron. (*Tim McLelland collection*)

was then taken out on to the airfield for a final systems shake down and then test flown, still wearing its patchy undercoat of green etching primer. After being flown and evaluated the aircraft then returned to the factory and brought back to the head of the assembly line where it was given two coats of gloss white anti-radiation paint and once more subjected to thorough checks before being declared ready for delivery to the Royal Air Force.

Work on preparing the Vulcan for the RAF continued with huge enthusiasm at Woodford, rectifying the minor difficulties that had arisen as the aircraft was tested and evaluated. Even though there were problems, there were no fundamental flaws in the basic design and it was agreed by everyone that the Vulcan showed great potential. After having been officially released for service on 31 May 1956, the first Vulcan delivery to the RAF was made on 20 July 1956, when XA897, the ninth production aircraft, flew to RAF Waddington, joining the newly formed 230 Operational Conversion Unit (OCU). The delivery obviously marked an important step in the bomber programme, but was, in effect, merely a symbolic gesture and XA897 soon returned to Woodford to undergo a series

of minor modifications in preparation for a long-range 'goodwill' flight to New Zealand.

Even at the very beginning of the Vulcan's service life, the RAF was keen to demonstrate to the world (and the USSR in particular) that Britain now had a truly effective strategic bomber with a very clear global reach. The second Vulcan to arrive at Waddington was XA895, which was delivered to 230 OCU on 16 August as a follow-on to the first aircraft, but again its time at Waddington was only brief. It soon departed for the A&AEE and spent a significant amount of time based at Boscombe Down, assigned to Operational Reliability Trials. Vulcan XA897's flight to New Zealand was primarily a diplomatic flag-waving exercise, intended to showcase the Vulcan's abilities, although in more practical terms the deployment also presented an opportunity to test the aircraft's long-range operational capabilities for the first time. The bomber's captain was Squadron Leader Donald Howard, with a very distinguished VIP taking the co-pilot's seat in the shape of the commander-in-chief of Bomber Command, Air Marshal Sir Harry Broadhurst. The rear crew comprised Squadron Leaders Albert Gamble, Edward Eames, AFC and James Stroud, who was also

a qualified Vulcan pilot and therefore able to take turns on the flight deck with Broadhurst, sharing the tiring and tedious task of getting the aircraft so far south. The crew was accompanied by Fredrick Bassett, a technical representative from Avro who was accommodated inside the Vulcan's cabin on what became the infamous 'shelf', at the foot of the flight-deck ladder.

Although the Vulcan had only just entered RAF service and was therefore prone to many teething problems, the outbound flight went remarkably smoothly, via Aden and Singapore and then on to Melbourne, with a flying time of forty-seven hours and twenty-six minutes, including stopovers. After visiting Sydney and Adelaide, the crew flew on to Christchurch on 18 September to complete an immensely satisfactory exercise for Bomber Command, and a relatively enjoyable (but tiring) journey for the crew. The Vulcan inevitably caused a great deal of attention during its visit, and by the time of its scheduled departure, XA897 had become something of a media celebrity. For the long return trip, the aircraft was flown via Brisbane, Darwin, Singapore, Ceylon and Aden, departing the latter at 0250hrs on 1 October 1956 to begin a seven-hour

flight back to England. Rather than returning directly to Waddington, the Vulcan was to be the star exhibit at a VIP reception at London's Heathrow Airport, where representatives of the RAF, Ministry of Aviation (MoA) and Avro were waiting with the crew's families and the media. Typically, the weather conditions at Heathrow were poor and from inside the Queen's Building the airfield was barely visible, shrouded in dark cloud and heavy rain. Above the carpet of thick cloud XA897 approached the English Channel, and Howard called Bomber Command Operations at High Wycombe to receive the discouraging news that Heathrow's current weather status was 8/8ths cloud at 700ft, with 2/8ths cover at 300ft. The airfield was in rain and visibility was just over 3,000ft.

Although the VIP spectators were undoubtedly saddened by the prevailing conditions, there was no reason why XA897 still could not land at Heathrow, as normal airliner operations were continuing without difficulty. Howard did have the option of diverting to Waddington, where the weather was far better, but the decision was his, and in view of his extensive flying experience he saw no reason to divert. Broadhurst agreed, and rather than disappoint the waiting audience, they elected to proceed to London. The aircraft descended into the gloom and entered an instrument approach at 5nm from touchdown at 1,500ft. The spectators waiting on top of the Queen's Building ventured out into the rain, determined to brave the elements in order to see the Vulcan's arrival. The GCA talk-down began as normal, with glide path and centreline corrections being issued verbally from a radar controller until the aircraft was three-quarters of a mile from the runway, at which stage the ground controller instructed the captain that he was 80ft above the glide path. This was the last elevation advice received from the controller, and a just few seconds later the Vulcan's extended landing gear suddenly struck the ground. The first indication the assembled spectators had of the Vulcan's proximity was a sudden roar of engine noise as the Vulcan's four engines wound up to full power. XA897 then came into view, climbing steeply away from the runway with its landing gear still extended. Almost immediately the aircraft passed 800ft when the canopy was seen to jettison as both pilots ejected, leaving the Vulcan out of control, turning sharply to starboard before entering a 30-degree descent back to the runway. It ploughed into the ground with a sickening thud and instantly exploded. The four crew members still inside the aircraft had clearly been killed. The VIPs still waiting inside the Queen's Building were informed that the anticipated arrival had ended in disaster and that XA897 had been destroyed. When the crash rescue crews arrived on the scene they battled to extinguish the burning wreckage, which continued to burn for almost an hour.

Investigators quickly descended upon Heathrow and after only a cursory examination of the horrific scene it became clear that the aircraft's main wheels were missing. Even beyond the 300-yard scattering of wreckage, there was still no sign of the missing undercarriage, and Avro's chief aerodynamicist, Roy Ewans (who had been waiting for the Vulcan's arrival at Heathrow) drove along the runway towards the airport boundary, where still nothing more could be seen. He then drove out of the airport and began a careful search of the fields surrounding the runway approach. He eventually found two deep holes rapidly filling with rainwater. Ewans realised that the holes had been created by the Vulcan's main gear as it had briefly hit the ground, short of the runway by some 1,988ft (displaced to the north by 250ft). Ahead of the holes were two swathes of sprouts that had been flattened by XA897's exhaust gasses as the aircraft had climbed away. The main wheels were here, scattered across the field. Back in the 1950s only a very few aircraft were equipped with landing gear designed for landing on soft ground, and given the circumstances of the glancing blow which the Vulcan had made with the ground, it was not surprising that the wheels had broken free, but the loss of the Vulcan's lower leg assembly would not in itself have been too serious. However, the excessive backwards force created by hitting the ground had also caused the gear's drag struts to fail, allowing the legs to swing back on their main hinges to hit the lower surface of the wing, ahead of the trailing edge control surfaces. The gear assembly had penetrated the wing at a point where the aileron control rods were located, damaging them to such an extent that all lateral control of the aircraft was immediately lost. The brief contact with the ground had been sufficient to render the aircraft uncontrollable.

The following day an RAF Court of Inquiry was opened, headed by Air Chief Marshal Sir Donald Hardman. On 26 October the Minister of Transport and Civil Aviation requested that Dr A.G. Touch, Director of Electronics Research and Development at the Ministry of Supply, should conduct an independent investigation into the accident, looking particularly at the standards and procedures of the GCA facilities at Heathrow. The conclusions reached by Dr Touch's report were as follows:

The GCA equipment was correctly set up and calibrated. There is no evidence of malfunctioning or failure. The controller failed to warn the pilot of his closeness to the ground. During the last ten seconds of the approach the aircraft made a steep descent to the ground. The cause for this descent was probably due to the build-up of oscillations about the glide path. Poor talk-down by the controller contributed to things, but as the approach was subject to the overriding judgment of the pilot the controller was not to blame for events arising from the control. The critical phase was the first four seconds after the descent steepened, during which no height guidance was given to the pilot. It is very difficult

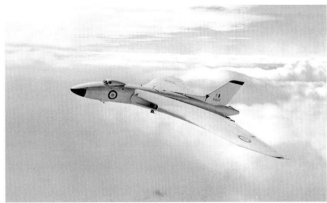

Far left: First production Vulcan B2 XH533 was the only B2 to carry serials under its wings. These were removed when the aircraft entered regular RAF service. (*Tim McLelland collection*)

Left: XH558 was the first Vulcan B2 delivered to the RAF. It was, of course, also the last Vulcan to be withdrawn from RAF service. Completed in white, it carried full-colour national insignia prior to being re-sprayed with disruptive camouflage. (*Rolls-Royce*)

to pass judgment on this matter, but in view of all the circumstances, I do not think the controller should be blamed. No warning was given during the final five or six seconds. It should have been, although it would have been too late. Although it cannot definitely be proved, the most likely theory is that the controller made an error of judgment, concentrating too much on azimuthal correctional and paying insufficient attention to the elevation error meter. Human errors are more likely to occur under stress or unusual circumstances. In my opinion, evidence exists to show that all the elements in the GCA 'servo-chain' were strained.

Dr Touch later explained that the term 'servo-chain' referred to the way in which the GCA information was acted upon by the pilot, in a kind of 'servo-loop' between the pilot and the ground controller. The post-accident technical investigation – part of the RAF Court of Inquiry – confirmed that the aircraft had not suffered any technical failures and was perfectly serviceable at the point of initial impact. The inquiry concluded that the Vulcan captain had made an error of judgement in selecting an unsuitable break-off height of 300ft and had been even more unwise to then go below that height, still out of visual contact with the ground. The ground controller had advised the captain that he was 80ft above the glide path just seven seconds

before hitting the ground, but no subsequent warning was given when the aircraft rapidly went below the glide path, indeed the talk-down continued after the Vulcan had first hit the ground, as if the approach was still continuing normally. Consequently, the RAF inquiry concluded that this failure to warn the pilot that he was below the glide path was the principal cause of the accident. This was a slightly different conclusion from that made by Dr Touch, but as it is RAF policy not to make Court of Inquiry evidence public, Dr Touch remained unaware of the RAF's view. At the inquest into the deaths of the rear crew members, another contributory cause became evident in the shape of altimeter error. In his summing up, the coroner, Dr H.G. Broadbridge, stated that there was nothing in the evidence to show criminal negligence on the part of anyone in the aircraft or on the ground and everyone seemed to be doing their duty as they thought appropriate at the time. Squadron Leader Howard said that before leaving Aden he had received a signal from Bomber Command saying that he was to land at Heathrow:

I was going to make an attempt to land, in view of the weather. If I could not, I was going to overshoot and go to Waddington, where it was promised that the weather would be very good. I decided to come down to 300ft on my altimeter, which represented to me a minimum approach altitude for London Airport of 150ft over the ground.

Howard continued, confirming that the talk-down from the ground controller proceeded as normal, and he acted on

A Vulcan B2 carrying a Blue Steel stand-off missile. The weapon was carried in a semi-recessed position over the aircraft's bomb bay. *(BAE)*

the verbal information as soon as he received it, but before the talk-down was completed he had inexplicably hit the ground. The last instruction he remembered hearing was that he was three-quarters of a mile from touchdown at 80ft above the glide path and he therefore increased the rate of descent. Continuing his account, Howard said:

> I asked the cc-pilot to look for the high-intensity lighting, which I was going to use for the landing. He told me he could see the lights over to starboard, and all this time I was looking at instruments and not looking out. I looked at the lights as he told me, and I did not recognise the pattern. They were not what l expected to see. Immediately I had looked I went back on instruments and he then told me I was very low and to pull up and so I did. At that precise time the aeroplane touched the ground and I decided to overshoot. This I tried to do, but as the aircraft accelerated it became obvious that I could

not control it any more. It wanted to roll over to the right. I used all the control I had but I could not stop it and I realised I could do no more. My altimeter was showing slightly below 300ft. I shouted to the crew to get out and when it was apparent that the aircraft was going to roll into the ground, I decided to eject.

Squadron Leader Howard was asked if the Vulcan's altimeter had been misleading him. He believed that it was, but he did not know how this could be accounted for. He stated that he held a Master Green instrument rating, the highest that an RAF pilot could have. Continuing, he said that his altimeter had a known error of 70ft, and he set 80ft as the height of London Airport above sea level. He agreed that if he had been on the glide path at three-quarters of a mile from touchdown, he should have been at about 260ft, and if the altimeter had been functioning correctly he would have aborted his attempt to land at that stage.

Air Marshal Sir Harry Broadhurst was also questioned by the coroner, and he commented that the talk-down was normal as far as he could recall: 'There was nothing in it to alarm you. It seemed perfectly safe.' After hitting the ground with a glancing blow, he was convinced that no damage had been done, and had even said 'if we turn slightly left we can still make it'. However, the captain had answered, 'No, I'm going to overshoot', but quickly added, 'I think we've had it'. Broadhurst tried the controls as Howard ejected, but failed to get any response, and so he also ejected. Returning to the altimeters, Broadhurst said that there was an error of between 50ft and 80ft between his and the captain's. The ground control tracker, Miss A.C. Maley, said that as she watched and advised on height and range, she could not recollect any rapid descent. When the Vulcan was about 2 miles from touchdown it appeared to drop roughly 100ft below the glide path, but she agreed that it must have recovered height, since later in the approach it was above the glide path again. Squadron Leader Howard was asked if it would be an abnormal rate of descent to drop 300ft in 500 yards. Howard said this would be 'fantastic, about 4,000ft per minute' and that he would certainly have known if they had been going down at that rate. Finally, as if to confirm the underlying cause of the accident, Wing Commander C.K. Saxelby from the A&AEE said that it had been discovered that the 70ft altimeter error could become as much as 130ft when close to the ground, added to which there was the 80ft for Heathrow's height above sea level to take into account. In addition, there could have been a further error of 70ft because of friction phenomena. Despite numerous investigations and a variety of theories, no single factor was ever identified as the principal cause of XA897's tragic accident. Clearly the crew members were not to blame, and as Dr Touch's report indicated, neither was the ground controller. The crash seemed to be the result of a culmination of errors. Sir Harry Broadhurst commented on the accident:

The whole thing is a puzzle to me. It seemed to me an absolutely normal glide approach until the ground appeared in the wrong place. If we had been coming down at an unprecedented rate we would have hit the ground, and the undercarriage would have been forced up into the wings. As it was, we touched so lightly we merely thought the aircraft had burst a tyre or something. We had no idea that the undercarriage had been ripped off. Until then the captain, obviously very experienced, imagined he was being talked down normally. The fact is they were still talking him down normally after he had gone up again. Obviously something went wrong. We cannot supply the missing links.

Although the rear crew lost their lives, it was something of a miracle that even the two pilots escaped. When XA897 returned to Woodford for modification, prior to embarking on the New Zealand trip, Avro had just designed a new system to interconnect the canopy release with the operation of the seat pull-down blinds that actuated the ejection sequence. Instead of requiring the pilot to make two separate actions – one to release the canopy, and the second to pull the seat handle – the single operation of either seat blind handle would now blow off the canopy and fire the seat in automatic sequence. Although the aircraft had been scheduled for delivery without this modification, the change was made prior to the overseas tour, and without it is questionable whether the pilots would have had time to eject safely. It is also interesting to note that despite the harrowing nature of his experience with the Vulcan, Sir Harry Broadhurst's confidence in the aircraft was undiminished and he later went on to become Managing Director of A.V. Roe, after retiring from the RAF.

The horrific accident was a major blow to both Avro and the RAF. The loss of a new and much-publicised aircraft, together with the loss of life, cast gloom over the Vulcan programme, even though there was no question of there having been any design of technical deficits within the aircraft. Ultimately, the crash seems to have been a result of a growing time lag between the radar picture, the ground controller's interpretation of it and the pilot's reaction to the controller's instruction. This mismatch grew until it resulted in a wildly varying approach path, which ultimately allowed the Vulcan to make contact with the ground. Of course, no such accident could have occurred in good weather and the only significant lesson to be learned from the accident was that events (particularly public and VIP receptions) sometimes create a desire to 'press-on' in a situation that might otherwise be aborted.

With the tragic story of XA897 eventually put to rest, safe in the knowledge that the Vulcan's design was sound, confidence in the bomber programme was restored and production continued. In January 1957, 230 OCU finally received two more Vulcans (XA895 and XA898), which were destined to remain at Waddington on a more permanent basis. Following a period of intensive flying trials, the task of training Vulcan crews began on 21 February. During March, April and May 1957, three more aircraft were delivered (XA900, XA901 and XA902) and it was on these machines that the personnel of the first OCU course qualified, graduating on 21 May 1957. Number 1 Course then re-formed as 'A' Flight of 83 Squadron, the first RAF Vulcan squadron, and following a short period in which the unit borrowed aircraft from the OCU as required, 83 Squadron's first aircraft – XA905 – was delivered from Woodford and handed over to the RAF on 11 July, the day on which the squadron was commissioned.

Although the OCU Vulcan B1s had been fitted with Olympus 101 engines, the five aircraft delivered to 83 Squadron were powered by 12,000lb thrust Olympus 102s – an interim standard until the Vulcan B1 fleet eventually standardised on 13,500lb Olympus 104 engines. The second OCU course also became a Flight within 83 Squadron and then the subsequent graduates transferred to Finningley, where 101 Squadron was formed on 15 October 1957. By the end of the year four Vulcan B1s had been delivered to Finningley and the last aircraft from the 1952 order (XA913) had finally been handed over to the RAF. At the start of the 1953, the first of a new batch of B1s was completed, as part of an order for thirty-seven aircraft placed in September 1954. Initial OCU and squadron flying proceeded surprisingly smoothly and no major problems were encountered during the Vulcan's introduction into RAF service. In fact, the Vulcan enjoyed one of the most trouble-free entries into RAF service that anyone could remember – an outstanding achievement for a large and complex strategic bomber. The Vulcan's strategic capabilities were exercised from the very start and these first aircraft were immediately operated far and wide across the globe, participating in exercises and goodwill tours which extended Bomber Command's reach to exotic locations such as the United States, New Zealand, Libya, Kenya, Rhodesia, Brazil and Argentina. Not only was the RAF acquiring the ability to deliver a devastating blow to any potential enemy, it was also demonstrating that it could deliver its power wherever it might be needed.

Bomber Command ordered two Vulcans (together with Comet support aircraft and crews) to be sent to the Strategic Air Command Bombing Competition at Pinecastle AFB, Florida, during October 1957, the RAF returning to the competition after an absence of several years. In company with a pair of Valiant bombers, the Vulcans and their crews made a considerable impression on their American counterparts (not least because their previous participation had been with Lincolns), but the Vulcan crews didn't enjoy any great success in the competition, being placed forty-fourth overall. The results were disappointing, but considering the fact that the Vulcan had only just entered service, it was probably something of an achievement just to have taken part. The RAF's relatively short experience of operating the Vulcan was undoubtedly a factor, as was the lack of suitable navigation and other equipment which the Vulcans didn't always have during the early days of the V-force. Air Officer Commander in Chief (AOCinC) Bomber Command Sir Harry Broadhurst said that, 'The results have rather hinged on the experience of the ground crews in maintaining the equipment rather than the aircrews using it', but other factors also conspired to create difficulties, such as the hot and humid conditions, which affected the Vulcan's electronic equipment, the operational heights used during the competition, which were lower than the altitudes at which the Vulcan crews had been training, and the lack of experience that even the air and ground crews had with their new aircraft. However, the competition was just part of a very long and enduring relationship between the RAF and USAF's Strategic Air Command (SAC), and marked the very beginnings of a degree of integration between America's and Britain's forces that had not been experienced since the Second World War and, as Sir Harry commented, it also demonstrated that Britain was 'back in the nuclear club'.

However, there were more setbacks. Most were of relative insignificance, but one particularly tragic accident marred the success of the Vulcan's early operational years, this being when 83 Squadron's XA908 was lost on 24 October 1958. The aircraft was flying on a Lone Ranger exercise

This page and overleaf:
XH535 was destroyed
after entering a flat
spin during a sortie
from Boscombe Down
on 11 May 1964. The
wreckage was strewn
across a field near
Andover in Hampshire.
(A&AEE)

from Goose Bay in Labrador to Lincoln AFB, Nebraska, when, at approximately 60 miles north-east of Detroit, its main power supply suddenly failed. Although the aircraft's four engines continued to feed the electrical generators, a short circuit in the main busbar blocked the power supply. This shouldn't have presented the crew with any major difficulty, since the aircraft had battery standby power for some twenty minutes of further flying, and the aircraft's captain requested an emergency descent to Kellogg Field in Michigan. However, the batteries supplied power for only three more minutes, after which the powered flying controls simply ceased to operate. The captain immediately requested directions to the nearest landing

field, but without any power the Vulcan's control surfaces were useless and the aircraft flew into the ground at a 60-degree angle, killing all but one of the crew. The co-pilot did manage to eject, but tragically landed by parachute in Lake St Clair, and as the only member of 83 Squadron who could not swim (and without a lifejacket) he drowned.

Following this distressing accident, the Vulcan B1 fleet was swiftly modified – the main busbar being divided in two – to prevent any such disaster happening again. However, this fleet-wide fix wasn't introduced quickly enough and history repeated itself when XA891 suffered an electrical failure on 24 July 1959. This Vulcan had yet to receive the electrical system modification and shortly after take-off from Woodford (where the aircraft was flying trials with Olympus 200 engines), the same lethal situation arose. This time, however, the batteries provided a greater reserve of power and the entire crew was able to parachute to safety, leaving the aircraft to crash on open land.

Despite these isolated and serious events, the Vulcan proved itself to be a very reliable aircraft, enjoying an excellent safety record that undoubtedly owed a great deal to Avro's passion for rugged design, reliability and simplicity. However, there was one particularly dark tragedy which inevitably cast doubt over the soundness of the Vulcan's design for some time. The prototype Avro 698 (VX770) remained active on test-flight duties and made an air show appearance at Syerston near Nottingham on 20 September 1958. In front of a crowd of astonished and horrified spectators the aircraft suddenly disintegrated and smashed into the runway, killing everyone on board. Investigation revealed that structural failure of the wing had been the cause of the accident, but a more detailed analysis confirmed that the aircraft had been flying outside its safe speed and g envelope. Its structure was clearly not at fault and the accident was attributed to the pilot's failure to keep the aircraft within the safety limits imposed upon it. In subsequent years there was much discussion over the possibility that the aircraft had in fact been overstressed during test flying prior to the Syerston display and that this may have been the root cause of its failure, but no conclusive proof was ever found to substantiate this theory, and it remained obvious to Avro that, whether the root cause was due to pilot error or damage which had not been identified and rectified, the accident did not indicate any previously undiscovered deficiency in the Vulcan's structural composition. However, the Syerston accident did emphasise that although the Vulcan was an astonishingly manoeuvrable machine, it was often all too easy to forget that it was also a very big and heavy four-engined bomber, which was just as susceptible to aerodynamic stresses as any other comparable machine.

The terrible loss of VX770 and its crew undoubtedly cast a shadow over the whole bomber project, but with no evidence to attribute the accident to the production-standard Vulcan, deliveries of the Vulcan B.Mk 1 continued. Nevertheless, even as the aircraft were slowly delivered to their squadrons, Avro and the RAF were already looking towards a second-generation Vulcan, based on the promise of even greater thrust output from Bristol's Olympus engine, which continued to benefit from development. By the first half of 1955, sufficient data was available to suggest that the Bristol B.01.6 engine would be capable of delivering 16,000lb thrust, with the prospect of even more powerful versions of the Olympus becoming available at a later stage. Analysis of the aircraft's structure indicated that with suitable modifications the Vulcan could accommodate these later engines within the existing wing framework, but that a Vulcan fitted with these more powerful engines would suffer from the high-speed and high-altitude buffet problems even with the Phase 2. Clearly this wing design would have to be revised again, and during September 1955 Avro submitted a brochure to the Ministry of Supply describing what would ultimately become the Vulcan B.Mk 2.

Avro had, in fact, been discussing the possibility of a Vulcan Mk 2 with the MoS for some time, and having gained a great deal of encouragement from the Ministry, funds had been made available within the company to initiate full-scale development of the new design. Although the revised wing layout was fundamental to the new variant, there were other external differences between the B1 and B2, and in many respects the Vulcan B2 was almost a completely different aircraft, both in terms of its overall design and the equipment with which it was fitted. The airframe was re-stressed to a gross weight of over 200,000lb, which was more than double the figure originally set by B.35/46. The landing gear was redesigned and strengthened to withstand much greater take-off and landing weights. The electrical system was changed to 200V AC and, instead of direct-drive 112V generators, each engine was given constant-speed drive and alternators. A gas turbine auxiliary power unit was installed, driven by a Rover 2S/150 engine and the flying controls were revised, the ailerons and elevators being replaced by inner and outer elevons (combined ailerons and elevators), each with independent power control units. The Vulcan B2's new Phase 2C wing extended the span by 12ft (to 111ft), while the thickness/chord ratio changed from 7.92 per cent to 4.25 and the wing area increased from 3,446 to 3,965sq ft. The compound taper of the leading edge was further increased (incorporating a significant concave 'droop') and the wing's trailing edge was also swept rearwards. It is important to note that the creation of the Vulcan B2 was not a simple linear continuation of the Vulcan's development process, and had political and military circumstances been any different, the B2 may well never have reached the production stage at all.

Governmental discussions on the projected size of the V-force (the Medium Bomber Force (MBF) that represented, in effect, a strategic capability) had been in existence since 1954 and the ultimate size of the force was continually the subject of much debate. It wasn't until 31 May 1956 that ministers agreed to proceed with the construction of more Vulcans and Victors, both types being of an improved 'second-generation' design. Initially, the plan was to order both types with Rolls-Royce Conway engines, since there was little enthusiasm for proceeding with Bristol's Olympus when the Conway was already proving successful and reliable. The MoS was invited to investigate whether the Olympus should be supported only as a civil programme, but Bristol – faced with the cancellation of the Olympus Mk 6 – offered to carry all further development costs and even offered to provide completed engines at the same price as Conways, if an order for 200 engines was placed. It was this act of desperation that ultimately saved the Olympus programme and resulted in further hugely successful developments that went on to power not only the Vulcan, but the still-born TSR.2 and eventually, the magnificent Concorde. Minister of Supply (Reginald Maudling) commented:

> There are at present 99 Vulcans on order and I am proceeding on the assumption that there is no suggestion that this number should be reduced. We have been re-examining the Vulcan programme and it now looks as if the Mk 2 version can be introduced at about the 45th aircraft. This means that 54 Vulcans should be the new and greatly improved Mk 2 version.

Despite this statement there was still a great deal of doubt as to precisely how many medium bombers could be comfortably afforded. Almost inevitably the Admiralty stepped in and stated that the force should not 'Cost so much inside the total resources set aside for defence as to make it impossible to finance the other forces essential to ensure the cohesion of Commonwealth, dependencies and alliances'. Today, the Royal Navy's Trident programme (which was developed years later) takes up a significant proportion of modern defence spending, and it is clear that the navy's attitude towards the Vulcan undoubtedly had little to do with sound military thinking and much more to do with inter-service rivalry. It was eventually decided that the MBF should comprise a front-line strength of 144 aircraft, of which some 104 aircraft would be Mk 2 Vulcans and Victors.

During March 1956, a production contract for one Vulcan B.Mk 2 prototype was placed and a further contract issued in June effectively converted the existing order for the final seventeen B1s into B2s, and added eight more machines to the total. Interestingly, these aircraft were covered by Specification B.129P Issue 2, which referred to this new batch of Vulcans as being a B(K).Mk 2 version, which suggests that the aircraft were to have had an inflight refuelling tanker capability. This option appears to have been dropped prior to the batch's completion, although design drawings for a Vulcan in tanker configuration certainly exist in Avro's archives. It was, of course, a quarter of a century later that the Vulcan was finally introduced into the tanker role, almost by chance.

The second B1 prototype (VX777) was selected for conversion as the B2 prototype, and on 31 August 1957 it made its first flight in the revised configuration, lacking some of the anticipated changes that would be incorporated into production B2s, but acting as an aerodynamic test vehicle for the larger and re-shaped wing. As the B2 development programme continued, Avro also received instructions to equip the Vulcan fleet with new electronic countermeasures (ECM) gear, reflecting the ever-increasing capabilities of Soviet forces. This required a fairly radical redesign of the rear fuselage in order to accommodate the bulky equipment, which couldn't realistically be placed elsewhere within the Vulcan's airframe. Until this stage in the V-force's existence there had been little need for an advanced ECM fit, thanks largely to the Soviet Air Force's notoriously rigid system of fighter control, which was well monitored by the West. Only a limited number of VHF channels were used

Vulcan B2 XL385 was destroyed on 6 April 1967 following an engine fire as the aircraft prepared to take off from RAF Scampton. (*Tim McLelland collection*)

XM576 veered off the runway after making a crash-landing at Scampton on 25 May 1965. It never flew again and was scrapped some months later. (*Tim McLelland collection*)

With VX777 back in the air following modifications, the new Phase 2C-winged Vulcan was displayed at the 1957 Farnborough show, where the aircraft's readily obvious external changes caused more interest, speculation and excitement. After the show the aircraft was put through a series of aerodynamic trials, while a further seven B1s were brought into the B2 development programme, ensuring that every aspect of the redesigned Vulcan could be properly explored prior to deliveries and entry into service. Early in 1958, XA891 was fitted with the first Olympus 200-series engines, each rated at 16,000lb. Meanwhile, XA890 was employed on avionics work and XA892 was assigned to weapons research. XA893 was fitted with the B2's electrical system, XA894 was allocated to development of the B2 and B1A ECM fit, while XA899 was also used for avionics research. Vulcan B1 XA903 was later employed as a Blue Steel missile trials aircraft, in support of the Vulcan and Victor Mk 2 programmes. Flight trials with the B2 prototype revealed a 25–30 per cent increase in range over the B1, effectively extending Bomber Command's projected target range by a corresponding amount. Certainly the predicted high-speed and high-altitude buffet problem had been avoided, and on 4 March 1959 the first production Vulcan B2 (XH533) reached an altitude of 61,500ft during a test flight. It had made its first flight on 19 August 1958, powered by 16,000lb Olympus 200s, but still fitted with the original, unmodified tailcone. It is interesting to note that the aircraft actually made its first flight long before production of Vulcan B1s had even been completed – the last B1 made its first flight during February 1959. Likewise, the second production B2 (XH534) took to the air ahead of the last B1 in January 1959, and this was the first aircraft to fly with production-standard Olympus 201s rated at 17,000lb, together with a full ECM fit (it should be noted, however, that the next three aircraft from the production line first flew with unmodified tailcones). As production of the Vulcan B2 got under way, the first seven aircraft (including the prototype) were all assigned to flight trials work, XH534 being dispatched to Boscombe Down where it was used to gain a CA Release, issued in May 1960.

Finally, on 1 July 1960, XH558 was ferried from Woodford to 230 OCU at Waddington, thereby becoming the first Vulcan B2 to enter RAF service. Ironically, XH558

to control Soviet fighters and the RAF possessed suitable jamming equipment, code-named 'Green Palm', which was deemed more than capable of blocking every frequency with a high-pitched wail. However, developments beyond 1960 suggested that something rather more sophisticated was now required, and a tail warning radar (code-named 'Red Steer') was created, to be fitted into the Vulcan, together with ECM equipment, including a flat-plate aerial installation (code-named 'Red Shrimp'), which was accommodated between the starboard jet pipes (and between both sets of jet pipes on some B2s).

Although the new ECM fit was intended primarily for the B2, a contract was also received to convert part of the existing B1 fleet to carry the same gear. Aircraft so equipped were redesignated Vulcan B.Mk 1A. Consideration was also given to the rather more ambitious concept of converting the B1 fleet to the full B2 standard, but as the cost of each aircraft conversion was estimated to be roughly two-thirds of the cost of a new-build B2, the idea was too expensive to contemplate seriously. However, some twenty Vulcan B1s from the 1954 contract were eventually converted to B1A standard, together with nine machines (those in the best condition) from the original 1952 contract.

also eventually earned the distinction of becoming the last Vulcan B2 to leave RAF service, thanks to a combination of circumstance and good luck. It was of course the very last Vulcan to continue flying, more than half a century later. Vulcan B2 XH559 was delivered during August, with XH560, XH561 and XH562 arriving at Waddington before the end of the year. XH557 was loaned to Bristol Siddeley for further engine trials and it was eventually fitted with what was to be the ultimate Vulcan powerplant, the Olympus 301, rated at 20,000lb thrust. Two engines of this standard were fitted, one in each of the port nacelles, flying for the first time in this configuration on 19 May 1961. Although these immensely powerful engines required a greatly increased amount of intake airflow compared to the early Vulcan B1 powerplant, the first production Vulcan B2s retained the same air intakes as the B1, but on later aircraft the lower lip of the intake was deepened (starting with XH557) and all subsequent B2s were manufactured accordingly to accommodate the increased airflow mass. XH557 was later fitted with a standard complement of four Olympus 301s before entering RAF service, and approximately half the Vulcan B2 fleet was completed or retrofitted to this standard, while the remainder continued to operate with 17,000lb Olympus 201s. The Vulcans fitted with the more powerful engines were sometimes informally referred to as the 'B2A' variant, although there is no evidence to suggest that this designation was ever officially applied, either by Avro or the RAF, and this dubious designation appears to have been no more than convenient slang that has gradually drifted into widespread use.

Although continued Vulcan production naturally enabled the RAF to form more squadrons, official policy dictated that the B2s should first be delivered to an established unit, which would then transfer its B1s to newly converted squadrons. Consequently, the crews of 'B' Flight of 230 OCU went on to 83 Squadron at Scampton, where transition to the Vulcan B2 began in November 1960. On 1 April 1961, 27 Squadron formed at Scampton on the B2 and the Scampton Wing was completed in September 1961, when 617 Squadron (the legendary 'Dambusters') started conversion from B1s on to B2s. Waddington standardised on the B1A variant, with 44 Squadron forming on 10 August 1960 using aircraft that had previously been operated by

Vulcan B2 XM654 was damaged in a landing accident during the 1970s, although a precise date for this incident has not been established. *(BAE)*

83 Squadron (the first B1A being delivered to 44 Squadron in January 1961). Number 101 Squadron relocated from Finningley during June and 50 Squadron formed on 1 August (using former 617 Squadron aircraft). The Vulcan OCU then relocated to Finningley, where it was divided into 'A' Flight with Vulcan B1 and B1As, and 'B' Flight with Vulcan B2s. Finningley also provided a home for the Bomber Command Development Unit, which operated a mixed fleet of Vulcans, Valiants and (occasionally) Victors for various trials work.

The second Vulcan B2 Wing was then established at Coningsby, where 9 Squadron formed on 1 March 1962, followed by 12 Squadron on 1 July and 35 Squadron on 1 December. The wing moved to Cottesmore in November 1964 and the last production Vulcan B2 (XM657 – the final Vulcan to be manufactured) was delivered there on 15 January 1965, when it joined 35 Squadron. Following the initial order for twenty-five B2s, a further contract had been issued for an additional twenty-four aircraft, followed by a final order for another forty machines. The final Vulcan B1A conversion was XH503, delivered to Waddington in March 1963, after which the remaining B1s were either withdrawn from use or transferred to the OCU and the Bomber Command Development Unit. From 1966 the Waddington Wing also began converting to Vulcan B2s, completing the transition at the end of 1967. At this stage the OCU then relinquished its remaining B1s and the RAF standardised on the Vulcan B2 from 1968 onwards, with just a handful of Mk 1 Vulcans remaining active on test duties, the very last machine being XA903, which continued flying on engine development work with Rolls-Royce until 1 March 1979, when it was grounded (and subsequently cut up) at Farnborough.

Vulcan B2s during an exercise deployment to RAF Finningley. The ORP at Finningley was unique in that it fed on to the runway from the right-hand side. *(BAE)*

7

ATLANTIC ALLIANCES

The varying degrees of American reluctance to share nuclear secrets with Britain had largely been due to pressure from some US politicians, who naively believed that America should endeavour to remain a nuclear monopoly, even though it quickly became clear that nuclear know-how was already in the hands of the Soviets. Some also believed that Britain simply could not be trusted to share nuclear knowledge, because of continual spy revelations and even because Britain could be invaded by the Soviets at some stage. None of these concerns bear close scrutiny, however, and it seems inevitable that America's isolationist stance was largely based on commercial interest rather than security. Despite the fact that many American officials, including a succession of presidents, firmly believed in the special relationship, it was not until the RAF received its first atomic weapons (and demonstrated that Britain would therefore be a nuclear power either with or without American co-operation) that the transatlantic friendship flourished once more. The very fact that Britain had successfully created its own atomic weaponry was sufficient to wipe away all further doubts at a stroke. It is also fair to say that beyond the corridors of political power, the strong working relationship between the RAF's Bomber Command and the USAF's Strategic Air Command had survived the political ups and downs of the early post-war years and, as the climate slowly improved, the possibility of co-ordinating nuclear strike plans became a reality. Moves towards co-operation in this field were first made by the British, and in September 1955 the CAS visited the USA with a briefing paper, which set out Britain's key objectives. It began by stating: 'The primary aim of the defence policy of the United Kingdom is to prevent war', and went on:

The main instrument for achieving this aim lies in the nuclear capability together with the means of delivery, which is possessed by the United Kingdom and the United States alone. We should achieve a closer association with the United States worldwide in the field of defence strategy This is particularly important in strategic air operations, where Bomber Command and the Strategic Air Command will be attacking components of the same vast target complex. It follows that unless there is a full exchange of information and a co-ordinated plan of attack, wasteful overlapping and dangerous omissions will result.

Many attempts were made by the chiefs of staff to persuade their American counterparts to embrace the concept of joint planning, but it wasn't until the RAF's V-bomber force was demonstrably in place that the SAC finally accepted that this was an inevitable and logical proposition. Formalised agreement was achieved in August 1956 and a team of senior USAF officers was sent to London to discuss the co-ordination of strike plans with Bomber Command. Additionally, in a remarkable volte-face, the USAF's once lukewarm attitude had now shifted towards wholehearted support, and agreement was made to supply the RAF with American atomic weapons as a stop-gap measure until sufficient British-made bombs could be completed to render Britain's deterrent posture fully effective. With the poisonous McMahon Act still in force, the US could not simply hand weapons to Britain, however, so the American bombs would be kept in USAF custody on RAF bases, from where they would be released to the RAF in a wartime emergency.

Trials with an ejection seat system for the rear crews in all three bomber types were conducted by Martin-Baker. The Air Staff concluded that the system was too complicated and expensive for introduction into a fleet of aircraft that was expected to be in use for little more than a decade. *(BAE)*

The detailed agreements made in London included references to the general concept of Allied atomic air operations, stating that, in a general war, atomic weapons would be used right from the outset. There was no question (at this stage) of a graduated response to Soviet aggression. It was established that if an atomic war began, it would probably begin with an initial phase characterised by an intensive exchange of atomic blows, followed by a subsequent exchange of 'indeterminate duration' at a 'reduced atomic intensity'. The *Brief Plan of Action* stated that the Allied counter air offensive would begin with heavy co-ordinated attacks against airfields, logistic facilities, control centres and command headquarters, creating a contraction of forces that would concentrate the surviving enemy aircraft on remaining airfields, enabling SAC and Bomber Command to exploit the vulnerability of such concentrations.

In January 1956, the British defence minister, Duncan Sandys, wrote to Charles Wilson, his American counterpart, with a detailed set of proposals. The reply from Wilson was positive, and agreed that arrangements should be made to furnish the Royal Air Force with United States atomic bombs in the event of general war, and to co-ordinate the atomic strike plans of the United States Air Force with the Royal Air Force so that the two forces could effectively operate as one decisive power. However, Wilson also added that 'the provisions of United States legislation must govern and that the United States cannot engage in a commitment to transfer custody of such weapons to the Royal Air Force other than by Presidential decision in strict accordance with his constitutional and legislative authority'. The supply of American atomic bombs (Project E) was discussed in detail by President Eisenhower and Prime Minister Macmillan when they met at the Bermuda Conference in March 1957. The 1956 Suez Crisis had been a turning point for Anglo-American relations, and the Bermuda meeting marked a significant improvement in mutual confidence between the two countries. After the conference, Eisenhower outlined his views, stating that:

The United States Government welcome the agreement to co-ordinate the strike plans of the United States and United Kingdom bomber forces, and to store United States nuclear weapons on RAF airfields under United States custody for release subject to decision by the President in an emergency. We understand that for the present at least these weapons will be in the kiloton range. The United Kingdom forces could obviously play a much more effective part in joint strikes if the United States weapons made available to them in emergency were in the megaton range, and it is suggested that this possibility might be examined at the appropriate time.

America's decision to co-operate with Britain, and even supply the UK with weapons, was a well-kept secret at the time, as the president indicated, by writing in his communication to Macmillan:

With respect to the item 'Nuclear bomb release gear for RAF bombers' I agree of course that you shall probably have to make some statement in order to prevent speculation in the press that might prove not only inaccurate, but damaging. However, as I explained to you verbally, the United States would prefer not to be a party to a public statement which might give rise to demands upon us by other governments where we should not be in a position to meet the requests. Consequently, I suggest the possible adequacy of a unilateral statement by yourself or by the British Defence Minister to the effect that Canberras are now being equipped to carry atomic bombs.

In fact, Project E covered the supply of atomic bombs not only to the RAF's Canberra tactical bomber force, but also to the V-force itself. An Air Ministry meeting in August 1956 reported that the US government had not given any indication of the numbers of weapons to be supplied, nor was it likely to, but it was believed to be almost certain that the numbers would exceed any delivery capacity that the UK was ever capable of developing. Records do not indicate when the first E weapons actually arrived in the UK, but US transport flights began towards the end of 1958 and both Honington and Waddington received the first suitably modified bombers in October that year. Approval was given for modifications to be made to seventy-two aircraft at Honington, Waddington and Marham, to carry American Mk 5 (6,000lb) bombs (and subsequently the Mk 7, Mk 15/39 and Mk 28).

This page and following three pages: Vulcan B1 XA894 did not enter service with the RAF. Initially assigned to engine trials with the A&AEE, it was subsequently transferred to Bristol Siddeley Engines at Patchway as a test-bed aircraft for the Olympus 22R engine being developed for TSR.2. Fitted with test pod under the bomb bay, the aircraft performed numerous test flights (and made an appearance at the SBAC show) before being destroyed on 3 December 1962, when the Olympus engine disintegrated during a ground run on the airfield at Filton. *(Rolls-Royce)*

Numbers 90 and 57 Squadrons at Honington, equipped with Valiants and Victors, respectively, were the first units assigned to Project E, during the spring of 1959, followed by 148, 207 and 214 Squadrons (with Valiants) at Marham and 83 Squadron (operating Vulcan B1s) at Waddington. In 1960, 7 Squadron (flying Valiants) and 55 Squadron (with Victors) at Honington, together with 44 Squadron (operating Vulcan B1s) at Waddington, also joined Project E and, finally, 101 and 50 Squadrons (both flying Vulcan B1s) at Waddington were assigned in 1961. The supply of American bombs enabled Bomber Command to equip the V-force with significant numbers of atomic weapons at an earlier date than would ever have been possible with British weapons. Had the US weapons not been supplied, there would have been an absurd situation in which the RAF possessed more bombers than bombs for quite some time.

However, Project E was a less-than-perfect solution to Britain's early problems, chiefly because of American restrictions on the deployment of the weapons. The E weapons could not be distributed throughout Bomber Command, nor could they be dispersed to remote sites from which clutches of V-bombers would operate during wartime, in order to evade enemy attack. Project E was essentially a political gesture, which served to convince the USSR that Britain's growing fleet of strategic bombers were not merely a bluff. Consequently, Project E was relatively short-lived, and the decision to begin a phase-out was taken on 7 July 1960. America was reluctant to disclose how many nuclear bombs were ultimately stored at RAF bases and it was equally ambiguous when revealing the nominal yield of each weapon. Eventually it was established that the bombs were largely of a type that would deliver only half the yield they had previously been thought to possess, which meant that once British equivalents were available, the greater flexibility they afforded (not least in being 'dispersible') would also be married to a much greater destructive capability. Valiants assigned to Supreme Allied Commander Europe (SACEUR) and RAF Germany's Canberras would continue to carry E weapons for some time, but in a matter of months the Vulcan squadrons no longer had any association with American weaponry.

Nevertheless, co-operation between SAC and Bomber Command had become increasingly intimate, as the CAS' comments relating to a November 1957 meeting indicate:

Examination of the separate Bomber Command and SAC plans has shown that every Bomber Command target was, understandably, also on SAC's list for attack and that both commands had doubled up strikes on their selected targets to ensure success. A fully integrated plan has now been produced, taking into account Bomber Command's ability to be on target in the first wave several hours in advance of the main SAC forces from bases in the US. Under the combined plan, the total strategic air forces disposed by the Allies are sufficient to cover all Soviet targets, including airfields and air defence. Bomber Command's contribution has been given as 92 aircraft by October 1958, increasing to 108 aircraft by June 1959. 106 targets have been allocated to Bomber Command as follows: a) 69 cities which are centres of government or of other military significance. b) 17 long-range air force airfields which constitute part of the nuclear threat. c) 20 elements of the Soviet air defence system.

The USAF's Strategic Air Command had a total of 380 B-52s and a staggering 1,367 B-47s by the end of 1958, but it would be wrong to assume that Bomber Command's contribution to the Allied counter air offensive plans was insignificant. Even though the RAF had a much smaller fleet of bombers at its disposal, the V-bombers possessed superior speed and altitude performance, and the RAF's training and technical expertise was at least as good as SAC's, if not markedly better. However, the key advantage that the RAF could always claim was one of geographic position; Britain was far closer to Moscow than the United States and a strike against the USSR would inevitably be spearheaded by the RAF's bombers, simply because they were already much closer to their planned targets. Just as significant was the fact that although RAF forces were obviously more vulnerable to air attack, Bomber Command had introduced a dispersal plan that would enable the V-force to deploy in groups of two or four aircraft to a total of thirty-six airfields scattered around the UK, from where the combined force would be capable of getting airborne in less than ten minutes. The performance of the V-bombers, together with Britain's geographical location, meant that Bomber Command's aircraft would be certain to reach their targets long before SAC's aircraft could cruise over the Atlantic or Arctic Circle, so even with fewer aircraft at its disposal, the V-force was quite literally at the forefront of the West's nuclear strike capability.

After the political embarrassment of the Suez Crisis, which had highlighted Britain's impotence in the face of American economic and political pressure, Macmillan was eager to restore the special relationship. Fortunately Eisenhower shared the same sentiments, as highlighted in a letter to Churchill, in which he wrote: 'I shall never be happy until our old-time closeness has been restored.' The 1957 Bermuda Conference had represented a historical turning point in Anglo-American relations where, as described, the US agreed to joint strike plans and the supply of nuclear weapons. Also, as first mentioned in July 1956, the supply of the Thor intermediate-range ballistic missile (IRBM) system to the UK was proposed, these nuclear-armed weapons being all-American but jointly operated by RAF personnel and located on RAF bases. Thor would ease American worries of a growing 'missile gap' between the USA and the Soviet Union, by placing missiles within striking distance of key Soviet targets, and at the same time it would 'give Britain a megaton rocket deterrent at least five years before we could provide it ourselves', as Macmillan later commented. He also added that the:

United States would provide weapons and specialised equipment, including anything costing dollars. Nuclear warheads would be held under the same conditions as nuclear bombs for British bombers. We would undertake site works and would provide general supporting equipment. United States estimate of the cost to us for the four sites [eventually there were, in fact, five sites] is £10 million, apart from the costs of personnel and their training and housing.

By this stage the UK government had already considered the possibility of manufacturing its own ballistic missile,

based on Air Staff Requirement OR.1139 of 8 August 1955. The Blue Streak missile was to be housed in a series of underground silos (a British concept that was ultimately adopted in other countries) scattered around the UK, whereas Thor would be a surface-housed weapon, stored horizontally in shelters before being erected for fuelling and launch. It was considered that Thor might provide useful experience in advance of Blue Streak, which was expected to enter service in 1964, whereas Thor would be operational by 1958. In January of that year agreements were made for the establishment of SM-75 Thors in the UK, with the first missiles arriving by July. Each squadron would be deployed on five sites, and each site would house three missiles. A White Paper issued on 25 February 1958 stated that the missiles would be 'manned and operated by United Kingdom personnel' and that any decision to launch the Thors would be a joint one between the two governments, that the 1-megaton warheads would remain in full United States custody, and that the Thor agreement would remain in force for not less than five years.

The first missile was delivered to 77 Squadron at Feltwell on 19 September 1958 and the first live firing by an RAF crew took place at Vandenberg AFB on 18 April 1959. Deployment was complete by March 1960 and a total of sixty Thors was ultimately deployed to the UK, all arriving on transport aircraft from the USA. Although Thor could be accommodated easily inside Military Airlift Command's huge Douglas C-124 Globemaster and Cargomaster aircraft, the task of delivering the missiles, and transporting some back to the USA for RAF live firings at Vandenberg, was far from simple. The transport aircraft had to operate within strict rate of ascent and descent figures to avoid pressure damage to the Thor's fuel tanks. Even more exacting was the need to transport the hugely expensive guidance unit gyroscopes, which were suspended in a lubricant that had to be maintained at a constant temperature. Control of the temperature required direct power from the transport aircraft's engines, so the crews had to keep the outboard engines throttled up to high power, even while taxiing, brake power being applied against the thrust. Once the missile was installed, however, it was regarded as being a very effective and reliable weapon. Its downfall was the fact that it was not mobile and could not be housed underground,

Vulcan B1 XA903 at Patchway, with an Olympus 593 engine that was tested on the aircraft as part of the Concorde programme. (Rolls-Royce)

rendering the entire Thor force vulnerable to a Soviet attack. Much consideration was given to the possibility of extending Thor's service life beyond the planned everyday period, but like Britain's Blue Streak it was accepted that a fixed IRBM system could not remain viable as a credible nuclear deterrent. The last RAF Thor complex to close was at North Luffenham, and on 23 August 1963 the component squadrons (Nos 144, 130, 218, 223 and 254) disbanded, marking the end of Bomber Command's brief IRBM era. CAS commented:

When Thor came into service we knew that we would be faced with many new and complex technical and administrative problems and we fully expected that one of the greatest of these problems would be the task of maintaining the morale of the officers and men allocated to the missile sites. In the event, the problems were met and solved with a degree of enthusiasm, skill and resourcefulness, which was in the finest traditions of Bomber Command and the Royal Air Force. The high morale, which was a feature of the Force from its inception, has never flagged, and Thor's fine record of serviceability and state of readiness over the years is a remarkable tribute to the loyalty and sense of duty of all the personnel who played a part. They will be able to look back with pride on a most valuable contribution to our deterrent force.

The Thor era ended in 1963, but the Blue Streak programme had closed in 1960, a Commons statement in April 1960 stating:

The Government have been considering the future of the project for developing the long-range ballistic missile Blue Streak and have been in touch with the Australian Government about it, in view of their interest in the joint project and the operation of the Woomera range. The technique of controlling ballistic missiles has rapidly advanced. The vulnerability of missiles launched from static sites, and the practicability of launching missiles of considerable range from mobile platforms, has now been established. In the light of our military advice to this effect, and of the importance of reinforcing the effectiveness of the deterrent, we have concluded and the Australian Government have fully accepted that we ought not to continue to develop, as a military weapon, a missile that can be launched only from a fixed site. Today, our strategic nuclear force is an effective and significant contribution to the deterrent power of the free world. The Government does not intend to give up this independent contribution and, therefore, some other vehicle will in due course be needed in place of Blue Streak to carry British-manufactured warheads. The need for this is not immediately urgent, since the effectiveness of the V-bomber force as the vehicle for these warheads will remain unimpaired for several years to come, nor is it possible at the moment to say with

XA903 pictured over the Bristol Channel while testing the Olympus 593 engine. The engine's test pod is attached under the aircraft's bomb bay and under the nose is a water-spray test rig. (Rolls-Royce)

certainty which of several possibilities or combinations of them would be technically the most suitable. On present information, there appears to be much to be said for prolonging the effectiveness of the V-bombers by buying supplies of the airborne ballistic missile Skybolt, which is being developed in the United States. Her Majesty's Government understands that the United States Government will be favourably disposed to the purchase by the United Kingdom at the appropriate time of supplies of this vehicle. The Government will now consider with the firms and other interests concerned as a matter of urgency, whether the Blue Streak programme could be adapted for the development of a launcher for space satellites.

Eventually, the Blue Streak design did indeed become part of the European Space Agency's rocket design process, but as a military weapon the fixed-site IRBM concept was obsolete. Britain was already looking towards American developments, most notably the aforementioned Skybolt and the sea-launched Polaris missiles, as possible future means of ensuring that Britain could successfully deliver its atomic warheads to their targets.

With the development of atomic weapons under way and a fleet of bomber aircraft being produced with which to

A rare image of a Vulcan B2 wearing the markings of 83 Squadron, on Finningley's ORP. XL426 is now preserved at Southend Airport. *(Tim McLelland collection)*

deliver them, the next step was to mate the atomic bomb with its carrier aircraft. The first ballistic trials of various bomb casings were undertaken using an Avro Lincoln (later casings were dropped from the Sperrin, after that type was separated from the bomber programme). The Lincoln was an appropriate choice, not only because the aircraft was readily available (and the only type suitable for the job), but also because it would have had to be modified to carry operational atomic bombs if the V-bomber programme had foundered. This would have been a far cry from the ambitions of the Air Staff, but if all else had failed it would have been the only alternative.

During 1948, Lord Tedder had suggested to the chiefs of staff that the RAF should begin training for the handling and storage of nuclear weapons, and a committee was subsequently established to explore the matter. It was known as the Herod Committee, an acronym of High Explosives Research Operational Distribution, and its first meeting took place on 22 November. The committee made a number of key decisions on operational activities, including the planning for the acceptance of nuclear weapons at Wittering and Marham. It also agreed that the first in-service bombs should be designed for inflight fusing, enabling the tube containing the fissile components and corresponding outer layers of the bomb to be inserted after take-off, as a safety measure. In November 1951, the Herod Committee decided that the RAF Atomic Weapons School should be located at the first RAF station where nuclear weapons would be stored (Wittering) and it was agreed that the Armament Training School should also be based there, after having first considered Honington, which was originally scheduled to be the first Valiant station.

Vintage RAF promotional photograph showing a Vulcan B1 crew dashing to their aircraft for a demonstration scramble. Waddington's rather agricultural perimeter fence contrasts with the security fencing that now surrounds the same area (now the base's E-3D apron). *(Tim McLelland collection)*

The Tornado's RB.199 engine pictured during a reheat test, slung under Vulcan XA903. *(Rolls-Royce)*

Beautiful 1965 image of XM600 painted in anti-flash white colours with 35 Squadron at Coningsby. This aircraft crashed just a few miles away at Spilsby in January 1977. *(Joe L'Estrange)*

Two fascinating images of Coningsby's operational readiness platform, taken during the 1960s. The white-painted Vulcans of 9 and 35 Squadrons are pictured just a couple of years later in the same position, painted in disruptive camouflaged, indicative of the switch to low-level operations. *(Joe L'Estrange)*

XM651 served with the Coningsby, Cottesmore and Waddington Wings, before being retired in September 1982. *(Godfrey Mangion)*

Perhaps the second most famous Vulcan of all, XM607 touches down at RAF Luqa after a flight from Waddington. Number 1 Group's panther emblem is visible on the nose, probably as a result of an overseas exercise detachment. *(Godfrey Mangion)*

A rare image of the markings applied to 9 Squadron's aircraft when they were camouflaged for low-level operations. The photographer's vantage point at the end of the runway at Luqa will be familiar to countless spectators on the island of Malta. *(Godfrey Mangion)*

XM653 roaring skywards as the undercarriage retracts. Based at Coningsby, Cottesmore and finally Waddington, the aircraft was retired to St Athan in September 1982 for scrapping. *(Godfrey Mangion)*

Under stormy skies at Luqa, XJ783 awaits another exercise sortie over the Mediterranean. It was operated by many Vulcan squadrons and the OCU at Finningley, as well as the Akrotiri Wing. *(Godfrey Mangion)*

XM603 basking in the sun at RAF Luqa. It eventually became the static trials aircraft for the K2 tanker programme and now awaits an uncertain future at Woodford, following the airfield's closure in September 2011. *(Godfrey Mangion)*

Number 617 was the only Vulcan unit to adopt this unusual colour-scheme variation. The black radome was repainted in camouflage colours, although the TFR remained in black. The scheme was quickly abandoned when low-visibility red/blue national insignia was applied to the whole Vulcan fleet and the white undersides were repainted light aircraft grey. (*Godfrey Mangion*)

Possibly the only surviving photograph showing a Vulcan dropping its full conventional load of twenty-one 1,000lb HE bombs. XM599 enjoyed a relatively uneventful service life, stationed at Coningsby and subsequently at Waddington. (*Tim McLelland collection*)

XJ784 wears a short-lived 'interim' scheme with low-visibility insignia, but still sporting white undersides and a black radome (mostly applied to Akrotiri's aircraft). It was assigned to the Akrotiri Wing when this picture was taken. *(Godfrey Mangion)*

XL446 pictured with the Akrotiri Wing, landing at RAF Luqa, Malta. It subsequently joined the Waddington Wing, before finally moving to Scampton. (*Godfrey Mangion*)

XJ782 serving with the Akrotiri Wing. It was retired in September 1982 for preservation. Sadly, its time at Finningley as a static display aircraft was short and it was scrapped just six years later. (*Godfrey Mangion*)

Unusually, XL391 sported what became the last of the Vulcan's 'standard' finishes, even before the fin-tip RWR set was fitted. It was subsequently equipped with the distinctive box-shaped fin-tip antennae and modified for Black Buck operations – but not used operationally. *(Godfrey Mangion)*

XH537 is shown carrying air-sampling pods. Unusually, some of 27 Squadron's aircraft wore soft-edged camouflage colours, as can be seen on this example on Malta. *(Godfrey Mangion)*

XM603 shortly after retirement at Woodford. There were hopes that this aircraft would be restored to flying condition, but after a great deal of work from dedicated volunteers (all former Avro people), it was abandoned, mostly because of BAE Woodford's lack of support for the project, a sad and rather ironic fate for one of Woodford's proudest creations. *(Paul Tomlin)*

Only ten Vulcans were repainted in overall dark grey and dark green camouflage, as part of the RAF's ongoing Red Flag deployments. XM575 is now preserved at the East Midlands Aeropark. *(Godfrey Mangion)*

Gear down and airbrakes out, XH537 approaches RAF Scampton's runway, proudly wearing the familiar Dumbo motif adopted by 27 Squadron. *(Terry Senior)*

Although Vulcans were once based at Coningsby, XH537 was not one of the station's aircraft – it spent most of its early life as a trials aircraft before joining the OCU at Finningley and, finally, 27 Squadron at Scampton. Seen here making a practice approach at Coningsby (the familiar shape of Tattershall Castle is in the background), the aircraft was a regular visitor to many bases in the UK and overseas. *(Terry Senior)*

XM652 was the first Vulcan repainted in overall wraparound camouflage. After retirement the aircraft was dismantled and transported to Sheffield for preservation, but after these plans failed, it was cut up as scrap. *(Terry Senior)*

XH558 just a few months before retirement from operational service, equipped as a K2 tanker with 50 Squadron, on approach to RAF Coningsby. (*Terry Senior*)

The last Vulcan built, XM657 was completed in January 1965. It ended its service life with 44 Squadron before being allocated to crash/rescue training at Manston in January 1982. It was eventually destroyed there – a sad end to the very last Vulcan. (*Tim McLelland collection*)

An unusual view of a very familiar aircraft and location. XH558 pictured on final approach to RAF Waddington, about to cross the A15 and photographed from an accompanying Jet Provost. (*Tim McLelland collection*)

XA903 carrying Concorde's Olympus 593 engine on a test flight over the Bristol Channel. *(Rolls-Royce)*

XM597 being towed into Goose Bay's hangar. The aircraft wears the 1960s-vintage markings of 9 Squadron and is finished in a very unusual dark grey (rather than the standard medium sea grey) and dark green camouflage finish, which appears to have been applied to only a handful of aircraft for a short period. *(AVM Ron Dick)*

An Akrotiri Wing Vulcan streaks over the perimeter fence at RAF Luqa during a cross-country flight over the Mediterranean. *(Godfrey Mangion)*

Down in the hills over Lake Windermere, XH558 performs for an appreciative public during 2011. (*Gareth Brown/lowflyingphotography.com*)

This page and following two pages: A peek inside the Vulcan, looking up through the entrance/escape hatch and across the flight deck, and a left and right view of the Vulcan's rear crew positions. (*Andy Tomlin*)

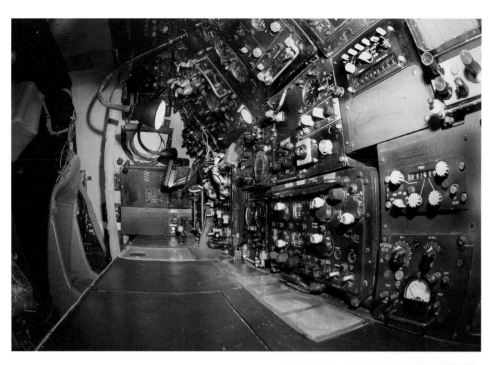

A rare movie clip still, showing XA903's unique water-spray system in operation, feeding a cascade of water over the Olympus 593's intake during engine trials from Filton. *(Rolls-Royce)*

XL391 was modified for Black Buck operations (hence the dark grey undersides), but was not selected for deployment to the South Atlantic. After retirement it was flown to Blackpool Airport for preservation, but was soon abandoned and after deteriorating over many years it was finally scrapped. *(Shaun Connor)*

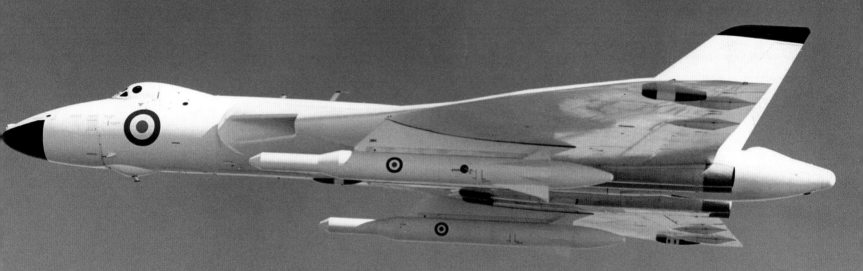

XH537 carrying two Skybolt rounds during flight trials in the 1960s. The aircraft also has camera fairings (painted black) under its wing tips to film missile releases. *(BAE)*

Above: Very rare image of Vulcans deployed to Yeovilton on a dispersal exercise. XL388 spent most of its operational career with the OCU, ending its service life with 101 Squadron at Waddington. *(AVM Ron Dick)*

A Vulcan from 9 Squadron visits RAF Luqa on the island of Malta, proudly wearing the unit's badge on its nose, together with anti-flash 'pastel' insignia. *(AVM Ron Dick)*

Inside the warmth of Goose Bay's hangar, an almost factory fresh Vulcan B2 shelters from the Canadian cold. This image clearly illustrates the B2's revised leading edge shape and the polished finish of the new-built aircraft, which didn't last for long. *(AVM Ron Dick)*

The venerable Hastings was a fundamental part of the Vulcan story. All rear crews were trained on the Hastings, initially at the BCBS (Bomber Command Bombing School), which became the SCBC when Strike Command absorbed Bomber Command, at Lindholme. The Hastings were later moved to Scampton, where they formed a Flight within 230 OCU. *(Tim McLelland collection)*

XM612, with 101 Squadron, climbs away from Waddington on a training sortie. This aircraft was retired in January 1983 and is now preserved with the Norwich Aviation Museum at Norwich Airport. *(Michael J. Freer)*

The switch to low-level operations resulted in a fleet-wide application of disruptive camouflage. This publicity photograph was arranged to demonstrate the new camouflage scheme on a pair of Vulcans from Finningley's OCU. *(Tim McLelland collection)*

Although many Vulcans were suitably decorated with 1 Group's panther emblem for overseas trips (particularly to the USA), this aircraft received reciprocal attention from its USAF hosts; a Strategic Air Command emblem is clearly visible upon its return to the UK. *(Michael J. Freer)*

Right: A sad end for XM651 at Waddington as the scrap merchants begin their work during November 1982. *(Joe L'Estrange)*

Below: A last chance photograph of XM651 awaiting the scrap merchant at Waddington. Unusually, the port wing control surfaces are fully deflected, illustrating the rarely seen actuating fairings. *(Joe L'Estrange)*

Below, right: Rare colour image of a Vulcan B2 crew door, carrying the badges of each component squadron of the Coningsby Wing. The Coningsby station badge is uppermost, with 9 Squadron to the left, 35 Squadron to the right and 12 Squadron in the centre. *(Joe L'Estrange)*

The initial operational V-bomber squadron, No. 138 (flying Valiants), would also be at Wittering and since it also housed the co-located Valiant Trials Flight, No. 1321, the station was at the very heart of the RAF's V-force build-up. The design of the first atomic bombs progressed well, although for some time it was still unclear if the bomb would be completed before the first Valiants, or vice versa. Dr Penney commented:

> My philosophy is that the RAF has handled aircraft for a long time and can fly Valiants as soon as they come off the production line. But the Royal Air Force has not yet handled atomic weapons. Therefore, we must get some bombs to the RAF at the earliest possible moment, so that the handling and servicing can be practised and fully worked out.

He also added that these first weapons would, in effect, be the same as later, further developed versions, but that they might require modifications to the In-Flight Insertion (IFI) cartridge and, if these first bombs had to be used, the cartridge might have to be loaded just before take-off, rather than in flight.

Planning was set in place for the storage of atomic weapons at Wittering, Marham, Honington and Waddington, and for a bomb depot to be completed at Barnham in Norfolk. The first of the completed atomic bombs were finally delivered to the RAF (the Bomber Command Armament School) on the nights of 7 and 14 November 1953, when a series of convoys arrived at Wittering. Trials with the Valiant were to begin during 1954, but the first aircraft could not be delivered to Wittering until the following year, and so it was not until 15 June that Valiant WP201 arrived. The MoS had formed 1321 Flight during 1954, specifically for the dropping trials, and the unit had completed some bomb delivery and handling training with Vickers at Wisley. It was decided that bombs would only be assigned to operational units so, following the initial drop trials, 1321 Flight became 'C' Flight of 138 Squadron in February 1956, changing to 49 Squadron on 1 May 1956.

The delivery of Valiant WP201 enabled the MoS flight trials to begin and the first ballistic store was dropped from 12,000ft at 330kt over the Orfordness range on 6 July 1954.

Vulcan B2 XJ824 pictured in service with 230 OCU at Finningley. The aircraft is now part of the Imperial War Museum collection at Duxford. (BAE)

Progress was satisfactory, but a setback occurred on 29 July when 138 Squadron's WP222 crashed shortly after taking off on a cross-country training flight. The Valiant entered a left-hand turn that continued through 300 degrees until the aircraft impacted at about 300kt just three minutes after take-off, killing the entire crew. Subsequent investigations revealed that a runaway actuator had fixed an aileron tab in the 'up' position, causing the uncontrollable roll. Fixing the potentially fatal flaw was simple, but the crash raised more concerns about the ability of air crew to abandon all three V-bomber types in emergencies. In fact, this controversial subject was never properly addressed for a variety of reasons. Most importantly it was accepted that the original concept of fitting each bomber with a jettisonable crew compartment would have created a design and engineering problem that would inevitably have delayed the aircraft's entry into service. Likewise, such a system would have been prohibitively expensive and as service experience on all three V-bombers began to grow, there was an understandable belief that the V-bombers were proving to be remarkably safe aircraft, which suggested that elaborate escape systems would be unnecessary. However, following the Heathrow tragedy, the whole question of V-bomber escape systems was inevitably raised once more and on the day after the accident the Air Minister asked the Air Staff to outline their policy on ejection seats. The DCAS (Deputy Chief of Air Staff) replied on 15 October, stating again that when the Valiant, Vulcan, and Victor were first conceived they were to have been fitted with jettisonable cabins that would separate from the aircraft and make a parachute-retarded descent:

As design and development proceeded it became clear that this facility could not be provided, and agreement not to have a jettisonable cabin was reached in the case of the Valiant in June 1948, the Vulcan in May 1949 and the Victor in October 1952. In all three bombers the layout of the cabin, which was operationally very satisfactory, made it impossible, for structural reasons, to produce ejection facilities for aircrew other than the pilots. It was, however, agreed to provide ejector seats for the pilots so that they could remain with the aircraft for longer and help other crewmembers to escape. Facilities for the other crewmembers were provided by means of side doors in the Valiant and Victor and through an underneath hatch in the Vulcan, which has virtually no fuselage. The result of this is that all three bombers and the developments of them will, according to present planning, have ejector seats for the pilots and escape by door or hatch for the three other crewmembers. A trained crew takes approximately 20 sec from the time the order to jump is given until the last man leaves the aircraft, but it is important to remember that it is unlikely that the three non-pilot crewmembers would escape in conditions where high 'g' forces are being applied through battle damage or loss of control, when the aircraft is at low level. On the other hand, when the first Valiant had a fire in the air, all live members got out of the aircraft successfully at high altitude – unfortunately the second pilot was killed by striking the fin. I have discussed a possible modification plan for the V-bombers with Mr James Martin (managing director and chief designer of the Martin-Baker ejection seat company) and with the Ministry of Supply, and am of the opinion that it is certainly not impossible to incorporate ejection facilities for the three non-pilot members of the crew of the V-bombers, but the implementation of such a policy would naturally raise very grave issues. The first issue is whether or not we would be right to go in for such a policy, and the second is whether we could afford to do so, both in terms of money and effort, as well as the delay of the V-force build-up. A retrospective modification programme would naturally be an immense undertaking, but it is not technically impossible, and if we do go in for it we must realise what may be involved. My own view is that we should not attempt to adopt such a policy.

In practice, it was always accepted that in most potentially catastrophic situations the rear crews would probably have sufficient time to abandon the aircraft simply by evacuating through the aircraft's escape hatch. This belief proved to be only partially correct and the notion of the pilot and co-pilot being afforded the luxury of ejection seats while the remaining crew had only parachutes was an issue that was never properly settled throughout the history of the V-force. It might have been addressed more thoroughly if the Air Staff had realised just how long two of the three V-bomber types would remain in RAF service. As it was, they were expected to be replaced by more advanced bombers (or other delivery systems) within a matter of years.

At Orfordness and Jurby, the Blue Danube bomb-dropping trials continued and it became evident that the Royal Aircraft Establishment (RAE) designers had produced a near-perfect ballistic casing for the atomic warhead and, in some respects, that the design was possibly too good – when the instrumented test specimens were released they often 'flew' beneath the Valiant's rear fuselage before falling clear (each test drop was tracked visually by theodolite). To counter this potentially dangerous tendency, the Valiant was re-equipped with strakes forward of the bomb bay, which created an airflow disturbance to push the bomb downwards, away from the fuselage. However, subsequent experience with the Vulcan and Victor confirmed a cleaner bomb release from both types. Equipped with six Valiant B1s, 49 Squadron was quickly assigned to Operation Buffalo, which would culminate in the first air drop of a live British nuclear weapon. Two Valiant B1s, WZ366 and WZ367, departed for Australia on 5 August 1956. Further training was to have been conducted from Wittering, but

This page and overleaf: XH557 was assigned to engine trials and was the first Vulcan to fly with the more powerful Olympus 301 engine. One engine was fitted in the inner starboard bay (as illustrated in the inflight image), before a second engine was fitted in the outer starboard bay. All four engines were eventually replaced by 301s. *(Rolls-Royce)*

poor weather and difficulty in obtaining sufficient weapons range access, among other reasons, meant that the crews could operate more effectively by using the Maralinga and Woomera ranges. The work-up towards Operation Buffalo did not proceed smoothly, however, as a report by Group Captain Menaul, commander of the Air Task Group, indicates:

The Valiants arrived at Edinburgh having completed part of a bombing training programme in the UK. It was planned to complete their training in Australia using the range facilities at Maralinga or Woomera as required. The main reason for the non-completion of training in the UK was the late delivery of aircraft and the lack of flight clearance for certain items of equipment, notably the bombing system, the automatic pilot and the radar altimeter. Unsuitable weather and difficulties in obtaining bombing ranges also added to the delays. During the training which followed, ten practice 10,000lb bombs and 60 x 100lb bombs were dropped in the UK by the two Valiant aircraft. The 10,000lb bombs were primarily to prove the weapon and aircraft systems and the 100-pounders to prove the accuracy of the aircraft's bombsight, particularly in the hands of inexperienced crews. On completion of this training programme in the UK, the results of which were not entirely satisfactory, it

was decided that the standard obtained, considering the time available, was adequate and the aircraft and crews were prepared to fly out to Australia. Technical defects discovered during the UK training phase were corrected, and modifications to the bombsight sighting head and the Green Satin radar output improved the system and gave considerably better bombing results at a later date. The whole of the training programme in the UK could have been considerably improved if more emphasis had been placed on overseas operations.

Valiant WZ366 took off from Maralinga airfield with the live nuclear weapon on board. The crew consisted of Sqn Ldr Flavell (captain), Group Capt Menaul, Flt Lts Ledger and Stacey, Flg Off Spencer and Pilot Off Ford. The aircraft climbed to 38,000ft in a wide arc, avoiding the range area until it reached the emergency holding area. The bombsight was levelled, contact was established with the air controller on the ground by VHF and HF and the aircraft then descended to 30,000ft ready to begin the fly-over sequences, using precisely the same drills and procedures as in the concrete and HE drops. At 14:25 the first fly-over, Type A, was successfully completed, with all equipment, both in the air and on the ground, working satisfactorily. Types B and C fly-overs were then completed in turn, and by 15:00 all was in readiness for the final Type D fly-over and the release of the nuclear weapon. The final D type fly-over was completed according to plan with all equipment functioning perfectly and the weapon was released at 15:27. Immediately after release a steep turn to starboard on to a heading of 240 degrees true was executed in order to position the aircraft correctly for the thermal measuring equipment to function. During this turn, 1.9g was applied. The weapon exploded correctly and the aircraft, after observing the formation of the mushroom cloud, set course for base, where it landed at 15:35. The operation had gone smoothly and exactly according to the plans drawn up during training. The bombing error was afterwards assessed at 100yd overshoot and 40ft right.

The explosive yield of the Blue Danube bomb had been fixed at 40kt, but for this drop the figure had been reduced to 3 kt in order to avoid the risks of extensive radioactive fallout, which would have been created if the bomb's barometric fusing had failed and the airburst had, in effect, become a ground burst. This was mentioned in a report sent to the Secretary of State for Air by Air Marshal Tuttle:

> The weapon, a Blue Danube round with modified fusing, in-flight loading and with the yield reduced to 3–4 kilotons, was dropped from the Valiant aircraft at 30,000ft. The weapon was set to burst at 500ft and telemetry confirmed that the burst occurred between 500 and 600ft. The bomb was aimed visually after a radar controlled run-up.

This first 'operational' air drop demonstrated to the world that Britain not only possessed nuclear know-how, but that the RAF now had a practical means of delivering nuclear weapons to their targets.

This first demonstration of how atomic weapons could be successfully delivered by the new V-bombers was another key moment in the creation of a national independent nuclear deterrent. However, by this stage the British government was already turning its attention to what was essentially a completely new means of creating destructive power and Britain was, essentially, a generation behind both the USA and the Soviet Union in terms of nuclear weapon development. The development of the thermonuclear (hydrogen) bomb represented yet another quantum leap in technology, which was almost as great as the initial development of atomic weaponry itself. Although the concept was essentially a development of atomic fission (and had been established as a theoretical possibility for almost as long as the atom bomb), the physics involved in the process are rather different.

In simple terms, hydrogen bombs use the energy of a fission bomb in order to compress and heat fusion fuel. In the most common 'Teller-Ulam' design (which accounts for all multi-megaton yield hydrogen bombs) this is accomplished by initially placing a fission bomb and fusion fuel (tritium, deuterium or lithium deuteride) in close proximity within a special, radiation-reflecting container. When the fission bomb is detonated, gamma and X-rays emitted at the speed

of light first compress the fusion fuel and then heat it to thermonuclear temperatures. The ensuing fusion reaction creates enormous numbers of high-speed neutrons, which can then induce fission in materials not normally prone to it, such as depleted uranium. Each of these components is known as a 'stage', with the fission bomb as the 'primary' and the fusion capsule as the 'secondary'. In large hydrogen bombs about half of the explosive yield comes from the final fissioning of depleted uranium. By chaining together numerous stages with increasing amounts of fusion fuel, thermonuclear weapons can be made to an almost arbitrary yield. Just six weeks after the first British atomic test at Monte Bello, the USA successfully detonated the first two thermonuclear (hydrogen bomb) devices at Eniwetok, the Soviets following with their own test on 12 August 1953. In 1954 British Prime Minister Anthony Eden said that the hydrogen bomb had 'fundamentally altered the entire problem of defence', and in February 1955 the government produced a paper that included the following:

> In the *Statement on Defence 1954*, HM Government set out their views on the effect of atomic weapons on UK policy and on the nature of war. Shortly afterwards the US Government released information on the experimental explosion at Eniwetok in November 1952, of a thermonuclear weapon many hundred times more powerful than the atomic bombs which were used at Nagasaki and Hiroshima in 1945. On 1 March 1954 an even more powerful thermonuclear weapon was exploded in the Marshall Islands. There are no technical or scientific limitations on the production of nuclear weapons still more devastating. The US Government have announced that they are proceeding with full-scale production of thermonuclear weapons. The Soviet Government are clearly following the same policy; though we cannot tell when they will have thermonuclear weapons available for operational use. The United Kingdom has the ability to produce such weapons. After fully considering all the implications of this step the Government have thought it their duty to proceed with their development and production. The power of these weapons is such that accuracy of aim assumes less importance; thus attacks can be delivered

by aircraft flying at great speed and at great heights. This greatly increases the difficulty of defence. Moreover, other means of delivery can be foreseen which will, in time, present even greater problems.

There is certainly no doubt that when the British scientists returned from the Manhattan Project, they possessed more than a little generalised knowledge of how a hydrogen bomb might be produced, and theoretical work on the hydrogen bomb appears to have begun in 1951. Nevertheless, early results were evidently disappointing; during 1952 Lord Cherwell, the prime minister's chief technical advisor, told Churchill that hydrogen weapons were 'beyond our means'. Despite this initial pessimism, Britain's thermonuclear weapon programme was remarkably successful. The initial decision to manufacture hydrogen bombs was made by a Cabinet Defence Committee on 16 June 1954 and was discussed by the full Cabinet during the following month. The final Cabinet decision was taken on 26 July, when approval was given to the proposal that 'the current programme for the manufacture of atomic weapons should be so adjusted as to allow for the production of thermonuclear bombs'. Churchill stated: 'We could not expect to maintain our influence as a world power unless we possessed the most up-to-date nuclear weapons.' Likewise, the Cabinet agreed that thermonuclear bombs would be more economical than their atomic equivalents, and that in moral terms the decision to manufacture these new weapons would be no worse than accepting what would amount to the indirect support and protection of America's hydrogen bombs. Towards the end of 1955 the Defence Research Policy Committee (DRPC) commented that: 'The earliest possible achievement of a megaton explosion is necessary to demonstrate our ability to make such weapons, as part of the strategic deterrent against war.' In fact, the main reason for the almost frantic development of hydrogen bombs was not directly due to any perceived deterrent policy or any immediate threat – it was simply a response to the growing pressure for an international ban on atmospheric nuclear tests which would effectively prohibit Britain from testing and eventually manufacturing a hydrogen bomb. Britain maintained what was perceived to be an even-handed diplomatic position by backing calls

for a test ban while maintaining an active developmental programme. Aubrey Jones, the minister responsible for the nuclear tests, said:

In the absence of international agreement on methods of regulating and limiting nuclear test explosions – and Her Majesty's Government will not cease to pursue every opportunity of seeking such an agreement – the tests which are to take place shortly in the Pacific are, in the opinion of the government, essential to the defence of the country and the prevention of global war.

Britain was effectively caught up in a race to develop and detonate a hydrogen bomb before being forced to accept a ban on nuclear testing. The DRPC said, 'It is essential that this first series should be planned in such a way as to safeguard the future by obtaining the greatest possible amount of scientific knowledge and weapon design experience as the foundation of our megaton weapon development programme.' The committee identified four basic requirements: a megaton warhead for a free-falling bomb; a similar megaton warhead for a powered, guided bomb (which eventually became the Blue Steel missile); a smaller and lighter warhead for a medium-range ballistic missile (which was to have become Blue Streak); and a multi-megaton warhead intended to demonstrate that Britain could match the devices which had been tested by America and the Soviets. As Britain's scientific knowledge of thermonuclear weaponry was at this stage restricted to theoretical analysis, the DRPC report stated that the most certain way of achieving a megaton explosion in 1957 would be to use a large, pure-fission assembly in a Mk 1 case, surrounded by sufficient fissile material to ensure a megaton yield (a so-called 'boosted' device). The bomb would consequently be big, heavy and extravagant in fissile material, but it would work, although it could only be developed into a free-fall bomb because of its size and weight. The government agreed to proceed with a series of test explosions, and on 5 June 1956 the Cabinet agreed that the prime minister should make a parliamentary statement about the tests. Two days later, Eden announced to the House of Commons that Britain was to conduct a limited number of test explosions, this time in the megaton range.

Vulcan B2 line-up during a press call. Just visible is the smaller B1-sized air intake fitted to XH554 (the third aircraft in the line), which was common to the first-production Vulcan B2s. The sixth aircraft is XH558, its early high-visibility insignia now replaced by anti-flash pastel colours. (Rolls-Royce)

Vulcan B2s at Scampton. The huge ECM fairing fitted to the Vulcan B1A and B2 housed a pack of large ECM 'dustbin' modules and required a large cooling vent, fitted to the port side, as can clearly be seen on XJ782. The upper fairing on the ECM cone housed the brake parachute. (Rolls-Royce)

8

MEGATON MIGHT

The crews of 49 Squadron at Wittering began training for Operation Grapple on 1 September 1956, using standard Valiant B1s until the first specially modified Grapple aircraft was delivered. Various modifications were made to the Grapple Valiants in order to equip them for their live-weapon trials. Most notably they were sprayed with an anti-flash white paint capable of withstanding 72 calories of heat energy per square centimetre. The control surfaces were strengthened to withstand the bomb's pressure wave, the flight deck and bomb-aiming positions were fitted with metal anti-flash screens and a number of sensors and cameras were installed.

Valiant XD818 departed for Christmas Island on 2 March 1957, via Aldergrove, Goose Bay, Namao, Travis and Honolulu, since it had not been fitted with underwing fuel tanks at this stage. It was followed by XD822, XD823, and XD824 at one-day intervals. Flown by 49 Squadron's CO, Wing Commander K.G. Hubbard, XD818 arrived over Christmas Island on 12 March, descending from a familiarisation circuit at 1,500ft to a rather more spectacular 50ft for a low-level fly-by over the airfield dispersal area before landing. After a settling-in period, the four Valiant crews began a series of training sorties, establishing a precise bomb-aiming capability and manoeuvres which would be used for each bomb drop. The training was completed by 5 April, despite the unexpected torrential rain which made life in Christmas Island's 'tent city' fairly grim for some time. Two aircraft, XD818 and XD823, were prepared for the first live drop, which was designed to test the 'Green Granite Small' warhead. This was a two-stage device weighing 4,200lb and was contained in a lead bismuth casing with a total weight of 10,000lb. It was a true thermonuclear fusion weapon, the spherical fission primary having a composite U235 and Pu239 core with a spherical secondary comprising U235 and a U238 tamper, all packed in lithium deuterate. Valiant XD818, flown by W/C Hubbard, was to be the drop aircraft for the first test, with XD824 acting as observer aircraft, flying a second crew to give them experience of flash and blast from a thermonuclear weapon. The historic two-hour twenty-minute sortie took place on 15 May 1957, as reported by Hubbard:

The aircraft became airborne at 09:00 V-time and all anti-flash screens were in position prior to the aircraft commencing its first run over the target. After one initial run to check telemetry, the Task Force Commander gave clearance for the live run. The bombing run was made at 45,000ft true, and as Green Satin drift was fluctuating badly, the set was put to Memory on average drift. The bombing run was steady on a course of 203 degrees and the weapon was released at 10:36 W-time. Immediately after release the aircraft was rolled into the escape manoeuvre, which averaged a turn of 60 degrees bank, excess g 1.8 to 1.9, airspeed Mach 0.76, rolling out on a heading of 073 degrees. The time taken for this turn was 38sec and at the time of air burst of the weapon, the slant range between aircraft and burst was 8.65n/ms. Neither crew nor aircraft felt any effect of flash, and the air blast reached the aircraft 2.5min after release; the effect of the blast was to produce a period of five seconds during which turbulence alike to slight clear air turbulence was experienced. Six minutes after release, all shutters in the aircraft were removed, and after one orbit to see the mushroom cloud effect, the aircraft returned to base and made a normal landing.

This description is typically business-like and fails to emphasise the drama of the test, although Hubbard later said that 'it really was a sight of such majesty and grotesque beauty that it defies adequate description'. Nick Wilson, an ableseaman on board HMS *Warrior*, witnessed the explosion from a distance of 30 miles:

Although more famous as the aircraft that performed the first bombing raid on Port Stanley, XM607 is pictured here during the mid-1960s, stationed at Coningsby with 35 Squadron. (*Joe L'Estrange*)

0.72Mt. Squadron Leader Roberts, captain of the release aircraft, XD822, was the most experienced Grapple pilot, but the 'Orange Herald' flight nearly ended in disaster, as his flight report explains:

My crew was detailed to take off at 09:00 on 31 May in Valiant XD822 to drop Orange Herald on the target area south of Malden Island. The forecast weather for the target area was one- to two-eighths of cumulus, and wind velocity 090 degrees/20kt at 45,000ft; conditions at base line. In view of this, fuel load was reduced to 5,000gal in order to give an all-up weight of 99,000lb immediately after release of the bomb. The crew reached the aircraft at 07.40 and completed cockpit checks by 08.10. AWRE (Atomic Weapons Research Establishment) had connected the bomb batteries by the time the crew entered the aircraft at 08.40, but then the take-off time was delayed on orders from JOC (Joint Operations Centre). At 09.00, permission was given to start engines and we were airborne at 09.07. The flight to the RV (radar vector) took 50min and was uneventful. Good contact on HF and VHF was established and maintained with the appropriate authorities throughout the flight. The first run over the target was navigation-type and the weather was found to be as forecast.

After the first run the remaining black-out shutters were fitted and we went straight round on the initial run. Shortly after completing this, permission was given to carry on with the live run. The run-up was steady and the bomb was released at 10.44, heading 202 degrees, IAS (indicated airspeed) 216, IMN (Indicated Mach Number) 0.75. After a slight pause I initiated a steep turn to port at 60 degrees bank. At this stage the second pilot should have started to call readings on the sensitive accelerometer, but on this occasion he was silent for a few seconds. I looked up and saw that the instrument indicated unity. Experience told me to believe the instrument, so disregarding my senses, I increased the backward pressure on the control column. At that instant the second pilot and I realised that the instrument had failed at the time of release; simultaneously, the aircraft stalled, and the bomb aimer, who was making for his seat, returned to the bomb-aimer's well with some force.

I felt my back warming up and experienced the flash, though I had my hands over my face and dark goggles on. Five seconds after the flash we turned round and faced the flash, but it was still bright so I replaced them. There in the sky was a brightly glowing seething ball of fire. This rapidly increased and became more cloudy. Soon it was looking like a very dark ripe apple with a snow-white sauce being poured over it. On the horizon at sea level a cloud appeared that must have been dust and spray from the island. The whole sight was most beautiful and I was completely filled with emotions.

Although the sight was undoubtedly very impressive, 'Green Granite Small' was not a perfect success. Yielding 0.3Mt (megatons) from a predicted yield of up to 1.0Mt, the lithium deuterate only partly ignited, but the test did at least demonstrate the warhead's potential (and an explosive force 100 times that of the Buffalo air drop), and it also provided the opportunity for another airborne test of a live Blue Danube casing. Despite the mixed results, Britain had visibly (and audibly) entered the thermonuclear age. The next drop, on 31 May, was Grapple 2, or 'Orange Herald', which tested Dr Penney's 'fallback' high-yield fission bomb, which was again contained in a Blue Danube casing. The warhead, which was developed into an operational physics package known as 'Green Grass', was, as on the first drop, detonated by barometric means at 8,000ft, and yielded

After regaining control, the manoeuvre was completed in 43 seconds, using the mechanical accelerometer. This instrument might have been referred to earlier had it not been so far from our normal instrument scan. At 53sec by the navigator's countdown, a bright white flash was seen through chinks in the blackout screens and the coloured glass in the first pilot's panel was lit up. At 2min 55sec after release, the blast waves were felt, first a moderate thump, followed a second later by a smaller one. I waited a further two minutes before turning to port to allow the crew to see what had happened. The cloud top at this time appeared to be some 10,000ft above our flight level, and it is a sight which will not easily be forgotten. The symmetry and the colours were most impressive, especially against the dark blue background provided by the sky at that height; as we watched, the upper stem and mushroom head started to glow with a deep peach colour. We then set course for base and landed at 12:47.

The third test, code-named 'Purple Granite', took place on 19 June. This time the air drop involved the 'Green Granite Large' warhead, an enlarged version of the 'Green Granite Small' with a total weight of 6,000lb, excluding the HE. Surprisingly, it was the least successful of the three drops, yielding just 0.2Mt after being dropped from XD823. The Grapple tests had been useful and spectacular, but they were rather disappointing in terms of results. The situation was summed up at a progress meeting on 16 July, when the development of 'Yellow Sun' (the code name for what would become the standard free-fall megaton weapon for the V-force) was discussed. While Grapple had been successful in providing data on the performance of two different types of megaton warhead, it had not provided sufficient data to enable a firm decision to be made regarding the warhead to be chosen for Yellow Sun. On the evidence of the trials, a 'Green Bamboo' type warhead had been chosen by the Air Staff for use in what would be an interim megaton weapon, pending deliveries of Yellow Sun.

Further trials ('Grapple X') were scheduled for November 1957, and 49 Squadron was again tasked with the provision of aircraft and crews. This time the bomb-drop at ground zero would be just 20 miles from Christmas Island (instead of almost 400), to avoid the expense and delays involved in setting up a naval task force to monitor the tests. Valiant XD825, captained by S/L B.T. Millett, made the fourth drop on 8 November, the weapon being fitted with another 'Green Granite Small' warhead. This time, however, the scientists were pleasantly surprised at the result when the bomb delivered a yield of 1.8Mt, the first true British megaton explosion. Sapper Arthur Thomas witnessed the test from Christmas Island:

> Then it happened, the blast, a lightning speed of wind and whistle of trees – a bang – it hit us all unexpectedly, lifting us off our feet and depositing us three to four yards away, landing on top of each other in a pile of bodies. We were not told to expect anything of this nature.

The clear success of this drop explains why just one test was made when the Task Force Grapple Air Plan had called for the 'air drop of two thermonuclear weapons with minimum risk to all concerned'. The records of 49 Squadron state: 'The results were entirely satisfactory, precluding the necessity for any further tests in this particular phase of Operation Grapple.' However, the test programme was far from complete, and 'Grapple Y' took place during April 1958. Valiant XD824, captained by S/L R.M. Bates, made the next (fifth) drop on 28 April. Evidence suggests that the warhead was a 'Green Granite Large' device and the resulting explosion delivered the biggest yield of any British nuclear tests, a tremendous 3.0Mt, which demonstrated that Dr Penney and his scientists could, if necessary, produce weapons which easily matched the destructive power of either the American or Soviet Union's hydrogen bombs. Further tests ('Grapple Z') took place during the summer of 1958, on a faster timescale, as Britain slowly moved towards an agreement to end nuclear testing. Number 49 Squadron's records stated: 'Due to the decision to accelerate the entire dropping programme for political considerations, the intensity of the high-explosive drops in preparation for the nuclear drops has been increased.' These (final) nuclear detonations took place in September, as the squadron's records describe:

> The month of September brought to fruition all the training for Operation Grapple Z, with the dropping of

An extremely rare photograph of an operational WE.177 tactical nuclear bomb. This particular weapon is on a loading trolley at Cottesmore, ready for attachment to one of the resident Vulcans. (*Tim McLelland collection*)

two more nuclear weapons by the squadron. On the 2nd Sqn Ldr G.M. Bailey and crew in Valiant XD822 dropped the first device of the series. This weapon was the first to be dropped by ground-controlled radar. A grandstand aircraft on this occasion, Valiant XD818 was flown by Flt Lt S. O'Connor and crew. On 11th September Flt Lt S. O'Connor and crew, in Valiant XD827, dropped a second nuclear device. This weapon was released on a visual attack. Sqn Ldr H.A. Caillard and crew in Valiant XD824 flew as grandstand. Immediately after the second air drop, the aircraft were prepared for the return trip to Wittering.

When the Valiants and crews returned to Wittering 49 Squadron continued training for an anticipated further series of test drops, but by the end of November 1958 Britain had effectively decided to abandon nuclear testing, and the government later stated that the United Kingdom would no longer carry out further nuclear tests, whether in or above the atmosphere, underwater or underground. Christmas Island was gradually reduced to a minimum holding state and HQ Task Force Grapple was disbanded on 3 June 1960. From 1 December 1958, 49 Squadron reverted to a standard

bomber role and the Grapple Valiants were de-modified and refitted with the standard radar navigational bombing system. Although the Cabinet decision to manufacture thermonuclear bombs had been taken more than five months previously, Churchill made no reference to this historic date in British history when he said:

> The advance of the hydrogen bomb has fundamentally altered the entire problem of defence, and considerations founded even upon the atom bomb have become obsolescent, almost old-fashioned. Immense changes are taking place in military facts and in military thoughts. We have for some time past adopted the principles that safety and even survival must be sought in deterrence rather than defence and this, I believe, is the policy which also guides the United States.

Designed chiefly as a scientific and operational test programme, Operations Buffalo and Grapple had obviously demonstrated to the USA that Britain was more than capable of producing thermonuclear weapons which were, if anything, more efficient than its foreign equivalents. It is hardly surprising, therefore, that relations between America and Britain gradually improved after the first nuclear tests (Operation Buffalo) in 1956, and even survived through the days of the McCarthy period. The Atomic Energy Act, effectively a revision of the infamous McMahon Act, was signed in 1954, permitting the transfer of data concerning the external characteristics of nuclear weapons – size, shape, weight, yield and effects. The USA and Britain agreed to co-operate within the terms of this act in a bilateral agreement signed on 15 June 1955. However, the real breakthrough came, rather ironically, after the huge transatlantic rift that developed during the Suez Crisis. Prime Minister Harold Macmillan and Eisenhower met twice in 1957. During their first meeting, in Bermuda during March, agreements were made for the deployment of Thor missiles to the UK, which would be under 'dual key' control. Eisenhower commented that this was 'by far the most successful international conference' he had attended since the war. When they met for a second time, in Washington during October, revisions were made to the Atomic Energy Act to allow scientific co-operation

Rare image of a
Blue Steel missile
undergoing engine tests.
Both Stentor rocket
motors are operating.
(Rolls-Royce)

between 'Great Britain, the United States and other friendly powers'.

It was no coincidence that the president's enthusiasm for restoring the special relationship came in the same year that Britain embarked upon the first Grapple tests, just months after the first operational hydrogen bombs had entered US service. Britain's thermonuclear advances had been remarkable, and the USA identified potential advantages for a new co-operative arrangement with Britain. Another important consideration was the launching of the Soviet Union's Sputnik satellite, which threw into question many assumptions of American technical superiority, and

Blue Steel attached to its (AEC) transporter and loading unit, inside the Blue Steel facility at RAF Scampton. (Rolls-Royce)

underlined the possibility that the Soviet Union might eventually be able to deliver nuclear weapons to targets in Europe and the United States, by missile. The Suez Crisis had also served to illustrate just how far apart Britain and America were and this too possibly served as a catalyst in repairing the faltering special relationship. Finally, in 1958 the Agreement for Co-operation on the Uses of Atomic Energy for Mutual Defence Purposes was signed, enabling both countries to exchange virtually all types of nuclear information. Britain quickly learned a great deal from American expertise in engineering and weapons assembly techniques. Conversely, American officials were amazed at the scientific and technical knowledge that Britain possessed, which in many respects was ahead of the Americans'. The intimate and totally reciprocal collaboration continued into the 1960s and beyond, long after America could possibly have hoped to derive any further benefits from the cc-operation. A British official illustrated the position in the 1970s when he stated:

> The United States has two laboratories and we have one; they spend five times as much as we do on these establishments; they have conducted some 870 tests – how many of which were really necessary I wouldn't say – and we have conducted 30. That gives, I think, a fair indication of the 'hardware balance' although in the idea end of the business, the relationship is rather more equal.

The completion of the Grapple tests eventually led to an Air Staff Requirement for a thermonuclear bomb (ASR OR.1136), which was issued on 6 June 1955. It called for a bomb which was not to exceed 50 inches in diameter (and would be made smaller if possible), and which was not to exceed 7,000lb in weight, capable of carriage internally by Valiants, Vulcans and Victors, for RAF service from 1959. When the Cabinet made its historical decision to proceed with development of hydrogen bombs during June 1954, the meeting agreed that work on the programme should be performed 'as unobtrusively as possible' and that it was 'desirable that costs be concealed as much as possible'. Before them was a memorandum from the chiefs of staff, based on a report by the Working Party on the Operational Use of Atomic Weapons, whose members included Sir William Penney, the deputy chiefs of staff and scientific advisors. The report concluded that hydrogen bombs would 'go a long way towards overcoming the difficult problems of terminal accuracy', simply by delivering a huge explosive force and that only a relatively limited number of bombs would be required, beyond which any increase of stocks would not offer any corresponding military advantage.

The chiefs of staff decided (during a meeting on 6 April 1955) to develop, as a first priority, a thermonuclear bomb with a yield of approximately 1 megaton, and ASR OR.1136

Vulcan B2 XL317 from 617 Squadron, carrying a Blue Steel training round. (*Tim McLelland collection*)

was accepted by the Ministry of Supply on 28 July, leading to the start of development work on the weapon called 'Yellow Sun'. During March 1956, members of the Operational Requirements staff visited Farnborough, where drawings and a wooden mock-up of Yellow Sun were prepared. The bomb carcass was 240in long, 48in in diameter and had small cruciform stabilising fins, similar to the Second World War 'Grand Slam' design (larger ones would have had to retract, to enable the weapon to fit into the Valiant's bomb bay). Unusually, however, the bomb had a flat nose, intended to slow it during free fall to increase the weapon's stability and simplify the requirements of the internal barometric detonation device, which would probably be unable to cope with a terminal velocity that exceeded supersonic speeds. The warhead weighed approximately 3,500lb and the completed weapon had a weight of around 6,500lb.

While Yellow Sun was being developed, a second weapon, Red Beard, was also evolving, primarily as a smaller tactical bomb, but also partly as a replacement for the first-generation Blue Danube which, as a relatively crude fission device, delivered a relatively low explosive yield of around 20kt, despite weighing a staggering 10,250lb. However, it was quickly accepted that if the development of these two new weapons proceeded smoothly (and much had depended on the outcome of Operation Grapple), the warheads would be ready before the bomb bodies

Four aircraft from 9, 12 and 35 Squadrons on Wittering's ORP during a dispersal exercise. (*Tim McLelland collection*)

being designed to carry them. Therefore it was proposed that an interim weapon should be manufactured so that the RAF could acquire a thermonuclear capability as soon as possible. Three warheads – Green Granite, Green Bamboo and Orange Herald – could be made available and incorporated into a standard Blue Danube bomb casing. A report prepared by the RAE in April 1957 described progress with the RAF's hydrogen bomb:

The Yellow Sun weapon to meet Air Staff Requirement OR.1136 will provide the first British bomb having a yield in the megaton range; as such it is the keystone of the offensive deterrent policy. It is intended for carriage in the V-class bombers and will have a diameter of 48in and a length of approximately 20ft. The weight will be about 7,000lb. The weapon is being designed around the Green Bamboo warhead under development at the Atomic Weapons Research Establishment. The means of making a warhead in this range wholly safe in storage and transport has not been finalised, but all schemes of providing inflight insertion of some part of the fissile material have been abandoned.

Consideration has also been given to the alternative warheads Green Granite and Short Granite, which are being tested at Operation Grapple. Both are fission-fusion-fission types and differ only in that Short Granite is smaller and lighter. Neither warhead requires ENI (External Neutron Initiations). Nuclear safety is ensured by some form of inflight insertion. Preliminary investigation indicates that if after Grapple Short Granite becomes the preferred warhead, no serious delay should occur, but the Green Granite would require a larger and heavier weapon, so that much of the ballistic and fusing work already well advanced would have to be repeated, and the in-service date would have to be set back at least nine months.

Subsequently, a second progress statement, issued later in 1957, included the following:

The Operational Requirement OR.1136 Issue 2 calls for the development of a megaton bomb, the type of warhead to be carried not being specified except that it shall be capable of use in both Yellow Sun and Blue Steel. The original requirement was for incorporation of the Green Bamboo warhead and much of the work done has been on the assumption that this warhead will be used. It has, however, been evident for some time that as a result of the Grapple trials another warhead might be preferred, and preliminary investigations were made at an early stage into the problems which would arise if one of the Granite-type of warheads were chosen. These have been followed by further work, especially in connection with the possible use of Short Granite. The general position now is that an early decision as to the type of warhead, and information on associated matters such as nuclear safety systems, is essential if development of the weapon is not to be held up.

The revised Operational Requirement stated that Yellow Sun would be carried by the Vulcan and Victor, the earlier requirement for carriage by the Valiant having been cancelled. Despite this decision, however, many of the Yellow Sun trials were conducted by Valiants, until Vulcans and Victors could be made available. The report continued:

'Yellow Sun is being developed as a fully engineered weapon to meet the requirements of the OR. The provision of an interim megaton weapon only partially meeting these requirements is planned for introduction into service considerably earlier than Yellow Sun.' A paper issued by the MoS in August outlined the indecision that had surrounded the choice of warhead for Yellow Sun:

The object was to give the RAF a megaton capability at the earliest possible moment. It was proposed to base the interim weapon on one of the bombs to be dropped in Operation Grapple and it was stated that the date of introduction to the Service of Yellow Sun would not be

affected by the interim missile. The results of Operation Grapple were such that none of the rounds dropped was immediately applicable to the interim weapon, but AWRE were satisfied that the principles had been cleared sufficiently for them to offer various alternative warheads to the Air Staff for consideration. The Air Staff, largely on the basis of numbers which could be provided, chose a warhead similar in outside shape to Green Bamboo but having a yield of half a megaton, known as Green Grass. Throughout the discussions on this interim megaton weapon the general approach has been that, in the interests of providing a megaton capability to the RAF at the earliest possible moment, the Service is prepared

XM595 at Scampton, carrying a Blue Steel. The missile's ventral fin-folded horizontally to provide ground clearance. (*Rolls-Royce*)

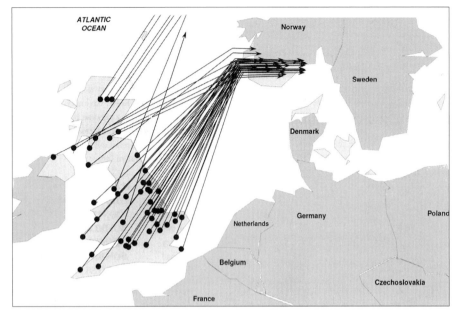

Above, opposite and overleaf: Series of diagrams produced by Southend's Vulcan Restoration Trust (based on information supplied by John Reeve), showing the inbound and outbound routes that would have been used by the RAF's Vulcans if they had attacked the Soviet Union. The routes from the UK dispersal airfields merge off Norway and run across to their targets. Aircraft then head back to the UK, or south to the Mediterranean.

to sacrifice rigorous testing, proofing, and clearance of the weapon and to introduce special maintenance procedures in association with AWRE. Furthermore, the Air Staff were willing for the same reason to discount many of the provisions of OR.1136. A reassessment of the Yellow Sun programme has recently been made primarily to examine the possibility of offering an earlier capability to the RAF in view of the successful progress of the development, but also taking into account the desirability of switching over to the Short Granite type of warhead if and when this is cleared by AWRE. This later type of warhead is very desirable because of the smaller amounts of fissile material needed.

After much deliberation it was agreed that an interim weapon (code-named 'Violet Club') would be brought into service until the first deliveries of a limited-approval version of Yellow Sun could be made. The Deputy Chief of the Air Staff commented:

We are anxious to get megaton weapons into service as soon as we can. We most certainly think it worthwhile to have even as few as five by the time the Yellow Suns come along. At the same time we are anxious to get Yellow Sun

as soon as we can because it does not have the serious operational limitations of Violet Club.

On 24 February 1958 the Assistant Chief of the Air Staff wrote to the AOCinC Bomber Command, stating:

I am directed to inform you that the first Violet Club, which is now being assembled at Wittering, is expected to be completed by the end of the month. A total of five of these weapons will be assembled on Bomber Command stations by July of this year, when deliveries of Yellow Sun should commence. Violet Club is still in some degree experimental and it will be subject to a number of serious handling restrictions. The extent of these and their effect on operational readiness are still under discussion with the Ministry of Supply. Until Violet Club has been formally cleared by the Ministry of Supply and it is possible to issue specific instructions on storage, handling, and transport, the weapon is to remain exclusively in the custody and under the control of the Atomic Weapons Research Establishment. It is possible that some such arrangement will continue throughout the life of these weapons as it is intended to replace them with Yellow Sun as early as possible. This will be done as soon as sufficient aircraft are modified to carry Yellow Sun. I am to say that the operational limitations of Violet Club, particularly those affecting readiness, are serious. Nevertheless, it provides a megaton deterrent capability several months earlier than would otherwise have been possible.

Although this 'interim' weapon retained the same bomb carcass as its predecessor, Violet Club was a completely different bomb, although it retained the same ballistics as Blue Danube and could therefore be used with the same bombing equipment, suitably adjusted for the appropriate detonation height. The Bomber Command Armament School (BCAS) Operations Records state that:

On 28 February a convoy from AWRE was stuck in a snow-drift at Wansford Hill at 15:00. An officer from this unit was sent to investigate. At 17:00 the vehicle was still unable to be moved. Rations and bedding were sent to the convoy and an officer and a team of airmen were detailed to stand by throughout the night to give help if required. It was not until the following day that vehicles began using the A1. The convoy arrived at the main guard room at 12:00. Personnel were sent immediately for a meal. Unloading was commenced at 14:00, when the convoy arrived at BCAS.

This bleak and wintry scene marked the arrival of the first Violet Club bombs and with it the very beginnings of the RAF's thermonuclear capability. By July a total of five bombs had been completed. Bombs 1 to 4 remained at Wittering, where personnel were trained by AWRE staff to install the Green Grass warhead at the relevant site. Bombs 5, 6, 7, 8 and 11 were dispatched to Finningley; and 9, 10 and 12 went to Scampton. Production of all twelve weapons was complete by the end of 1958. Violet Club was, as DCAS commented, 'rather delicate' and could only be assembled at the base from where it would be used. Likewise, road transport was limited to relatively short trips from the assembly point to the storage building. More details of Violet Club were contained in a document issued in July:

In view of the very small number of Violet Clubs being made available to the Service, and the difficulties of clearing the Victor for the carriage of this weapon, it has now been decided to limit its carriage to the Vulcan. Vulcan aircraft modified to carry Yellow Sun are now being returned to service and it is desirable to transfer the warheads from all Violet Clubs to Yellow Suns as soon as possible, and at the same time to redeploy the weapons to Scampton and Finningley.

In November 1958 a further report stated that:

Bomber Command wish to get rid of Violet Clubs as soon as possible, but they are anxious to have a number of Yellow Suns in store before they do this. As the obvious time to change over is at the six-monthly inspections, it is suggested that Violet Clubs should start to phase out at the rate of about one a month from April or May, providing the Yellow Suns are not late.

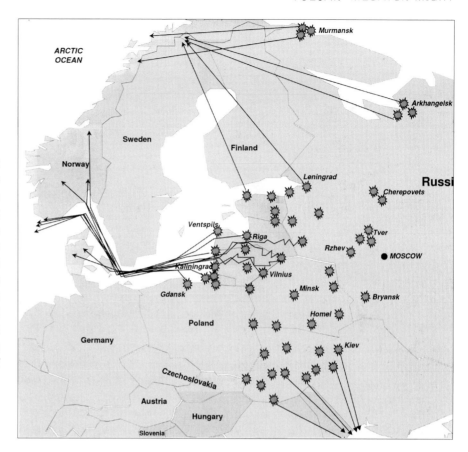

At the end of 1958 the RAF possessed a force of fifty-four Valiants, ten Victors and eighteen Vulcans, the Vulcans being capable of carrying the 12Mt-range Violet Clubs. The remaining V-force aircraft remained equipped to carry the smaller kiloton-range Blue Danubes.

Throughout the story of the Vulcan's development, many other vital projects were being pursued in an effort to ensure that Britain could retain a credible deterrent capability. The concept of guided nuclear missiles had already been established, and by 1954 the Air Staff had issued OR.1132, calling for a propelled air-to-surface missile for the V-force. Capable of being launched at up to 100nm from its target, the missile would rely on the parent aircraft's Navigation and Bombing System (NBS) for aiming, and would use Green Satin Doppler equipment to determine ground speed and drift, and to provide an accurate heading reference. Responsibility for the weapon,

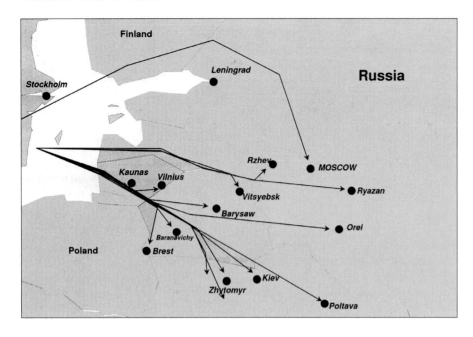

named Blue Steel, was divided between the MoS and Avro's Weapons Research Division, which had completed a design study for a stand-off bomb that resulted in a development contract being awarded in March 1956. Tests of a two-fifths scale model of the guided bomb were conducted in 1957–58, a series of drops being made from Valiant WP204 over the Aberporth range off the Welsh coast.

Designing Blue Steel was time consuming and extremely difficult, not least because virtually the entire programme represented a move into completely unknown territory as far as technical knowledge was concerned. In essence, Blue Steel was an aeroplane and Avro treated it as such. Some 35ft long, with small delta foreplanes, rear-mounted 13ft-span wings and vertical fins, it was powered by a hydrogen peroxide and kerosene Armstrong Siddeley Stentor rocket motor. Guided by inertial navigation and with automatic flight control and trajectory decision-making, the missile manoeuvred at supersonic speeds before delivering a 1Mt ('Red Snow') warhead to its target. The all-up weight of the bomb was about 17,000lb, which included 400Imp gal of high-test peroxide (HTP) fuel and 80Imp gal of kerosene. After release at 40,000ft the weapon would free-fall to 32,000ft, at which stage the motor would ignite and it would climb to 59,000ft, where the speed would increase to

Mach 2.3. The missile would then cruise-climb to 70,500ft, where the engine would burn out and a steady dive towards the target would begin. Bearing this very complicated system in mind, and the fact that Avro had no previous experience of designing and manufacturing guided missiles, it was not surprising that the development programme timescale began to slip, especially when the MoS was unable even to supply a Valiant test-bed aircraft on time. The Air Staff's hope that Blue Steel would be operational by 1960 was quickly discounted, despite the fact that it was already looking for a missile that could fly up to ten times further.

In May 1958 Air Staff Requirement OR.1159 called for an extended-range air-to-surface guided missile, stating that:

> By 1963 it is expected that the Russian SAGW (surface-to-air guided weapons) and the fighter defences will be so improved and expanded that the V-bombers, even with Blue Steel and ECM, will find it increasingly difficult to penetrate to many of their objectives. In order to maintain an effective deterrent during the period commencing with the decline in effectiveness of Blue Steel and continuing during the build-up of the RAF ballistic missile force, it will be necessary to introduce a replacement for Blue Steel having a range for attacking targets from launching points outside the enemy defence perimeter. It is envisaged that V-bombers equipped with this missile should be able to supplement the ballistic missile deterrent for several years. Missile range of 600 nautical miles will be acceptable as an initial operational capability but a range of 1,000 nm is desirable.

Minister of Aviation (Duncan Sandys) recognised that it would be foolish to distract Avro's efforts to get Blue Steel into service by adding the complication of a long-range Blue Steel development, so the subsequent cancellation of both Blue Streak and Blue Steel Mk 2 enabled Avro, the RAE and the Royal Radar Establishment to concentrate on getting Blue Steel Mk 1 into service at the earliest opportunity. On 28 April 1961, Minister of Aviation Peter Thorneycroft reported that:

> Blue Steel was accepted as a requirement in January 1956. It was then thought that the first delivery of

missiles would be made to the RAF in 1961/2. By the end of 1960, however, it had become apparent (owing to delays in the development programme) that the number of trial firings that could be expected to have been made by early 1962 would not be sufficient to enable the early deliveries of missiles to the RAF to be approved for normal operational use. It is, however, expected that by mid-1962 the functioning and safety of the weapon (including its warhead) will have been sufficiently improved to enable the missile to be used in an emergency, if required, thus providing a deterrent capability. Further trials will continue during the succeeding months to enable approval to be given for normal operational carriage and use of the missile.

He also added that the delays in the programme were due to 'detailed engineering faults and problems which are a normal part of the development process and may be expected to continue'. An order was placed for fifty-seven missiles, made up of a unit establishment of forty-eight operational rounds, plus four backing rounds and four proof rounds. Additionally, there would be sixteen training rounds, ten of which would be manufactured from light alloy and six with steel carcasses. During 1959, Vulcan B1 XA903 joined the Blue Steel programme and a variety of full-sized missile test bodies, mostly powered by de Havilland Double Spectre engines, were dropped from both the Valiant and Vulcan. Most of the later test flights were made over the Woomera range in Australia, where two Vulcan B2s (XH538 and XH539) were employed on test drop and monitoring duties.

Blue Steel was perpetually dogged by a series of relatively minor problems, which led to increasing frustration on behalf of the Air Staff. Avro was accused of poor management and of wasting time on projected plans for a long-range Blue Steel, when it should have devoted all of its efforts to completion of Blue Steel Mk 1. In reality, Avro simply suffered from a combination of initial over-optimism shared by the Air Staff and a whole range of new technical problems, which, as an aircraft manufacturer, the company had never before encountered. Considering that the typical development period for a conventional military aircraft could be anything up to ten years, it was perhaps

The Red Shrimp ECM plate aerial was fitted between the starboard jet pipes on the Vulcan B2. A handful of aircraft also had a second aerial plate fitted between the port jet pipes. *(BAE)*

unrealistic to expect a system as complicated as Blue Steel to be completed in a significantly shorter timescale. The Minister of Aviation also said in 1961 that:

Blue Steel was a fully navigated cruise-type missile with a range of 100nm designed for launching from Mk 2 Victors and Vulcans. It was intended to provide the main deterrent weapon between the time when bombers equipped with free-falling bombs were likely to become less effective against enemy defences, and the introduction of Skybolt which would replace it. Its cost was currently estimated at £60 million for R&D and £21 million for production; of this total, some £44 million had been spent or committed. Trial firings had proved disappointing in some respects, but it appeared that the difficulties were caused by teething troubles rather than by any basic fault which might invalidate the concept of the weapon. Further trials were proceeding at Woomera and it should be possible to make a comprehensive review towards the end of the year.

Early in 1962 the project's progress was evaluated and the Cabinet Defence Committee learned that the firing of W.100A rounds, closely representative of the final production version, was about to start and that by August or September enough preliminary information would be

Vulcan B2 XH533 at altitude. Just discernable is the original unmodified tail cone profile (no ECM equipment being fitted at this stage) and the smaller B1-sized air intake. *(BAE)*

available from launchings to enable the Air Ministry to assume an emergency capability. Finally, in July 1962 a production-model Blue Steel was successfully fired after being air launched from a Vulcan over Woomera, and on 25 July the Minister of Aviation, now Julian Amery, wrote to the Air Minister, stating:

> I am glad to be able to inform you that Sir George Gardner (Controller of Aircraft, Ministry of Aviation) has today forwarded to DCAS a CA Release for Blue Steel to be carried on Vulcan aircraft, complete with its operational warhead, in a national emergency. The clearance does not specifically authorise the launching of the missile because the required trials to prove the safety of the systems are not yet complete. However, no difficulties have been experienced up to date which affect the safety after launch and we are confident that further trials will provide the necessary proof. We expect to issue the operational launch clearance in December 1962. We have issued the present clearance on the understanding that, should a national crisis occur which warrants the carriage of the operational Blue Steel with its warhead, limitations as to its use could be overridden. In effect this means that you could declare an operational capability with Blue Steel as soon as you consider that you are in a position to do so.

The first unit to be declared operational on Blue Steel was 617 Squadron at Scampton. A great deal of time was spent discussing when the RAF should officially declare that the squadron had an operational capability, since Bomber Command wanted to arrange a press facility to show the Blue Steel system to the public. It was feared that a premature display of Blue Steel might lead to embarrassing questions as to the true extent of the RAF's capability at that time and so the date of the press day was continually delayed until 14 February 1963, by which time the squadron was fully operational with at least six missiles available. Unfortunately, by this time the Skybolt programme had been cancelled and the press were more concerned with plans for the V-force's future than with the event being celebrated at Scampton.

However, 27 and 83 Squadrons subsequently re-equipped with Blue Steels at Scampton, followed by 139 Squadron on Victors at Wittering, their conversion beginning in October 1963, followed by 100 Squadron. On 21 August an Air Ministry Nuclear Weapon Clearance for the use of Blue Steel on quick reaction alert (QRA) standby was issued, although the weapons were to be unarmed and unshelled except in an emergency. Clearance for a fully armed and fuelled Blue Steel on QRA was finally issued on 16 April 1964.

The final delivery of the last of Handley Page's Victor B2s in 1962 represented the culmination of Britain's long-established plans to equip the RAF with a fully effective nuclear deterrent. By 1961, with a combined force of 144 Valiants, Victor B1s and B2s, and Vulcan B1s and B2s, Bomber Command possessed awesome striking power beyond anything imaginable during the Second World War. The first-generation 20kt Blue Danube fission weapon was gradually withdrawn during 1960, Red Beard temporarily replacing it as the RAF's preferred fission weapon. Red Beard was essentially a tactical bomb, however, developed into Mk 1 (15kt) and Mk 2 (25kt) versions to be carried by RAF and Fleet Air Arm tactical strike aircraft (the Canberra, Scimitar, Sea Vixen and Buccaneer), although Valiants, Vulcans and Victors were capable of carrying it, but only as a potential 'second strike' bomb, which could have been used for repeat attacks following a first strike with megaton-class weapons (assuming there was any need for a second strike after the first exchange). The Yellow Sun Mk 1, with a yield of 500kt, was superseded by Yellow Sun Mk 2 from February 1962, initial stocks going to Waddington. The Red Snow warhead, which was also fitted to Blue Steel, was manufactured to deliver one of three different yields and it is likely that both the Blue Steel and Yellow Sun warheads were largely of the 1-megaton variety, the remainder being 500kt.

For much of the 1960s the Yellow Sun Mk 2 was the standard free-fall nuclear weapon for the Vulcan squadrons, while the Scampton Wing concentrated on Blue Steel operations. The government's unease at the prospect of relying on fixed-site ballistic missiles, which could take at least fifteen minutes to prepare for launching, prompted a search for a more suitable nuclear delivery system to replace Blue Steel towards the end of the 1960s. The difficulties and costs associated with the production of Blue Steel Mk 1 effectively killed off the Mk 2 project before it started and, with the Thor missile system as a stopgap, Britain seemed destined to rely upon the far more advanced Blue Streak missile as its main nuclear deterrent for the late 1960s, although the system (similar in concept to Thor) was likely to be obsolete even before it entered service.

It was at this stage that Britain had again looked towards America, where the Douglas GAM-87A Skybolt missile was being developed. This air-launched, nuclear-tipped guided weapon was to be capable of delivering a sizeable warhead from a range in excess of 1,000 miles, far beyond the capabilities of Blue Steel. In essence, it was everything that the Air Staff had wanted from Blue Steel Mk 2. Talks with the US president at Camp David suggested that there would be no American objection to the British purchase of Skybolts if necessary, and it was also indicated that the sea-launched Polaris might be made available, should Britain be interested. The ever-increasing cost of the Blue Streak programme and the pressing fears that the weapon would be very vulnerable to Soviet attack, led to the conclusion that an updated V-force, equipped with Skybolts, would be a much cheaper and much more credible option than relying on another non-mobile IRBM that would be an easy target for Soviet attack. Consequently, Blue Streak was abandoned. Skybolt was originally designed in response to a USAF requirement for an air-launched, strategic-range nuclear missile to be carried by SAC Boeing B-52s and Convair B-58s. It was quickly established that development of the weapon would be completed to enable the first Skybolts to enter RAF service in 1966, although a new carrier for the weapons would probably be required by 1970, because the Vulcans and Victors would reach the end of their useful life at that time. Macmillan was keen to place a provisional order for 100 Skybolts, but the chancellor was rather more cautious, not least because the missile was only just beginning development. However, following the meeting between Macmillan and Eisenhower in March 1960, a minute was issued by the US government, which stated:

> In a desire to be of assistance in improving and extending the effective life of the V-bomber force, the United States, subject only to United States priorities, is prepared to provide Skybolt missiles minus warheads to the United Kingdom on a reimbursable basis in 1965 or thereafter. Since Skybolt is still in the early stages of development, this offer is necessarily dependent on the successful and timely completion of its development programme.

The minute also made mention of the emerging Polaris submarine-launched missile programme, stating:

> As the United Kingdom is aware, the United States is offering at the current NATO Defence Ministers meeting to make mobile Polaris missiles minus warheads available from US production to NATO countries in order to meet SACEUR's requirements for MRBMs (medium-range ballistic missiles). The United States is also offering to assist joint European production of Polaris if our preference for United States production proves unacceptable.

Given that Britain and France were the only NATO countries outside the USA with a nuclear capability (and therefore the only countries able to operate the missiles), this offer was of particular significance to Britain, which effectively had the luxury of a choice between two weapons systems. However, Britain continued to pursue the Skybolt project, even though American concerns over the possible success of the development programme were being expressed as early as 1961. With more than 150,000 component parts, some 60,000 of which had to function perfectly in order to launch the missile, Skybolt was a very complex piece of hardware. The first live launches in 1962 ended in failure and the US Secretary of Defense advised his British counterparts that, although they did not believe Skybolt was a technical failure, they did believe that continuing the programme would be a waste of money in view of the emergence of other delivery systems at that time, such as Hound Dog and Minuteman. It was pointed out that Skybolt was essentially a research programme at the time when Britain first requested it, rather than being a production weapon. Consequently, the path would be open for Britain to continue development of Skybolt in association with a scaled-down American effort, or to develop Skybolt in isolation, albeit by using American technology.

The only other available option would be to adopt the Hound Dog missile, or to participate in a multilateral force of sea-launched (Polaris) missiles, under the terms being offered in March 1960. The Hound Dog option was quickly discounted because the weapon could not be carried by V-bombers and the Ministry of Defence (MoD) concluded that the real options for Britain were to acquire Polaris, complete Skybolt in America, complete Skybolt in the UK or produce a ballistic weapon in co-operation with France.

It had already been agreed that the V-force dispersal concept, whereby the bombers would leave their home bases in a wartime emergency and relocate in groups of four or two to thirty-six dispersal airfields scattered around the UK, would not be a credible option for very long without improvement, since the increasing sophistication of Soviet attack forces meant that bombers on the ground in any location would be at risk from attack. The best alternative to a dispersal policy would be to mount a continuous airborne alert, with Skybolt-equipped bombers maintaining a round-the-clock airborne presence, immune from attack. It was an expensive and technically difficult concept, but one which America was pursuing at the time. If Skybolt was abandoned, Britain would have to choose one of two expensive alternatives – either adopt an Anglo-French ballistic missile system, which would mean accepting all the disadvantages of Blue Streak again, or buy Polaris missiles and a submarine fleet from which to launch them. When Prime Minister Macmillan met President Kennedy at Nassau in the Bahamas during December 1962, Macmillan pressed Kennedy to continue with the Skybolt programme, but as a post-talk report stated, Kennedy, who was fairly ambivalent towards British interests, wanted to abandon the project:

> The President and the Prime Minister reviewed the development programme for the Skybolt missile. The President explained that it was no longer expected that this very complex weapon system would be completed within the cost estimate or the timescale which were projected when the programme was begun. The President informed the Prime Minister that for this reason, and because of the availability to the United States of alternative weapon systems, he had decided to cancel plans for the production of Skybolt by the United States. Nevertheless, recognising the importance of the Skybolt programme for the United Kingdom, and recalling that the purpose of the offer of Skybolt in 1960 had been to assist in improving and extending the effective life of the British V-bombers, the President expressed his readiness to continue with the development of the missile as a joint enterprise between the United States and the United Kingdom, with each country bearing equal shares of the future cost of completing development, after which the United Kingdom would be able to place a production order to meet its requirements.

This was a very generous offer to Britain, bearing in mind that Kennedy had little practical reason to provide any further funds for the Skybolt programme, and was not even a great believer in the special relationship. Macmillan recognised the value of Kennedy's offer, but the continuing doubts over technical difficulties, rising costs and delays in the delivery timescale prompted him to decline the opportunity to divert more financial responsibility on to Britain. Likewise, Macmillan could not accept Hound Dog because of the time and expense that would be involved in modifying the Vulcan and Victor to carry it. Instead he opted for Polaris, and Kennedy agreed that America would provide Polaris missiles, minus warheads, for British submarines. Consequently, Skybolt was officially cancelled by America on 31 December 1962, just a few days after a test round had made a perfect launch from a B-52 over the Eglin weapons range. As far as the RAF was concerned the programme officially ended on 3 January 1963 and, with Skybolt abandoned in favour of Polaris, the future of the RAF's nuclear force had been sealed; the British nuclear deterrent was to be transformed into a seaborne system.

XM605 out in the cold on a typically snowy day at Goose Bay in Canada. Vulcan crews regularly deployed to Goose Bay to train at low level over the sparsely populated areas surrounding the base. *(Tim McLelland collection)*

9

LOW LEVEL

Of course the choice of Polaris didn't immediately spell the end of the V-force. Developing and manufacturing the missile (and the submarines required to launch it) would require years of work before they became available, therefore the V-force would have to remain viable for the time being and the Air Staff turned its attention to ways in which Bomber Command could maintain a credible nuclear deterrent until the end of the 1960s. The Air Staff concluded that, beyond the mid-1960s, improvements in Russian air defences would mean that it would be practically impossible to penetrate Soviet airspace at high level. The V-force would have to attack at low level if it was to survive. Soviet radar systems had been geared towards the detection of high-flying bombers and, although the range and sensitivity of Soviet equipment was continuing to improve, radar detection was not effective at heights of around 3,000ft or lower, where aircraft radar returns began to merge with ground-generated clutter. If the V-force was prepared to attack at low altitude (500ft or lower), the Soviet radar systems would probably be unable to detect its bombers at all. Fears were naturally expressed that the V-bombers would not be capable of performing a low-level penetration role, bearing in mind that they were designed for high-altitude operations, but the Bomber Command Development Unit (BCDU) at Finningley flew a series of tests to prove that low-level sorties could be conducted safely, while a Vulcan and a Victor were sent to Libya to perform a series of ultra-low flights over the desert to demonstrate the capability still further.

In any case, the Valiants that had been assigned to SACEUR had already begun low-level operations without experiencing any significant problems (although, of course, serious problems were encountered later). The Vulcan B1A squadrons at Waddington (44, 50 and 101), and the Victor B1A squadrons at Honington (55 and 57) and Cottesmore (10 and 15), were assigned to low-level operations in March

1963. Training flights were normally made at 1,000ft, a conservative figure aimed at preserving aircraft fatigue life, but every third sortie was flown at 500ft. The Mk 2 Victors and Vulcans assumed a low-level role as of 1 May 1964.

Blue Steel also had to be re-roled, as outlined in a revised version of the original Operational Requirement: 'The Air Staff requires the further development of the Blue Steel missile to enable it to be launched from Mk 2 V-bombers flying at the lowest possible level in the height band 250ft-1,000ft.' After a series of trials in the UK and at Woomera, the Blue Steel missile was found to be readily capable of being launched at low level. After release, its motor was ignited and Blue Steel comfortably zoom-climbed to 17,000ft, before beginning a terminal descent to its target. Having been designed for high-altitude launch and then having had new operational profiles developed around it, Blue Steel entered RAF service primarily as a low-level weapon, requiring a completely different training programme to that first envisaged. The V-force's main nuclear weapon, Yellow Sun Mk 2, was incapable of low-level delivery, however, and bomber crews assigned to Yellow Sun delivery were trained to make low-level

XM572 was one of five early B2 aircraft from a batch ordered in January 1958 that were completed with Olympus 201 engines. The rest of the forty-aircraft order was equipped with Olympus 301 engines. (*Tim McLelland collection*)

Busy scene at Scampton as a Blue Steel missile is brought into place under the Vulcan's bomb bay, ready for loading. *(BAE)*

penetrations followed by brief pop-up ascents to medium altitude, from where the bomb could be released. This was a far from ideal situation and the Air Staff accepted that a completely new weapon would be required to suit the low-level delivery environment. Joint Naval/Air Staff Requirement NASR.1177 gave the details:

Because of envisaged enemy counter measures and the need to change aircraft approach and delivery tactics, the existing British nuclear bombs Yellow Sun, Blue Steel and Red Beard will be unsuitable as primary weapons beyond 1975. Moreover, with the cancellation of Skybolt as the planned replacement for Yellow Sun and the introduction of Polaris unlikely to become effective before 1970, an urgent need exists for a new bomb to maintain the United Kingdom independent deterrent during the interim period and as a supplementary capability thereafter. By 1966, the manned bomber aircraft may survive enemy defences in the European theatre and deliver a successful strike only by flying at high speed at very low level. Yellow Sun and Blue Steel are designed for release at medium/high altitude where the delivery aircraft and/or bomb is vulnerable to interception, while Red Beard cannot withstand the low-level flight environment, is limited in method of fusing and delivery, and possesses some undesirable safety restrictions when held at readiness in

an operational state. Early replacement is essential. The replacement bomb must be multi-purpose by design. It must satisfy joint Naval and Air Staff requirements for carriage and delivery in current medium-bomber aircraft and planned high-performance aircraft, to exploit fully their low-level strike capability against strategic and tactical, hard and soft targets, with corresponding different warhead yields. Research and development studies show clearly that such a bomb can be produced fully within the timescale. However, to maintain an effective United Kingdom nuclear deterrent during development of the Polaris weapon system, priority is given to production of the high-yield version for the RAF medium bomber force.

This design, which became the WE177 bomb, was to be used as a lay-down weapon, either by ballistic/loft mode or by retarded (parachute) delivery. It was also to be as small and light as possible, the Type B version not to exceed 1,000lb (in fact it weighed 950lb, while WE177A weighed 600lb). The A and B designations referred to different yields of 200kt and 400kt, respectively; they were 144in long and had a carcass diameter of 16.5in, and a tail fin span of 24in. Deliveries of WE177A began in September 1966 and trials were conducted with a Vulcan B2 at Cottesmore. WE177C was a 10kt naval derivative of the weapon, carried by Buccaneers and then by Sea Harriers, until it was withdrawn in 1992.

The aircraft in the re-roled low-level Vulcan and Victor force were modified with an updated ECM fit, sidescan radar, roller maps, ground-position indicator equipment and terrain-following radar. The all-white, anti-flash paint was replaced on their upper surfaces by a disruptive grey/green camouflage, the first aircraft so finished being Vulcan XH505, which emerged from Hawker Siddeley Aviation's Bitteswell plant on 24 March 1964. Thus the V-force was assigned to high-low-high (hi-lo-hi) delivery profiles, with a low-level phase of up to 1,000nm in the extreme case (for training sorties this would normally be 350–500nm). All-weather operations were practised and the height of the low-level phase of an operational sortie would be left to the discretion of the aircraft captain – in poor visibility conditions this might be 1,000ft, but in good weather

it could be as low as an incredible 50ft. For delivery of Yellow Sun, and possibly of Red Beard if required for a second strike, the captain would fly a pop-up manoeuvre to 12,000ft. Consequently, the unmistakable shape and sound of Valiants, Vulcans and Victors became a more regular part of rural life in the UK as the V-force crews descended from above the clouds and began to thunder over Britain's hills and valleys at 500ft, or even lower in specific low-flying areas, much to the surprise and occasional annoyance of those who lived underneath the new low-level air corridor that was set up for V-force training.

The V-force's key objective was to demonstrate its potential ability to successfully destroy its allocated targets in the heart of the Soviet Union. This was the fundamental basis of deterrence. Mutually Assured Destruction

ensured that both East and West would not and could not contemplate nuclear warfare. However, the concept of deterrence could only work if both sides were able to maintain continually a credible means of destroying each other. If either side had failed, or if either side had been steered into a political situation from which there was no means of escape without resorting to warfare, a global disaster could have easily ensued. The Cuban Missile Crisis illustrated just how easy it was to drift into a situation from which the only logical escape seemed to be an armed conflict. However, deterrence demonstrably did work, and the V-force's very existence ensured that Britain and the West remained secure. Nevertheless, this security was never taken for granted and the following account (based on material produced by John Reeve and other former Vulcan

XL321 illustrates the markings of 617 Squadron (fluorescent orange lighting strikes on the fin), which were initially applied to the unit's Vulcans when the fleet was repainted in disruptive camouflage. The more familiar diamond-shaped tail marking appeared a few years later. (*Tim McLelland collection*)

149

A Vulcan B2 gets airborne. The Vulcan's smoky exhaust emissions were eventually reduced significantly, but never eradicated completely. (*Joe L'Estrange*)

crews) provides a fascinating look at how the Vulcan crews operated during training exercises and therefore illustrates how the Vulcan would have been used operationally, if the 'unthinkable' had happened and Britain had gone to war:

The alert status of the V-force was largely dependant upon our surveillance systems, particularly the BMEWS (Ballistic Missile Early Warning System) at Fylingdales. But it was reasonable to assume that the war would not just come out of nowhere, but would reflect a steady build up of tension over a period of time – the Cuban Missile Crisis being the obvious example. The Force therefore had a series of measures to progressively increase its readiness in response to the international situation and these were regularly practiced on generation exercises. These generations were either ordered by Command under the code names Exercise Mickey Finn or Exercise Mick, or (by the Ministry of Defence) under the Taceval (TACtical EVALuation) programme. As part of these exercises, the aircrew and ground crew would be recalled to base, and Engineering Wing would 'generate' (i.e. prepare for use) as many aircraft as possible. This was taken seriously enough for aircraft in deep servicing to be

re-assembled and placed on the flightline. Crews would meanwhile be changing into flying kit and as a particular aircraft became available they would be detailed to check it by running the normal checklists, up to and including engine start. Once declared as fully serviceable the aircraft was handed back to the engineers and the armourers were free to load the nuclear weapon, which would be a Yellow Sun free-fall bomb or a Blue Steel missile. While this was being done the crew would report to the Operations block where, behind double locked doors in 'The Vault', the station had begun allocating crews and aircraft to targets. Reconnaissance photos and navigational details for a wide range of targets were retained here, together with detailed maps, which outlined suitable routes. The choice of allocation was complicated by the priority given to certain targets that had to be covered first and also because some targets were so far away that they required bomb bay fuel tanks to be fitted. Because there were not enough tanks to equip all aircraft, obviously only certain aircraft could be allocated to those longer-range targets. Moreover, crews were not allocated targets simply at random. Each crew had previously studied and memorised only a very small selection of the potential targets and so they were familiar with, and therefore able to fly, only a very small proportion of the overall range. Matching crews, targets, and aircraft was the job of the station weapons team, who were usually very experienced navigators on a ground tour, and it required close liaison between the engineers, squadron planners, and individual crews, in order to get it right first time.

While this was being done, the armourers would have loaded the nuclear weapons into each aircraft. From the beginning of the 1970s, when the RAF's strategic role had ended, the weapon used was the WE177B, a 400-kiloton device that replaced the Yellow Sun, Blue Steel and Red Beard weapons, which had provided the Vulcan's nuclear capability during the 1960s. That these bombs are now on display in museums (and no longer in RAF service) must be good news. On most exercise generations, the WE177B was simulated by loading a 'shape' – a dummy weapon that gave all the right electronic indications as the relevant switches were 'made'. These switches were the preserve of the navigators, with the Nav Plotter reading the special checklist that was subsequently actioned by the Nav Radar. With a 'shape' this usually took about ten seconds. However, on some exercises you occasionally found a genuine 'live' nuclear weapon had been loaded and with this it was very noticeable how much more steadily and slowly the checks were done. Also – as you cannot be too careful with a nuke – the Nav Radar would inevitably lean back very slightly when he moved a switch, and especially the arming key, just to be that bit further away in the event of a nuclear detonation!

The crew would then place the target and route material inside the aircraft, stow the inflight rations where they could be easily reached, lock the aircraft entrance door and retire to their nearby accommodation. Armed RAF Police would then mount guard with an access list of names and photographs – the list being specific to that particular aircraft – and instructions that nobody, not even the Station Commander, was ever allowed into the restricted area unless accompanied by another authorised person – the 'No Lone Zone' policy. What the Americans call the Use of Deadly Force would be invoked to enforce this rule. The weapon system – the aircraft, crew and weapon – could now be declared to Command as At Readiness State 15. If this sounds like a highly organised and totally secure system, the illusion is somewhat spoilt by the fact that there was actually only one key for all Vulcan aircraft, reference number FA501 which could be, and often was, bought at Halfords in Lincoln High street to replace the keys that occasionally got lost. WE177B arming keys were also not as unique as we had hoped, a similar design being used in 'one-armed bandit' fruit machines to change the payout percentage. Readiness State (RS) 15, as you might imagine, required the crew to be airborne within 15 minutes of the order. This was not too onerous to achieve – the crew had to stay together, usually at their squadron or the Mess and be within a few minutes reach of their allocated transport. It was perfectly possible to sleep and live a relatively normal life at RS 15, so it could be held for 28 days if necessary and, in reality it would probably have been longer. RS 15 also required good communications. The line from Command utilised what were called the

XM607 during an exercise deployment to RAF Luqa, Malta. *(Godfrey Mangion)*

'Bomber Boxes', comprising small public address system speakers, that beeped every ten seconds to prove that they were alive and would be used by Command to raise the Readiness States. They were fitted in the Operations Room and from there the Operations Staff could use phones or the station tannoy to pass the message on.

At this stage on an exercise there would be a Command decision and on an actual alert a political decision too, as to whether to disperse the V-force. On an exercise, any genuine nuclear weapon would be downloaded and returned to the bomb dump before the aircraft actually flew. Groups of up to four aircraft would then disperse to a whole range of UK airfields (the 'live' bombs would be flown to dispersal in a real wartime situation). You can still recognise some of these former dispersal fields even today, by the four (or two) concrete fingers close to, or at the end of the runway. These were the Operational Readiness Platforms (ORPs) where the aircraft would be parked. Dispersal on a genuine alert would be a very public action, which might raise tension and it was therefore a very high level decision, but obviously once dispersed the force as a whole was far less vulnerable to attack. On arrival at the dispersal the aircraft would be refuelled and declared back at RS 15 as soon as possible. After dispersing to their allocated sites, the

XM653 shortly before
touchdown at RAF Luqa.
The huge Beverley/
Shackleton servicing
hangar is visible in the
distance, together with
the tail fins of numerous
Lightning interceptors.
(Godfrey Mangion)

next stage of a an exercise generation (reflecting the
path that would be taken in a real war scenario) was to
go to RS 05, obviously to be capable of being airborne in
just five minutes. This would be ordered by the Bomber
Controller over the Bomber Box in a standard format:

Attention, this is Bomber Controller for Bomblist
Charlie. Readiness State Zero Five for Bomblist
Charlie. Readiness State Zero Five for Bomblist
Charlie. Readiness State Zero Five. Bomber
Controller Out.

Although most communications were obviously
authenticated, this particular message was not
authenticated on the assumption that there was no
advantage in any enemy sending the V-force to RS 05.
Crews would run or drive to their particular aircraft, be
admitted by the RAF Police and board the aircraft in a set
order. The captain would go first to get ready to start the
checks, the air electronics officer (AEO) would be next,
to start the APU (auxiliary power unit), the co-pilot would
follow him, and then the Nav Plotter and Nav Radar. The
door would be then closed and checks completed to get

the aircraft to RS 05, which was everything up to, but not including, engine start. With no fuel being burned – apart from the APU – RS 05 could be held for up to five hours, the limit being, essentially, crew fatigue. It's quite likely that it would have been a flexible limit if necessary, however, depending on the seriousness of the situation. The next stage was RS 02, which was ordered in a similar format to the RS 05 message and involved the starting of all four engines, probably using the rapid start system, which could spin an Olympus up to self-sustaining speed in about five seconds (a modern big turbofan engine today will take up to a minute to achieve the same steady state). The message could be passed over the radio or over a dedicated external intercom plugged into the Vulcan between the engine jet pipes – the telescramble. If the aircraft was not on an ORP it would be taxied to the runway and lined-up for take-off. As the aircraft was now burning fuel, RS 02 could only be held for a short time and would only be ordered if the aircraft were almost certain to be scrambled. The requirement to get airborne in two minutes was obviously linked to the four minutes warning that Fylingdales could provide and the crews would now be waiting for the scramble message, ready to go. The final order to scramble would be authenticated, as a false launch of the V-force would require time to recover to base and the aircraft would be off readiness for some time. The navigators would have a sealed envelope containing the authentication codes and be ready to confirm the order, which would be in the following format:

Attention, Attention. This is Bomber Controller for Bomblist Charlie. Scramble. Authentication Echo Two Bravo, Echo Hour One Nine Four Fife Zulu for Bomblist Charlie. Scramble. Authentication Echo Two Bravo, Echo Hour One Nine Four Fife Zulu for Bomblist Charlie. Scramble. Authentication Echo Two Bravo, Echo Hour One Nine Four Fife Zulu. Bomber Controller Out.

This order would be repeated constantly by the Bomber Controller and relayed by ATC (air traffic control) on any and all airfield frequencies. The message also implied take-off clearance. The ATC might announce that the aircraft were clear to take-off, which was certainly polite, but once ordered the Vulcans were going anyway.

The E Hour was a time datum and if the crew were scheduled to bomb at, for example, E plus 3 hours 10 minutes, then the time on target was 22.55 Zulu. Achieving this should deconflict each aircraft from other 'friendly' nuclear weapons, although there was obviously no opportunity to predict when and where any enemy bombs might arrive. Once airborne the aircraft would climb rapidly and be turned swiftly towards the northeast, continuing to climb up to high level. At this stage the force had been ordered airborne, but it had not yet been given clearance to proceed on its mission. Therefore a Positive Control Line was established at a position over the North Sea known as 8 East and the force would, if necessary, orbit at this position until the fuel situation dictated a return to base. Obviously the Russians would be aware of the scramble, as their satellites would have picked up the mass of radio traffic ordering the take-off. In effect this was part of an increasing diplomatic and military pressure that would hopefully generate some common sense at political levels, bringing the situation to a conclusion without any exchange of weapons. Equally the scramble might have been to get the aircraft airborne in response to incoming weapons, but without a political decision to retaliate, the force would not continue into the USSR. The Vulcans thus headed northeast in hope of a recall, but to avoid giving any additional information away, all aircraft transmissions were minimised. There would be no radio transmissions and once in the holding positions at 8 East the radar would only be used when facing west – away from Soviet listening devices – to update the navigation kit. Each crew would, however, be listening out on all relevant frequencies, which would include base RT (radio transmitter) frequencies, the long range Bomber Command high frequency radio net and even the old BBC Light Programme and Home Service, which used the powerful transmitters at Daventry. The Positive Release Message would be in the format:

… Is Now In Force

The Nav Radar would open another envelope to confirm that the codeword was correct and once this was received it was irrevocable and Armageddon was inevitable. The crews would now turn east and, with a few exceptions, head towards Norway and Sweden, the exceptions being the aircraft going to the Kola Peninsula. Strict emission control (EMCON) would hopefully hide each aircraft from the Soviet air defence system until they penetrated their long-range early warning (EW) line, which was based on the use of 'Tall King' radar. This was a large, immobile radar, whose locations the RAF knew. It had a range at altitude of some 250 nautical miles and so, well before this range, each crew would start a descent to low level so as to stay out of its coverage. The assumed EW lines included radars based in Finland, as the V-force calculated that by this time in any real conflict Finland might well have been over-run and their radars linked back to the Soviets' via the Finnish TV system, which was compatible with Soviet radar data. Norway is, of course, in NATO and knew the V-force's proposed routing, but the Vulcans' routes would also have taken them over neutral Sweden, which had – and still has – a first class air defence system. It is assumed that the Vulcans would have made their transit over Swedish territory without incident and then settled down over the Baltic, flying as low as common sense and captaincy would allow. There would be a final visual or radar position update based on Oland or Gotland Islands, scanning backwards to the west with the radar to conceal its emissions from the Soviets. The only radio emission would be from the Vulcan's radar altimeter, which pointed straight down and its transmissions should not have been detectable at great ranges – or so the RAF believed.

The forward-looking terrain-following radar would definitely be off while over the sea and would only go on as the aircraft approached the southern Baltic coast. The crews would also switch off cabin ventilation and go to 100 per cent oxygen to avoid breathing any contaminated air, which might be present if enemy weapons were being detonated. Also at this point, the pilots might put on the infamous eye patches, which have become a part of V-force folklore. The cockpit blinds would be up, and if a pilot had to look out he wore a patch over one eye

so that any nearby nuclear detonation would cost him only one eye. If any more blinding detonations occurred it is unclear how each crew could have proceeded, but in such a desperate situation it is likely that even without any ability to see, the crews would have endeavoured to press home their attack. The pilot would continue to fly the aircraft and the remaining two-eyed pilot (if there still was one) did any necessary look out … or at least that was the theory.

Traditionally, Soviet defences were shown on the RAF's maps marked in red. In the 1960s the defences were a solid red line down the Baltic, but at least it was a fairly thin red line. By the 1980s it was (as crews often wryly commented) 'as if somebody had suffered a nosebleed over the East German and the Baltic States coast lines', such was the increase in known defensive positions. Whatever else the V-force was, it was an effective economic weapon against the Soviet State, because all of these defences were largely there chiefly because of the V-force; bombers from the continental USA would come over via the North Pole, not via the Baltic.

The first line of defence would be elements of the Soviet fleet thrown forward in the Baltic to provide an early warning line. They would have to operate their radars to be of any real use and V-force hoped to detect their emissions and aim between the gaps. In principle, they would not jam these radars as they might effectively give away more by active jamming than they might gain by remaining silent. Of course, by day there was nothing they could do to prevent the visual detection of a large triangular aircraft that trailed a long line of black smoke, so they hoped that if a real wartime mission was ordered, it would be by night. Indeed, on one Vulcan squadron (No. 9) that was their official motto – 'Per Noctem Volamus' and their crews hoped it was an omen. The main line of defences would be at the coast. The first major problem would have been the 'Barlock' ground control radars and the 'Thinskin' height finders that controlled the Soviet fighters. 'Barlock' had a low-level range of about 30 miles. These radars would have to simply be accepted as inevitable and on the same logic as with the Soviet fleet, the crews would not jam them,

Vulcan B2 XL360 on a Sunflower exercise deployment in Malta. The 200-series engine jet pipes are clearly evident, together with the small TFR thimble radome on the nose. XL360 now resides at the Midland Air Museum, Coventry. (Godfrey Mangion)

as they did not, in themselves, constitute a hazard to the Vulcans. They would, however, jam any Soviet fighter radar that locked on to the force, deploy Type 22 chaff and flares, evade violently and hopefully fade away into the darkness to continue the mission. Another tactic would be to penetrate in substantial numbers just south of Riga, giving the defences in that area too many targets to engage at once – the old Bomber Command stream principle. However, the crews had to expect to be illuminated by the 'Fire Can' radars that controlled the anti-aircraft artillery and the 'Fan Song' radars

associated with the SA-2 missile system. Despite the earlier 'nosebleed' comment, the crews took comfort from the fact that the Baltic has a long coastline and the defences could not physically be everywhere at once. Also, the guns had a fairly short engagement zone, although they could shoot at very low-level targets. The SA2 missile, however, with a much longer range, had little capacity against such targets. The SA-3 was more capable, but also more thinly spread. In principle the V-force crews would jam any radar that directly controlled a threat system while manoeuvring to stay

XM569 was the first Vulcan B2 in a batch of forty aircraft ordered on 22 January 1958. It served with the Scampton, Waddington, Cottesmore and Akrotiri Wings. (*Godfrey Mangion*)

outside of the engagement zone of that weapon. There was a formalised evasion plan for skirting missile sites, called the Veronica Manoeuvre, an impressive name for basically turning away and flying around them.

Having evaded the many defensive systems, the Vulcans proceeded into Soviet airspace, but the sheer size of Russia meant that even the Soviet military could not provide low-level radar coverage of the entire country, except around high value military or civilian sites. Routes would be planned to avoid such areas except, of course, that the V-force's targets would, by definition, be high value sites. The routes were also designed to avoid being hit by other 'friendly' nuclear

weapon detonations, so major deviations from the planned route were considered to 'invalidate your Lloyds flying risk insurance policy'. The original Vulcan weapons – Blue Danube, Red Beard, and Yellow Sun – had to be dropped from altitude, but WE177B could be dropped from just 50ft. Therefore, the WE177B plan was to go straight in and straight out of the target area with little manoeuvring and as swiftly as possible, partly to counter Soviet defences and partly to avoid the effects of the Vulcan's own weapon. There was a problem here in that the Vulcan was designed for high-level flight where the airspeed is quite low, even when the Mach number or groundspeed is quite high. The aircraft structure was therefore not designed for very high airspeeds. The general wartime low-level speed would have been only 375kt, with a once-only acceleration to 415kt. This speed of 415kt was not based on scientific calculation, but largely on the RAF's rough guess of how fast VX770 was flying when it broke up in mid-air over RAF Syerston – not a comforting thought. Still, with this subject of comforting thoughts, in the 1960s when the V-force had to climb to altitude to release its weapons, the crews were somewhat concerned that SA-2s and 3s would shoot them down in the climb. Not so they were told, because the Soviets need 112 seconds to detect and engage a target. The good news was that the bomb would detonate 103 seconds after the Soviets first detected the Vulcan; this would burn out the ground radars and thus the missile would loose guidance 9 seconds before the planned impact, and therefore miss! Another comforting thought was that if the politicians could not make up their minds about Positive Release, there was, in certain cases, an option to hold until the Vulcan was down to a planned 1,000lb of fuel – roughly 5 minutes flying over the target. In that case, standard operating procedure darkly stated that the recovery plan would be at the 'captain's discretion'.

On the run to the target the Nav Radar would arm the nuclear weapon. There were two fusing systems and if they did not work the crew had to check the fuses (fuse 616 in panel 3P and fuse 1167 in Panel 4P). The captain would also activate the Bomb Release Safety Lock, which allowed the Nav Radar to release the weapon. The bomb could be released by radar or, if visual, the 'TLAR' system would be used, lining up the AAR (air-to-air refuelling) probe with the target. TLAR stood for 'That Looks About Right'. On release, the WE177 bomb would be retarded by a parachute and for Vulcan operations it would be detonated by a 32-second timer that allowed the Vulcan to reach a relatively safe 5.5-mile distance. The term 'safe' meant not only that the aircraft would not be blown out of the sky, but also that the shockwave would not rush up the engine jetpipes and flame-out the engines. Assuming that the crew survived, they would then send a message estimating their aiming accuracy and weapon yield. The message was in the format 'Call

Sign … Alpha Alpha' – the first letter being accuracy and the second yield. Command would then decipher this as a Category 1 accuracy and Category 1 yield, so the crews effectively had a code for a code. The crews never found out why they just couldn't say 'Call Sign One One' instead … the Russians would know all about the yield and accuracy by this stage. They also never found out how they were meant to actually estimate a weapon yield, never having experienced one before.

Depending on which dispersal airfield the Vulcan started from, the ToT (time over target) would vary because of the different distances involved. More distant dispersals were often given targets that were not time critical – perhaps cities with a military function, rather than bomber bases. For example, a typical profile flown from Ballykelly in Northern Ireland against Kiev would require bomb bay tanks and a high-level phase after bomb release. It had the small advantage that the Soviet defences should, by the time the bomber got there, have been severely degraded. The bomber's route after bomb release at Kiev would include turns that would be put in every 90 seconds, to break lock on SA-2 missile radars. The targets covered by the V-force extended across much of western Russia. The recovery routes were just as detailed as those planned towards the USSR and most were designed to bring the Vulcans back to the UK, but others were drawn-up to head for Cyprus and elsewhere. What the crews would do after landing was of course unclear and obviously could not be planned. The crews vowed that their reaction would be to go home, but would they have had a home to go to? It seems very unlikely. It is also quite likely that many of the Vulcans would have failed to reach their targets and would have been destroyed. As the crews often stated, any half decent Soviet fighter pilot who saw a Vulcan would have simply rammed it if all else failed. By night or in bad weather, however, the V-force stood a good chance, especially if the Soviet defences had been softened up by earlier strikes.

Like many of the Royal Air Force bomber aircraft that preceded it, the Vulcan was very much a multi-man machine and designed to be operated by a crew of five (pilot, co-pilot,

XH538 enjoyed an unremarkable service career, performing flight trials with the A&AEE before joining the Waddington and Scampton Wings. It was scrapped at St Athan in 1981. (*Tim McLelland collection*)

air electronics operator, navigator radar and navigator plotter). A former member of the V-force, Alan Steel, provides a fascinating account of the navigator radar's role:

The best way to begin describing the role of the Nav Radar is to describe the radar itself. We viewed the radar through something called the Indicator 301. It gave a True North presentation, which means simply that north was always at the top of the picture and the on-board compass system kept that so. The reason that it was designed like this was a belief that it made it easier to interpret the radar. Other radars are heading orientated, like the radars looking out the front of the aeroplane, scanning left and right. There would be no point in having a True North picture there because you might be heading east, in which case you wouldn't see very much. Some of my colleagues would have found that a help on some occasions! The radar normally scanned 360 degrees and by convention we had it scanning clockwise; the engineers told me (after, out of sheer devilment, I had flown for five hours with it scanning anti-clockwise) that the reason it should go clockwise is because that's the only way you get any lubrication on the thing, and the scanner was now completely ruined. Still, you live and learn! The aircraft position was normally the centre of the screen. It did not have to be, but it normally was. We called that the Origin and we had the line, known as the

Time Base, sweeping around the screen and you would pick up an almost map-like presentation of the ground underneath, ahead and to the sides of you. Readers who have looked carefully at the Vulcan will be thinking that you can't see behind you because somebody's put a great big aeroplane there. Very true, but at high level you could tilt the antenna down towards the ground and by doing that you missed out maybe as little as 5 or 10 degrees directly behind you and effectively you had a full 360-degree sweep. The screen was 9 inches across and there you have it – that was the 301.

I said that normally the origin would be in the centre of the radar displays, but sometimes you could move it off and you did that by moving the little joystick in front of the indicator. When you moved the origin away, the system produced a range as a curved marker and a bearing marker, and when you wanted to define a point on the ground that you were going to use to fix your position, you used to put that point underneath the intersection of the two markers. Effectively you drove the marker intersection around using the joystick in front of the radar display. The range marker was compensated for altitude such that it produced plan range to the system, in a wonderful piece of very adult Meccano. The whole navigation and bombing system was actually called NBS, the Navigation and Bombing System, but those of us that knew it and loved it called it Navigation by Bits of String! The reason for this was that inside the equipment were all these wonderful electromechanical devices, the best of which I always thought was something called the Triangle Solver. This piece of kit did what it said on the box – it solved triangles. The short side was your altitude and had a little runner, which tracked your altitude. One of the other sides was slant range – the distance from where you were to the object on the ground; but that's not what you want to know when you're going drop a bomb – you want know your actual plan range. Now, when you're at low level, the plan range and the slant range are exactly the same, but when you're 7 miles above the Earth, then that starts to change, and that is why the marker was height compensated. Instead of actually using bits of string, it used the equivalent of metal measuring tape. It may seem as if I am taking the mickey out of the technology and although it was almost a case of having to wind the thing up before flight, it did work incredibly well.

Now we come to Offset Aiming Technique. In our war role, where we were meant to go across into the Soviet Union and bring some heat and light into their lives, you might have been required to drop a bomb, for example, on the middle of Red Square in Moscow. Unfortunately, on the radar it is impossible to distinguish such a target. You could just go for the middle of the town, because if you were going to nuke somebody then you did not really need to be terribly accurate. However, the Royal Air Force insisted that our aim needed to be refined, and that was done through a technique called Offset Aiming. To do this, you use an easily recognisable point on the ground that is close to your target and you aim at that, but you effectively tell the bombing computer that you don't want to take out this place, 'I want you to bomb 2,000 yards to the south and 15,000 yards to the east'. And that is exactly what we did, and there were two sets of offsets, one in the table to the right of the radar display with the little joystick and this allowed offsets of up to 40,000 yards in any direction, and the other was inside the control unit in front of that table, but this only allowed offsets of 20,000 yards. The idea was that the Nav Radars would go off and they would be studying their targets well before flight and they would work out (guess) what would show on the radar that they could easily identify. You were looking for something nice and big to get you into the target area. A power station springs to mind – something that big. So you could start your aiming on the power station and as you got closer to the target, you were looking for something a lot smaller. Choosing the offsets was very difficult and one way you could do it would be to steal somebody else's ideas. There were some very generous Nav Radars around, particularly experienced ones, who used to leave the maps on which they used to pick offsets lying around. So as new boys we used to sneak in and copy them! However, later on, when we got a bit more experienced, we used to pick up any old map, stick a few random pinholes in it and then leave it lying around for just this very same purpose. All's fair in love and war! Having calculated the values,

you loaded them into the offsets; the internal offsets were 20,000 yards or 10 miles north, south, east and west and the external offsets were 40,000 yards, which is around 20 miles. On the bombing run you selected the appropriate offset aiming point into the system and you started aiming on that. Now this was not a foolproof method and the unwary amongst us had been known to bomb the offset! That normally resulted in you wearing your best blue uniform with your heels together and your hat on, in front of the squadron's commander!

The Nav Plotter (the guy who sat in the middle of the aeroplane) was tasked with checking the actual values that the Nav Radar had set in. Now, the external offset box, hidden in the desk, had only a tiny little scale and it was very easy to enter the offsets incorrectly. The Nav Plotter also had the task of making sure that I was not going to drop a bomb on the offset. For instance, if I was saying that the range to the target was 15 miles and his calculations gave it as 18 miles, it was a clue that something had gone wrong. I used to blame him anyway! When it came to choosing the offsets, operationally, you were very limited as to how you would approach the target. For instance, if you were doing a 'round-robin' of the Soviet Union, you tended to come from the west and you wanted to go back home to the east, so you were reluctant to vary your track to come at it from the south or the north. There might well have been one, or indeed a whole cluster of surface-to-air missile (SAM) sites that you wanted to route around as far away as possible – always considered a good idea! The upshot was that we maybe only had a 10- or 15-degree flexibility in how we could change our attack track. For training missions we chose whatever was going to give us the best result. A large external offset like a power station was ideal. You would not be terribly accurate aiming on the middle of a power station, but hopefully that would get you a lot closer to your release offset, which ideally was nice and small.

To give an example, we used to practise 'bombing' Lincoln, using a target that was the middle of a little bridge, which is now in the middle of the shopping precinct. You could not see the target directly on the radar, so we had to use offset aiming points. Somebody had built a nice big power station to the west and to the

Right and opposite: Vulcan B2 XL361 suffered a minor mishap on exercise at Goose Bay. Incorrect fuelling resulted in the aircraft's centre of gravity being exceeded, causing it to tip on to its tail. Damage was minor and the aircraft was repaired. I suffered another accident at Goose Bay in 1981 and it remains there on display. *(BAE)*

east, and somebody had built a sugar beet factory at the little village of Bardney, so if you came in from the north west, tracking to the south east, you would easily see the power station and at around 6 to 10 miles you would start to pick up the return from the Bardney sugar beet factory. Having defined the target very precisely to the radar system on the aeroplane, we needed to tell the pilots up front what we wanted them to do to take us over the target. The same marker system that produced the aiming markers also produced a steering signal, compensated for the wind effect. All the pilots needed to do was fly exactly down this steering signal and we would go right over the target.

The plan range that my dear old friend the triangle solver had worked out would be fed into the bombing computer which would, in turn, calculate how far away from the target you would have to release the bomb for it to hit. You cannot release the bomb when you are directly overhead the target because when you release anything from an aeroplane, at the instant of release, it still has the same speed as the aeroplane. Once released it will start to slow down at a rate determined by its shape. The distance between release and impact was known as forward throw. Before talking about this further, let me briefly return to the steering problem. The steering signal did not just tell the pilots to go left or go right – it actually indicated a bank angle to zero the steering signal. It was

really a 'feed the monkey' system for the pilots! I could control how many degrees of deflection the steering signal would give the pilots on a little control down by my left knee, but normally that was set to something like 2.4 degrees. Normally, at high-level we would prefer to use the autopilot, because then you did not even have to wake the captain up! When the pilots selected bomb function on the autopilot it linked my little joystick to the autopilot. The maximum angle of bank it would ever give you was 45 degrees, I think but the pilots used to chicken out well before it got anywhere near there. It would only control the aircraft in azimuth – you could make it go left or right but not up or down. So the Nav Radar could actually be flying the aeroplane in azimuth using his little joystick and, when we were totally serviceable, the captain would select the bomb door opening switch to automatic, and at a pre-determined time interval before release, the bomb doors would open up and we would get an automatic weapon release. While this system guaranteed maximum accuracy, there was also some psychology going on, as it saved you personally having to press the release button to nuke Moscow (or the little church which is just off to the north).

Returning to forward throw, there was a computer under the co-pilot's chair called the Calculator 3 and that used to work out how far away from the target you would have to drop the bomb for it to hit. At low level, to stop the Vulcan being blown up by its own bombs, someone had the clever idea to fit a parachute to the bomb, effectively dragging it behind you quite a way before it went bang on the ground. Very safe, but incredibly boring, because you don't hear the bangs – well hopefully you don't! I was assured by the armourers that if the parachute did not open, the bomb would not be live. That's a bit like the assurance from the guy that gives you the parachute and tells you to bring it back if it doesn't work. Each weapon type was loaded into the ballistic computer using a 35mm film strip and that computer sat on top of the Calc 3 underneath the co-pilot's seat. To give us great reassurance that it had worked out how far away to drop the bomb, the system displayed the forward throw to us. A smooth 1,000lb bomb would typically fly for about 6 miles if dropped at

40,000ft at a cruising speed of Mach 0.84 – and that's a fair old way. For low level, where we tended to overfly the target, drop the bomb, big parachute and on our way, a 1,000lb bomb with a parachute has a forward throw of 800 yards – about half a mile, when dropped from 300ft at an attack speed of around 350kt. As you can appreciate, there is a fair difference in distance there. Once you knew the distances, height, speed and forward throw, you could introduce a set time interval at which to open the bomb doors before release and that was done as late as possible to keep the bomb nice and warm, before you threw it into the -56° air temperature; you did not want your nuke to freeze up until it absolutely had to. It was normally set at 8 seconds on the Vulcan, which was fine, but operationally there was a snag. If you had unknowingly taken some damage from, say an air-to-air missile and this had affected the hydraulic system, and therefore the bomb door operation, the first you would know about it would be when you tried to open the bomb doors – and they didn't. You would then have to start up the emergency hydraulic power pack, but that took something like 30 seconds to get the bomb doors open. So, here's the situation: you've got Moscow in your sights – eight seconds to release – and the pilot says the bomb doors aren't working. Tell you what, why don't we use the hydraulic power pack? He does that, and 30 seconds later the doors open – 22 seconds after you wanted them open. Unfortunately, you only get one shot at the release signal so you have to grab the button and release the bombs manually. But you are 22 seconds further down the road – not a good idea. In practice, most crews would open the bomb doors manually, probably about 4 or 5 miles from the release point, to make sure the damn things were open before it came to the crunch.

Another little problem we had was when dropping a stick of conventional bombs – maybe a stick of 21 x 1,000lb bombs – was that you would always be aiming the middle bomb at the target. This meant that you had to release the first one extremely early, the middle one at exactly the right time and the last one very late. You could actually programme the stick length into the aeroplane and this length could be maybe a mile. To get your stick length, you could drop the bombs at a different time

interval between each bomb, and that was the Nav Radar's job to work out. This was done on the Weapons Control Panel on the left hand side. It was called a Ninety Way because there were ninety ways of dropping the bombs. Depending on the bomb type, you could set the release interval from 0.24 seconds up to around 5 seconds, and the time interval gave you the distance between individual bombs. During peacetime, dropping bombs is normally to be avoided, however. In fact, the rules said that if you had practice bombs on board you were not even to open the bomb doors over populated territory – unlike the crew I witnessed doing a flypast at a display in Manchester in the early 1970s. They flew past on a wingtip, showing off the lovely delta shape, and then someone decided to open the bomb doors to show all the nice people all the practice bombs on board! There was a wonderful photograph in the *Manchester Evening News* of sixteen practice bombs, all rattling and itching to get out!

The Air Force decided that they would have to introduce an accurate system of no-drop bomb scoring. This resulted in something called the Radar Bomb Scoring Unit (RBSU). Effectively, a very accurate radar picked up the Vulcan coming in on its attack track and followed it all the way through. At about 10 seconds to release, the Nav Radar would switch on a tone on the radio and at the instant of release the computer

Close-up of a Vulcan B2, illustrating the air intake splitter plate next to the fuselage, and the TFR radome. Also just visible is the port wing leading edge, illustrating how the upper-surface camouflage extends on to the undersides. (*Godfrey Mangion*)

switched the tone off. The Nav Radar would then lie through his teeth, telling the operatives on the ground about the Vulcan's airspeed, altitude and other details, and he would also tell them, in a highly secret code, what bomb type was being used. Depending on how the bomb run went, I used to like to change that at the last minute – sometimes it was advantageous, but sometimes you'd get it the wrong way round and create an even bigger error. The ground operatives would calculate your track over the ground, your precise distance at the instant of release and your flight parameters, and work out your bomb score. They would then pass the bomb score back

to you in code. I always liked the wag on the ground who passed you 'M ... I ... S ... S ... E ... D'! The RAF code was actually eight letters long and when we used to go out to America, doing the low-level competitions, their code was something like twelve letters long. I think included your inside leg measurements! Unfortunately, the score went on the telephone and the fax machine back to your base, so if you missed by quite a bit, people knew about it before you got back on the ground. There were RBSUs at RAF Lindholme near Doncaster (now a prison), RAF Coningsby and down in Devon. For some of the UK bombing competition work, they used to take the RBSUs on the road and take them to somewhere where you'd never bombed in your life, nor indeed had all the experienced guys, so you really had to pick good offsets. I reckon that legions of V-force Nav Radars paid people like Wimpey to build power stations where they did – we needed those power stations! If the RBSU was not available, then we could still score bombs by assessing the photographs that the system took. Right above the Indicator 301 screen was the R88 Radar Camera, which had a wonderful headrest – or was it a lens cover – on it. When you went into a bombing run, this thing took a photograph every 7 seconds and a little lamp illuminated at the instant of release. From this your bombing run could be reconstructed on the ground and your score calculated.

For low-level attacks we used to use a conventional vertically mounted camera in the visual bomb-aimers position. In fact I have to thank one of those for giving me my worst ever bomb score. It was something like 12 miles – we weren't even in the right country – we were supposed to be bombing England, the target was on the border and I let it go around 12 miles to the north! It was heels together on the squadron commander's carpet for that one! Bombing accuracy was always very contentious amongst V-force people. At high level (40,000ft and above), the overall accuracy was in the order of 400 yards – not very good. However, when you bear in mind that we were doing it with Meccano and navigation with bits of string, and the primary weapon was a big one, it was perfectly acceptable. A lot of system errors contributed to this inaccuracy: incorrect airspeed, incorrect ground speed and the forward throw calculation could be out by plus or minus 0.2 miles (400 yards). But the main problem really was caused by the Nav Radar not aiming at the right radar response, which might seem like a damning thing to say, but it wasn't that easy, especially if you were a new boy. At low-level the accuracy was the same, because we were still using the same system, but you could cheat a little bit by asking the pilots to resolve the track problem. To do this, you told the pilots not to follow the bomb steer totally, but to compensate for the wind, putting the target either right or left of the nose, which would allow the bombs to drift on to the target.

The other good thing the pilots could do, after nose probes were fitted to the Vulcan, was to use it for range marking. A point exactly halfway down the nose probe as seen from the average pilot's sitting position, would be 800 yards in front of the aircraft. That worked between 300 and 500ft and speeds of around 350kt. In fact, the Near East Air Force Wing out in Cyprus from the mid- to the late 1970s used to put fluorescent tape round the nose probes. 'Just going to calibrate the nose probes' we used to say! It was a remarkably accurate, if unorthodox system. As for system problems in the air, an experienced crew never had a system problem in the air because they would always spot it on the ground and throw the aircraft back at the ground crews, asking for another aircraft. Generally speaking, when we got airborne, we were committed to carrying out all the attacks we had planned and all those attacks would count towards your crew rating at the end of the year. The major prize was Command Rating, and the big advantage of that, other than getting a lovely bright badge for your flying suit and the undying respect of your brother aircrew, was that next year you had to drop less bombs to maintain your rating. To achieve something like Command Rating, you had to drop six bombs within 400 yards of the target, which is tricky when you are working with an overall system accuracy of 400 yards! For every bomb dropped outside 400 yards, we'd have to drop two inside to bring our average back down – quite a challenge.

Graduation ceremonies at Swinderby became synonymous with flypasts from Vulcans from nearby Waddington. As seen in this image, some of these flypasts (particularly those performed by accomplished Vulcan pilot Joe L'Estrange) were particularly impressive! (*Joe L'Estrange*)

10

INTO ACTION

The Vulcan's long and distinguished service career began to draw to an end during the early months of 1982. Although the aircraft's key role had ended in 1970 when Britain's independent nuclear deterrent had shifted to the Royal Navy, the Vulcan soldiered on, tasked with tactical strike duties armed with the WE177. No longer at the forefront of the country's offensive capabilities, the Vulcan was often regarded as a redundant relic of the Cold War, destined for a well-earned retirement. In fact, it continued to play a key part in the RAF's offensive capabilities. Still very much in the nuclear delivery business, the Vulcan squadrons (distributed between Scampton and Waddington) also had a conventional bombing capability and, with their arsenal of WE177s, the Vulcan force presented the East with a formidable presence, assuming a pseudo-tactical role that fitted neatly between the capabilities of the navy's Polaris long-range strike missiles and RAF Germany's tactical strike Buccaneers (later replaced by Phantoms and Jaguars). Additionally, a handful of Vulcans were modified to undertake a maritime radar reconnaissance role, enabling the Victors that had been performing that task to be withdrawn and converted into refuelling tankers. More than twenty years elapsed before any prospect of a replacement for the Vulcan's capabilities finally emerged.

Finally, by the early months of 1982, the end of the Vulcan's long story was in sight. The first Panavia Tornado strike aircraft had been delivered to the RAF and the process of replacing the Vulcan could begin. During April the first Tornado to carry 9 Squadron's unit markings appeared at Waddington, ceremoniously placed adjacent to one of the squadron's Vulcans, which it was now reluctantly dispensing with. The Vulcan units at Scampton also slowly wound down their operations, their aircraft gradually disappearing to museums, other RAF stations (for crash and rescue training) or to end their days being dismantled for scrap. Even 27 Squadron's reconnaissance Vulcans flew their last missions and, with the only surviving Vulcans at Waddington, it would be only a matter of weeks before the mighty Vulcan was replaced in its entirety by the Tornado. However, while the steady progress to retirement was taking place, events were unfolding thousands of miles away in the South Atlantic, which would have a remarkable last-minute effect on the Vulcan's story.

When Argentina invaded the Falkland Islands, it seemed unlikely that the RAF would play any significant part in their recapture. Prime Minister Thatcher's immediate response had been to send a huge naval task force which – at least superficially – looked more than capable of re-claiming Britain's territory. However, the Royal Navy's aircraft carriers didn't actually carry much of a punch. They were equipped only with Sea Harriers, aircraft primarily assigned to the fighter role (protecting the fleet) and with only a rudimentary offensive capability. RAF Harriers were also assigned to the Task Force, but they were relatively few in number and best suited to support of land forces. There was nothing within the Task Force that offered the ability to make a decisive strike against Argentina's occupation and, as the ships sailed south, the British government agreed that if it was somehow possible, the islands should be attacked prior to making any attempt to re-take them by re-invasion.

Most importantly, there was an urgent need to destroy (or at least disable) the airport runway at Port Stanley, which Argentina was using to resupply its occupation. The Royal Air Force had the answer – an aircraft that had been designed for long-range strategic bombing. Due to of the extreme remoteness of the Falkland Islands, only a bomber with truly 'long legs' could conduct a land-based strike against them and, with the aid of air-to-air refuelling, it looked as if the Vulcan would do the job with ease, even though it would require an extremely complex, risky and

Pictured over Cyprus, XM647 remained with the Akrotiri Wing until the early 1970s, when it was re-assigned to Waddington. It was finally retired to Laarbruch in 1982 and subsequently scrapped. *(Tim McLelland collection)*

expensive level of inflight refuelling support. Ironically, the Vulcan was in the process of being withdrawn from RAF service at the very moment that it was actually needed and, although the withdrawal process continued, the RAF turned its attention to those Vulcans that remained active at Waddington, with a view to equipping them for an operational role in the last few weeks of their long careers.

On 5 April ground crews at Waddington began the difficult task of restoring an air-to-air refuelling capability in ten selected Vulcans, to enable air crew to begin training in refuelling procedures as soon as possible. The Vulcans had retained their bolt-on refuelling probes since they were first fitted during the early 1960s, but the fuel system had not been necessary since the aircraft had switched from strategic strike to tactical-bombing operations and the internal fuel-transfer system had either been deactivated or, in the case of many aircraft, the seals and valves had deteriorated to such an extent that the system could no longer be used. Indeed, the refuelling system had been redundant for nearly two decades and when the RAF was suddenly required to provide both transport and maritime aircraft to support the Falklands operations, the

Vulcans had provided a solution. The refuelling probes of retiring Vulcans were removed and used to equip Hercules and Nimrod aircraft with a long-range capability. This serendipitous programme had been useful for the RAF's requirements, but resulted in many of the remaining Vulcans being without the refuelling capability that they now needed. A desperate, urgent search began for Vulcan refuelling probes, nozzles and equipment. Crews were dispatched far and wide to rob the recently withdrawn Vulcans of their refuelling gear. Museum aircraft (including those in the USA) duly became donors and a fortuitous discovery was also made at RAF Stafford, where a batch of 'new' refuelling non-return valves was found in storage.

From the ten aircraft that had their refuelling systems restored, five machines were selected for conversion to full operational conventional bombing standard, XL391, XM597, XM598, XM607 and XM612. These were all equipped with 300-series Olympus engines and the only Vulcans remaining in service with the full fore and aft Skybolt missile attachments. Under the code name Operation Black Buck, these Vulcans would be prepared for attack missions over the Falkland Islands, each carrying twenty-one 1,000lb HE bombs over the staggering distance of 3,900 miles from the nearest operating base at Ascension Island. Preparing the aircraft for a conventional mission was a fairly simple task, since although the Vulcans had been operating primarily in the tactical nuclear role for more than ten years, they retained a conventional capability that crews practised fairly regularly, and only a change in bomb carriers and cockpit control panels was required. A Delco Carousel inertial navigation system (INS) was also installed. This was purchased off-the-shelf from British Airways, which used the same INS in its Boeing 747s, and some gear was also taken from former British Airways Super VC10s in storage at RAF Abingdon, awaiting conversion to tanker standard for the RAF. The first trial INS fit was made at Marham, where the resident Victor fleet had already been equipped with Carousel and Omega, but although the idea of fitting Omega in the Vulcans was considered, the modification was not made.

Five crews were selected (although only four were eventually fully trained) for Black Buck duties, two from 50 Squadron, one from 44 Squadron, one from 101 Squadron and one from the recently disbanded 9 Squadron. Some of these crews had recent Red Flag exercise experience, which it was felt would be of value when faced with a real combat situation. Aerial refuelling training sorties began on 14 April – catching up on thirteen years of inexperience in thirteen days. It quickly became apparent that the Vulcan's refuelling nozzle was prone to fuel spillage and leakage, and various short-term fixes were improvised to prevent fuel flowing back over the windscreen, almost totally obscuring the pilot's forward view. No perfect solution was found and two rows of flat plates were eventually attached to the nose behind the refuelling probe in an effort to direct the stream of fuel away from the canopy. Eventually, after a great deal of trial and error, the system was fixed to an adequate standard and on the evenings of 16 and 17 April the crews flew night-refuelling sorties with Victor tankers. Indeed, even the Victor crews had to familiarise themselves with the skills necessary to refuel from other Victors at night, since until now there had been no requirement for such operations for many years.

The Vulcans selected for Black Buck were all equipped with Olympus 301 engines, which, in an effort to extend their service life and reliability, had been fitted with a restriction device during RAF service. This effectively gave them a maximum thrust of 18,000lb, saving on fuel burn and engine fatigue caused by intake resonance. The engine inhibitors were now removed and the engines restored to their original full-power status, which – as far as the regular Vulcan crews were concerned – effectively gave the them an additional 8,000lb of thrust per aircraft.

As the Argentine Air Force was known to be operating a Boeing 707 in a reconnaissance role over the South Atlantic, and because ground-to-air radar had been positioned in the Falklands, it was also decided to equip the Vulcans with additional ECM protection and the only readily available equipment was the Westinghouse AN/ALQ-101 pod normally carried by Buccaneers. Fortunately, Avro's Skybolt modifications now proved to be invaluable, since the wing hardpoints incorporated for Skybolt carriage provided a suitable location from which to attach the ECM pod and the ducting through with the pod could be wired to the flight deck. More good fortune revealed the presence of some mild steel girders

XH537 pictured at Woodford during Skybolt flight testing. This aircraft later entered RAF service and ultimately became a B.Mk 2(MRR), operated by 27 Squadron. (BAE)

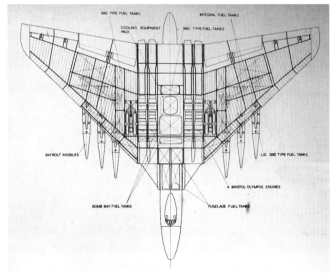

Avro drawing showing just one of the proposed developments for the Vulcan. This variant (which might have become the B.Mk 3) would have carried six Skybolt missiles and probably operated on a continuous airborne alert system, similar to that used by SAC. The concept was dropped when Skybolt was abandoned in favour of Polaris. (BAE)

at Waddington, which had been mistakenly ordered some time previously. When suitable sections were welded together, a near-perfect weapons pylon was produced. The electric cables necessary for operating the pod were run through the Skybolt coolant pipes and connected to a control panel fitted in the air electronics officer's position. XM645 had also originally been selected for Black Buck modification, but because it was a late-production machine, manufactured after the Skybolt programme had been abandoned, it was devoid of the appropriate ducting, so no further modifications were made to it.

The Black Buck Vulcans retained their normal service camouflage, although all squadron markings were removed

XH563 from 230 OCU in company with a Spitfire, posing for the camera over RAF Finningley. Another OCU Vulcan can be seen on the apron below. Interestingly, this is now the very same location from where XH558 – the last flying Vulcan – operates, more than forty years later. (*Tim McLelland collection*)

and the undersides were hastily painted dark sea grey. As the British Task Force sailed towards the Falklands, the Vulcan crews continued intensive training, flying night missions down to 200ft above ground level (AGL) – much lower than ever before. The first two Vulcans (XM607 and XM598) left Waddington for Ascension Island at 09.00Z on 29 April, with XM597 taking off as a reserve, but later returning to base. Supported by Victor tankers, the two Vulcans made their 4,100-mile journey to Wideawake Airfield on Ascension without difficulty, arriving at 18.00Z.

The first mission (Black Buck One) was to be an attack on the airfield at Port Stanley, which the Argentine Air Force was using for transport flights and which Britain expected Argentina to use as a forward base for Mirage, Skyhawk and Super Étendard fighters. Destroying the runway would be unnecessary and foolish (Britain would need it once the islands were recaptured), but disabling it was an important priority. A single Vulcan would be used for the mission, since the tanker support required for just one Vulcan on such a lengthy mission was phenomenal and the RAF simply didn't have sufficient Victors or crews to support anything more than a single aircraft. Wideawake

Airfield was also far from ideal for the RAF's operations, with barely enough space to accommodate the Vulcans and Victors assigned to the mission. Worse still, the runway did not have a serving taxiway, which meant that if the wind direction shifted, the aircraft would have to back-track along the single runway.

On 30 April the wind direction was favourable, however, and just before midnight two Vulcans (XM598, with XM607 as spare) taxied from the airfield apron on to the threshold of Wideawake's runway, accompanied by four Victors (including a spare). At one-minute intervals, in radio silence and with all navigation lights off, the fearsome and magnificent gaggle of V-bombers thundered into the air in a cacophony of sound and a haze of smoke. Each Vulcan carried twenty-one 1,000lb bombs (at an overload take-off weight of 210,000lb, compared to the normal maximum of 204,000lb), while the Victors were heavily laden with transfer fuel required for each other and the Vulcan. Shortly after their noisy departure, a second wave of seven Victors (one a reserve) roared skywards and the huge thirteen-aircraft formation began heading south, climbing to 27,000ft.

The crew of the primary Vulcan (XM598) encountered continual problems with the aircraft's port direct-vision window, which refused to seal properly, thus preventing them from pressurising the cabin. Consequently, XM607, captained by Flight Lieutenant Martin Withers, became the primary aircraft for the mission and as XM598 returned to Wideawake the formation climbed at 260kt to 30,000ft, a compromise altitude between the optimum cruising heights for each aircraft type. The plan was for the Vulcan to make five refuelling contacts ('prods'), but six were actually made, since the Vulcan's unusually high operating weight, together with the additional drag of the ECM pod, required more fuel than envisaged. The long haul south was maintained at heights varying between 27,000ft and 32,000ft, severe thunderstorms and turbulence being encountered along the way, making the task of formatting and refuelling even more difficult and hazardous than usual. Thirteen V-bombers in a severe storm, at night, was no place for the fainthearted. Most of the supporting Victors gradually peeled off and headed north, eventually leaving just two Victors and XM607 to continue to the Falklands.

XL446 was the last in a
batch of 24 Vulcan B2s
ordered in February
1956. Its flying days
ended in March 1982
and it was scrapped at
Waddington a few months
later. *(BAE)*

A familiar sight for motorists on the A15 and countless enthusiasts, as a Vulcan (XM571 from 101 Squadron) streaks over the perimeter fence at Waddington while the road vehicles wait at the traffic lights. (*Shaun Connor*)

Unbeknown to the Vulcan crew, the Victor tasked with the Vulcan's final pre-attack refuelling prod had flown into severe turbulence while refuelling from the second Victor (XL189), causing contact to be broken. This made it necessary for the receiver to head back to base, leaving XL189 to refuel XM607. Squadron Leader Bob Tuxford, captain of the Victor, was forced to wave the Vulcan off (using signal lights) before its tanks were completely topped up, otherwise there would have been no way in which the Victor could have returned to Ascension safely.

At 300 miles from the target, the final stage of the attack began and XM607 descended to approximately 250ft for an under-the-radar approach to the target, the co-pilot re-taking his cockpit seat from an air-to-air refuelling instructor (AARI), who had sat there temporarily while the prods were being made. At 40 miles from the target, Flight Lieutenant Withers hauled the Vulcan back up to 10,000ft (the necessary 'pop-up' manoeuvre) and turned on to a heading of 235 degrees, directly towards Port Stanley's airfield. Some initial difficulty was encountered in establishing a radar picture, since the H_2S airborne radar system had been switched off for most of the flight (the nose probe fuel pipe runs through the radar bay and the mixture of electrical activity and fuel was judged to be a potentially dangerous combination), but a good picture of the Falklands was eventually secured. At least one Argentine radar illuminated the Vulcan en route to the target, but it fell silent when the AN/ALQ-101 pod was activated. Withers

intentionally steered the Vulcan across the airfield runway diagonally, ensuring that at least one bomb stood a good chance of hitting the tarmac, as the long 'stick' of bombs straddled the target. In just five seconds (although the crew later said that it seemed like an eternity) the twenty-one bombs dropped from the bomb bay and a few seconds later the airfield erupted into a brief blaze of light. A few of the bombs were fitted with thirty- and sixty-second delay fuses, adding to the confusion of the occupying Argentine forces, who had been enjoying a peaceful night until XM607's dramatic appearance. At 07.46Z the code word 'Superfuse' was relayed to base, signifying the success of the attack (a 1982 equivalent of the Dambuster's famous 'Nigger' code word). This finally enabled Squadron Leader Tuxford in Victor XL189 to radio for another Victor to be scrambled from Ascension, so XL189 would not run out of fuel some 400 miles from Wideawake.

Turning northwards, the plan had called for an initial outbound height of 300ft, but to conserve fuel XM607 began to climb towards the first refuelling rendezvous, which was eagerly awaited, the Vulcan already being some 8,000lb short on fuel. As the time for the Victor rendezvous came and went, the Vulcan crew began to worry, but thirty minutes later contact was made, thanks to the assistance of a Nimrod crew, who directed the two aircraft towards each other. With roughly one hour's worth of fuel remaining, the refuelling was complicated by a considerable amount of leakage, making forward vision difficult. This prompted the Vulcan's nav radar to stand halfway up the pilot's access steps, to peer through a small portion of the lower windscreen that remained clear, in order to co-ordinate the task. The rest of the flight back to Ascension was long and tedious, but thankfully uneventful and XM607 touched down at Wideawake at 14.52Z to complete what was (at the time) the longest bombing mission ever flown by any aircraft. To this day it remains as the longest bombing mission in the history of British military aviation.

The attack was successful; the oblique approach to the airfield had virtually ensured that one bomb would fall on the runway and one such bomb did indeed produce a 115ft crater (84ft deep) on the runway, almost midway along its length. Additional damage was caused to other parts of the airfield, including the destruction of a hangar – pretty

Squadron Leader Joe L'Estrange brings XM597 in for a low and slow flypast at Greenham Common. (*Paul Tomlin*)

A rare photograph of
the Vulcan B2 (MRR)
equipped with air
sampling pods, pictured
at Luqa, ready to embark
on the long flight home to
RAF Scampton. (*Godfrey
Mangion*)

impressive for a crew that had been trained for the task
of delivering nuclear bombs on to rather larger targets.
The Argentinians were denied the unrestricted use of the
airfield, limiting the aircraft types able to use the strip
for the rest of the conflict. Although the huge crater was
repaired, Argentina's forces failed to prevent the area from
regularly subsiding and the attack had permanently halved
the useable length of available runway. Some attempts
were reportedly made to build decoy craters on the runway
in order to deter further attacks, but there is little evidence
to substantiate these claims, and of course a decoy crater
would be just as effective as a real one in denying the

runway's use. The attack had been extremely difficult
to accomplish, but it was undoubtedly a huge success.
Not only did it render the airport runway almost useless,
it also demonstrated to Argentina that even its mainland
bases were not invulnerable from attack, prompting the
allocation of fighter resources away from the Falklands, in
defence of these airfields and providing a greater degree of
local air superiority for British Harriers and Sea Harriers.

In fact, the practicalities of attacking Argentina directly
were never actively considered by the RAF, since the task
would have been too ambitious to contemplate seriously.
However, the seeds of doubt had been sown, and the Vulcan

raid achieved everything that had been required of it. A second mission (Black Buck Two) was flown on 3 May with the same aircraft, effectively making a repeat performance of the first sortie. However, the attack altitude was raised to 16,000ft, and sadly no bombs hit the runway, even though significant damage was caused to surrounding parts of the airfield. A third mission (Black Buck Three) was scheduled for 16 May, but forecast winds would have reduced fuel reserves beyond an acceptable limit and the mission was cancelled before take-off. In the meantime, XM607 had returned briefly to Waddington, where the port pylon was removed (the crews thought, erroneously, that it would

cause excessive drag), and XM598 had been replaced by XM612. Flight Lieutenant Withers was certainly satisfied with the results of Black Buck One:

Thanks to the massive team effort involving twenty aircraft [sic] and about 200,000 gallons of fuel, we managed to put a bomb on the runway, which was the aim of the exercise. We thus denied its use to high-performance aircraft and showed the Argentinians that we had the capability to attack their mainland – a threat which they certainly took seriously, because many of their Mirages which had been deployed south

XH558 in service as a K2 tanker with 50 Squadron. The starboard air-sampling pod is pictured with the nose filter cap removed, revealing the internal structure of the pod. *(Mike Jenvey)*

XM575 from
44 Squadron, above
what became a familiar
landmark for Vulcan
crews over three
decades, as well as
countless Second World
War bomber crews
– Lincoln cathedral.
(Joe L'Estrange)

were recalled to defend their own bases. This must have considerably helped the Harriers to attain air superiority.

Following the attacks on Port Stanley's runway, attention turned to Argentine radars, in particular the Westinghouse AN/TPS-43F and a Cardion TPS-44, plus Skyguard and Super Fledermaus units that were also in use. Back at Waddington, plans were made to equip the Vulcan for anti-radar attacks. The AS.37 Martel anti-radar missile was selected as a suitable weapon, since the RAF already had these missiles in good supply for its Buccaneer squadrons. Requiring roughly eight times as many wires to be attached than an ECM pod, the engineering crews at Waddington worked long and hard on the Martel fit until, on 4 May, XM597 flew with a Martel for the first time. The weapon was mounted on its port wing hardpoint, with an ECM pod to starboard.

A live firing was made over the Aberporth range the next day, after a cold-soak at altitude. Although the test firing was successful, there was some concern over the reliability of the missile after a long flight south at high altitude. Now the US government stepped in and offered to supply the AGM-45A Shrike, soon after the Secretary of State (Alexander Haig) had ended his infamous 'even-handed' mediation between Britain and Argentina. The Vulcan's pylons were reconfigured to accommodate a Shrike under each wing and more trial flights began; the pylons were subsequently adapted to carry twin-missile launchers. On 26 May, XM596 flew to Ascension, followed a day later by XM597, which was fitted with missiles at Wideawake.

The first operational anti-radar mission (Black Buck Four) was launched on the night of 28 May, but the attack was aborted five hours into the mission when one of the supporting Victor's HDUs (hose drum units) failed. Black Buck Five began the following evening and everything went well, with XM597 descending to 300ft approximately 200 miles from the Falklands. At 20 miles the aircraft climbed to 16,000ft and quickly picked up signals from the primary target, the AN/TPS-43F radar, although the unit was quickly switched off. It was later learned that the Argentine operators were attempting to make the radar's signal strength weaker than normal in order to fool the Vulcan crew into thinking that the radar was further away than it really was, and thus lure the Vulcan within the range of anti-aircraft guns. However, forty minutes later the radar was re-acquired and two Shrikes were launched at 08.45Z on 31 May. One of the missiles caused damage to the radar, but it was quickly repaired and a revetment constructed to protect it from further damage.

Black Buck Six was launched on the evening of 2 June, this time with four Shrikes, and the same radar unit was again identified during the run-in to the Falklands. After spending forty minutes in the area waiting for that or any other radar to illuminate the Vulcan, the crew made a dummy run towards Port Stanley's airfield and a Skyguard radar was quickly identified. Two Shrikes were launched and made a direct hit; four Argentine soldiers were killed. As the Vulcan's fuel state deteriorated, XM597 began the long journey north, making a rendezvous with a Victor with assistance from a Nimrod crew.

The Vulcan's refuelling was not without incident, however, and during the prod the aircraft's probe broke off at the tip, leaving XM597 without sufficient fuel to reach Ascension. The only alternative was to divert to the nearest airfield, which was Rio de Janeiro in Brazil. Even so, there was little chance of reaching the Brazilian coast if the Vulcan remained at the refuelling height of 20,000ft, so a climb to 40,000ft was initiated to conserve fuel. The two remaining Shrikes were fired off, but one hung up; there was no other way to jettison the missile and it remained attached to its pylon. Various sensitive documents were collected and loaded into a holdall bag, before being dumped through the crew entrance. In order to open the door at 40,000ft, the cockpit was first de-pressurised while the crew breathed oxygen. At a distance of around 200 miles a Mayday call was made to the airport at Rio. Contact with Brazilian ATC was difficult at first because XM597's crew attempted to keep their identity concealed for as long as possible, while diplomatic staff contacted embassy officials in Rio. However, an initial descent to 20,000ft was eventually cleared and, with the runway just 6 miles away by this stage, a straight-in approach was initiated, involving a dramatic steep spiral descent, with airbrakes out and throttles closed. Thanks to some careful flying by the captain, Squadron Leader Neil McDougall, XM597 straightened out at 800ft, just 1.5 miles from touchdown (at twice the normal speed) and then made a gentle landing with only 2,000lb of fuel remaining – less than that necessary for just one airfield circuit. After landing, the hung Shrike was made safe before Brazilian authorities impounded it. The Vulcan crew was well treated and although they were soon allowed to leave, they elected to stay with XM597 until it too was cleared to leave, minus the Shrike. On 10 June the aircraft returned to Ascension and on the 13th flew home to Waddington, complete with a new refuelling probe.

Black Buck Seven took off from Ascension on the evening of 11 June, with Vulcan XM607 flying a bombing mission against airfield facilities at Port Stanley. The British forces anticipated capturing the airfield, so there was no desire to cause further damage to the runway itself. Apart from an engine flameout that required three relight attempts the mission was completely successful, and a full load of 1,000lb HE and anti-personnel airburst bombs was delivered over the airfield.

Four days later the Argentine forces on the Falkland Islands surrendered and no further Vulcan missions were undertaken. The Vulcans made their way back to Lincolnshire and the bizarre story of the Vulcan's

Waddington Wing Vulcans preparing to perform a demonstration scramble for HM the Queen during the 1977 Jubilee review of the RAF at Finningley. *(Tim McLelland collection)*

last-minute reprieve came to an end – almost. A variety of weapons options for the Vulcan were considered while the Black Buck operations were being carried out, including the use of Sidewinder AAMs and laser-guided bombs (LGBs). Indeed, LGB trial flights were made in the UK, but none of these options was used operationally. After the Vulcans had returned to Waddington, conventional bombing training flights continued, together with some anti-radar defence suppression sorties; XM597 and XM607, among others, were noted carrying Shrike training rounds until 44 Squadron disbanded on 21 December 1982, finally marking the end of Vulcan bomber operations. However, even this sad event was not the end of the RAF's long association with the Vulcan, since 50 Squadron remained in business, operating Vulcans as AAR tankers.

As a direct result of the Falklands conflict, the RAF suddenly had a huge requirement for air-to-air refuelling tankers to support the seemingly endless supply flights to and from the Falklands (and Ascension Island), while maintaining day-to-day activities refuelling the fighter, and offensive support squadrons back in the UK. The Victors were heavily committed to this AAR task and although the conversion of VC10s into tankers was now under way, there was a short-term requirement for even more tankers. While the USAF was supporting RAF operations in the UK with its Boeing KC-135 tankers, it was decided to convert a number of Hercules and Vulcan aircraft swiftly into single-point refuelling tankers. The initial proposal, sent to British Aerospace at Woodford, was to install a hose drum unit in the aft section of the Vulcan's bomb bay, the Vulcan then being designated B(K).Mk 2. However, this idea was dropped, mainly because of the resulting proximity of the receiver to the tanker aircraft. It was felt that for safety reasons the HDU should be placed as far aft as possible. The ECM bay was therefore identified as being a suitable location (the internal equipment being unnecessary for tanker operations) and this would also allow an additional fuel tank to be installed in the bomb bay. XM603, which had been delivered to Woodford after retirement for static display, was used as a mock-up platform but, as J.J. Sherratt (BAE's assistant chief designer for Victor tanker systems) explains, the task of fitting the HDU was far from simple:

Sunday morning saw a group of us standing around a crated HDU, thinking that if it was anything like the size of the crate, we wouldn't stand much of a chance of fitting it. Even with the crate removed it looked big, but by this time we had resolved to get it into the Vulcan even if it meant restyling the back of the aircraft. There was no way of straight-lifting the five-and-a-half foot wide HDU through the existing ECM opening of four feet, but we noticed that the top part of the HDU could be separated from the bottom, and that we might be able to get the top half through the opening, leaving the bottom half to be straight-lifted in. A piece of wood the same size as the top section was called for to investigate the possibility. The verdict was that there was plenty of room if we had

a good shoehorn, and if necessary we could put the odd blister here and there to cover any awkward bits. After a design team meeting in the afternoon, we agreed to tell the MoD that we could do the job and, in the general euphoria, a target of three weeks to first flight was set. On Monday, two representatives from Flight Refuelling arrived to advise us on splitting the HDU and at around midday we received authority from MoD to proceed to the conversion of six aircraft. The first aircraft, XH561, arrived on Tuesday, by which time a whole army of workers had been mobilised to work all the hours it needed to do the job. Seven weeks to the day, on Friday 18th June, the first converted aircraft made its first flight at 12.32 p.m. An interim CA release was granted on June 23rd, and the first aircraft was delivered to the RAF on the very same day.

Greatly valued at the time, the Vulcan K.Mk 2 did not enjoy a particularly long career with the RAF, since although the Vulcan proved to be an excellent tanker aircraft, the hose drum units had been out of production for some time, and the Mk 17 HDUs fitted to the Vulcans had already been allocated to the VC10s being converted as tankers. As the VC10s were slowly completed, the HDUs were removed from the Vulcans, starting with XJ825 on 4 May 1983. Finally, on 31 March 1984, 50 Squadron, the last operational Vulcan unit, disbanded at Waddington, leaving its fleet of six K2s and three B2s to be delivered to museums and fire dumps.

XM597, which had been used for anti-radar strikes during the Falklands conflict, was ferried to East Fortune in Scotland, where it remains to this day with the Museum of Flight. XM652 was dismantled at Waddington and moved by road to Sheffield, where a private purchaser planned to house the aircraft in a leisure complex. Sadly the new owner failed to establish the precise proportions of the Vulcan's airframe and decided that it was simply too big. The aircraft was therefore offered for re-sale and it was subsequently scrapped, with only the nose section surviving with a private collector. A happier fate was in store for XL426, as the MoD decided to retain the aircraft on a temporary basis for air display appearances. Of the Vulcan tankers, XM571 was flown to Gibraltar,

Martel missile attached to XM597's port-wing pylon during launch trials performed in 1982. (*Tim McLelland collection*)

where it was placed on display next to the runway and quickly became a popular attraction for thousands of passing tourists. It didn't survive for long and a change in command eventually led to a decision to remove the aircraft and it was scrapped on site during 1989. XL445 was flown to Lyneham, where it was used for crash rescue training until 1991 when it too was scrapped. XJ825 remained at Waddington, in use as a crash-rescue and battle damage repair airframe until 1992, when the scrap merchant arrived to dismantle it. XH561 was flown to RAF Catterick and served as a crash and rescue trainer for a few years, until its wrecked carcass was finally

removed as scrap. XH558 was flown to RAF Marham on 17 September 1984 and in a matter of hours the aircraft had been abandoned, awaiting the eventual attention of the station's fire crews, who would slowly destroy the airframe during rescue exercises. XH560's future appeared much brighter, however, and it was designated as a replacement for XL426 (which was running out of hours) on the air display circuit (it was already used as a reserve aircraft for this purpose). However, as a crew from Waddington began to remove all usable items from XH558 over at Marham, a study of XH560's paperwork revealed that only 160 flying hours were left before a

Twin-rail Shrike missile
fit on Vulcan XM597.
(*Mike Jenvey*)

major service was due. After examining the logs of the other recently retired aircraft, it was discovered that, by comparison, XH558 had 600 hours left until its next major service was due. It seemed obvious that the aircraft should be swapped and so the hapless XH560 was flown to Marham (where it was eventually scrapped during 1992) and XH558, looking rather battleworn, was restored to a basic flying condition and ferried back to Waddington during November.

The next major task was to convert XH558 back to standard bomber configuration. A draft SEM (Service Embodied Modification) was compiled by Chief Technicians Brian Webb, Al Hutchinson and Bob Leese. This was submitted to both the MoD and British Aerospace at Woodford for approval and in February 1985 the conversion began. The HDU housing, associated fuel pipes, air pipes and huge quantities of wiring were removed and the original electrical system was restored. After two months (and roughly 1,200 man hours) XH558 was once again a B2, albeit in a slightly modified state since the ECM equipment was not replaced in the tail fairing because of structural modifications made by BAe during tanker conversion. The associated cooling duct on the starboard side of the tail cone was not replaced either, but this was the only external difference between XH558 and a standard B2. Internally, however, some tanker systems were retained, and one of the three bomb bay fuel tanks was also left in place, to counterbalance the missing ECM equipment. Following minor servicing, the aircraft departed for RAF Kinloss, where it was stripped and re-sprayed in an unusual wrap-around camouflage paint scheme that certainly looked smart, but certainly didn't look authentic. Emerging from the paint shop at Kinloss in November, XH558 made its public debut the following year.

With XH558 now regularly appearing at air shows around the country, XL426 was retired and sold. Stored temporarily at Waddington and Scampton, it was purchased by Roy Jacobsen, a businessman who had the means and will to fly a Vulcan under civilian ownership. He had already purchased XM655, which was duly delivered to Wellesbourne Mountford and plans were made to fly the aircraft at a limited number of shows during 1985. However, the CAA (Civil Aviation Authority) ultimately refused to give the aircraft a Certificate of Airworthiness (its rules and regulations being complicated and very demanding), and despite a great deal of discussion and debate, XM655 was destined to remain grounded at Wellesbourne. Undeterred, Jacobsen successfully bid for XL426 and, after having secured the co-operation of Heavylift Engineering to restore the aircraft for civilian operation, he had it flown to Southend Airport. Unfortunately, Jacobsen's relationship with the intransigent CAA deteriorated and despite attempts to secure a viable engineering arrangement with various companies at Southend, the Vulcan's future seemed increasingly bleak. British Air Ferries eventually performed a $5,000 survey on the aircraft and estimated that some $500,000 would be needed to restore it to the CAA's standards. This was sufficient to convince Jacobsen that flying a Vulcan would be impossible and, after a long period of inactivity (and more than a little acrimony), Jacobsen agreed to abandon his interest in XL426 and it was transferred to the care of the Vulcan Restoration Trust. This group of volunteers subsequently worked tirelessly to maintain it in good condition and XL426 is now a well-known exhibit at Southend Airport, occasionally making full-power runs along the runway on special open days (as does XM655 at Wellesbourne).

XM612 pictured after
having arrived at
Wideawake Airfield
following a long ferry
flight from Waddington.
(BAE)

11

BEYOND THE END

When Vulcan B2 XL426 was sold and flown to Southend, the RAF was left with only one Vulcan, XH558. It's short-term future seemed assured, since it was a major attraction at every event it attended, but the continuation of the RAF's Vulcan Display Flight at Waddington (XH558 actually belonged to 55 Squadron at Marham for administrative purposes) was regularly reviewed by MoD. While XH558's countless fans watched with delight as Squadron Leader David Thomas and Flight Lieutenant Paul Millikin put the aircraft through its paces every summer weekend, there was continual doubt as to how long the aircraft could actually remain in RAF service as an expensive, non-operational asset. Sufficient airframe hours remained to allow XH558 to fly a full 1992 display season and possibly a more restricted number of venues during 1993, but no official decision on the aircraft's subsequent fate was announced until shortly before it was offered for sale.

This final act of disposal by the MoD prompted a number of campaigns and petitions to keep XH558 flying. The Vulcan Association (VA) was formed in 1987, dedicated to publicising the uncertain future of XH558 in the hope that continual public support would encourage the MoD to keep the Vulcan flying. Sadly, internal politics befell the group and despite its many thousands of members, the VA effectively disappeared long before the aircraft it was supposed to be supporting. The future for XH558 continued to be just as uncertain as it ever was. There was no official statement from the Secretary of State for Defence, just a bewildering range of varying statements from MoD departments. The cost of maintaining XH558 was doubtless a major factor in the decision to ultimately ground the Vulcan, but the biggest factor appears to have been the cost of refurbishing the aircraft for another five to ten years of display flying, combined with the projected costs of continued operation and support. Cost estimates

from the MoD varied wildly from £750,000 to more than £2 million, depending upon who was asked.

Petitions continued to be signed (estimated at over 100,000 signatures) and MPs continued to be questioned, but the final disposal of XH558 remained in the balance. In November 1992 the MoD announced that XH558 was, at least for the time being, no longer for sale. In addition, the RAF confirmed that the aircrew had been instructed to remain current and that the Vulcan's ground crew had not received postings to new units. Consequently, there was great optimism within the many enthusiast communities that XH558 would be retained for further display flying and the possibility of civilian sponsorship began to look like a workable proposal. Most notably, the Save the Vulcan 558 Campaign made great efforts to convince the MoD that XH558 could be operated by the RAF on a no-cost basis, with civilian finance, and the future began to look a little brighter. But sadly the MoD had evidently decided to dispose of the aircraft almost regardless of any sponsorship proposals that might have been organised given sufficient time. The final blow was the announcement that the RAF would not be able to provide suitably qualified manpower to service the Vulcan beyond the end of 1993. The MoD based this statement upon the fact that the remaining Victor tankers would be retired at that time and consequently the RAF would no longer retain any technicians with V-bomber experience. Whether this really was a valid point is open to question, since the RAF continued to train crews for similarly sized aircraft, such as the VC10 and Nimrod, and the predictable reaction of the Vulcan's supporters was that the MoD was simply washing its hands of the whole affair and looking for a suitable excuse to cease operations. However, whatever its reasons, the MoD stood by its view that XH558 was a public expense that simply could not be afforded any longer, and early in 1993 it was announced that XH558 was once again for sale. This was, perhaps,

Sketch drawn up by RAF Victor crews showing the complicated aerial refuelling arrangement that was necessary in order to get Vulcan XM607 to and from its target at Port Stanley. *(Tim McLelland collection)*

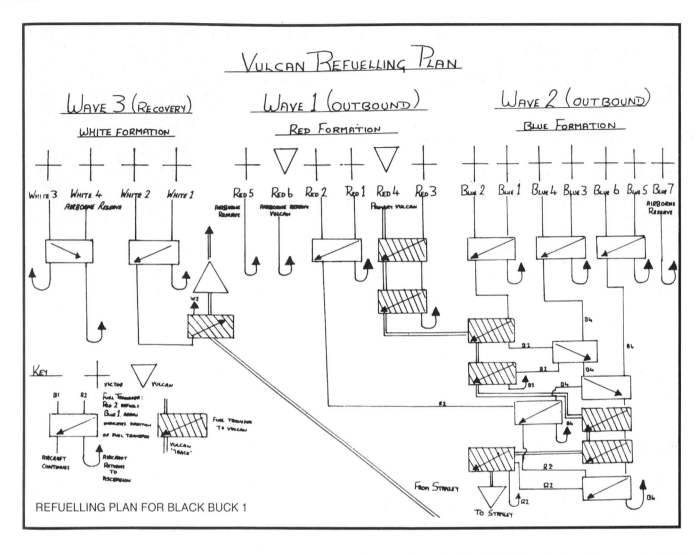

inevitable, but the debate as to whether it was the right decision will doubtless continue for many, many years. It was estimated by some commentators that the Vulcan had become the RAF's most popular air show attraction and yet the MoD had decided to end XH558's career, merely authorising monthly continuation flights to keep its crew current, until a final delivery flight could be made to a permanent resting place.

For some time the final fate of XH558 was unclear, but while the aircraft continued to make occasional crew continuation sorties from Waddington, there appeared to be some hope that it might be kept airworthy once the RAF had finally disposed of it. However, romantic notions of seeing a Vulcan operate under civilian ownership seemed a little unrealistic when the CAA made its position very clear. As far as the CAA was concerned, the Vulcan was a 'Complex' aircraft, which could not be permitted to fly on the civil register, at least not without the direct support of its manufacturer (British Aerospace, which was equally unenthusiastic). There were various bids made to the Ministry of Defence for the aircraft, including a bizarre plan to turn the aircraft into a restaurant, but among the

A post-Falklands celebratory formation of four Vulcans that participated in Operation Black Buck. XM607 leads the formation. (*Tim McLelland collection*)

XM597 pictured after returning from operations in the South Atlantic. The aircraft is still devoid of unit markings and retains the dark grey undersides applied for the Black Buck missions. *(Tim McLelland collection)*

Opposite: Laser-guided bombs were trial fitted to Vulcans in anticipation of their use over the Falklands, but they were never dropped operationally. *(Tim McLelland collection)*

interested parties was David Walton, head of a profitable family business based at Bruntingthorpe in Leicestershire. Among Walton's business interests was a huge airfield at Bruntingthorpe, once used by the USAF as a B-66 and B-47 base, and now used primarily as a car storage and test facility. A number of preserved aircraft had already arrived on the site and Walton was persuaded to put in a bid for XH558. His offer was accepted and on 23 March 1993 the aircraft was prepared for the relatively short ferry flight from Waddington to Bruntingthorpe. Not surprisingly, the

event caught the attention of countless aviation enthusiasts and a large number of spectators assembled around Waddington's perimeter to see the Vulcan's very last flight. Although there was plenty of optimism surrounding the aircraft's future, almost everyone believed that this would, indeed, be the last time that a Vulcan would fly.

Shortly after 11 a.m., XH558's four engines were started and the assembled crowds (which by now resembled a small air show audience) prepared to witness the historic event. Although there was a great deal of excitement, there was a also a tangible feeling of sadness and more than a few tears were wiped away as XH558 made its way to the runway threshold for the very last time. Finally, the Olympus engines gave out their ear-splitting roar and XH558 thundered skywards, heading west to begin a short tour of some familiar Vulcan sites, including Finningley, Coningsby and, of course, Woodford. Returning via Scampton, the Vulcan was steered above Lincoln Cathedral for the last time, before heading directly over Waddington, bomb doors open (with the legend 'Farewell' painted inside) for a final salute, a gentle wing rock signifying the very end of the Vulcan's long and illustrious RAF career. Just a few minutes later, XH558 arrived overhead Bruntingthorpe before making its final touchdown on the airfield's 10,000ft runway.

This would have been the end of the story, but David Walton's enthusiasm prevailed, and he continually maintained contact with both the CAA and British Aerospace, carefully exploring the many and varied concerns that the authorities expressed as being good reasons to keep the Vulcan grounded. Months of inactivity began to run into years, and although XH558 was occasionally treated to a full-power take-off run, its wheels remained on the runway, the aircraft seemingly doomed to remain flightless forever. However, Walton's dedication and persistence was rewarded, and after the Vulcan had effectively been transferred into the care of the VTTS (Vulcan To the Sky) Trust, the CAA agreed in principle that a Permit-to-Fly could be given to the Vulcan (now registered as civilian aircraft G-VLCN) if a whole series of very detailed but vital steps were taken. Initially, a feasibility study was undertaken, revealing that the project was indeed viable, and this led to a technical survey, specifying the actual maintenance and restoration that would be required to make the aircraft fit to fly again. Both British Aerospace (now BAE Systems) and Marshall Aerospace were heavily involved in this task, and following a very thorough investigation, it was concluded that XH558 was in remarkably good condition and that restoration could begin.

XH558 now disappeared into its hangar at Bruntingthorpe, before being slowly disassembled into its main component parts. Many of these items were outsourced to companies appointed to undertake specific

An interesting
photograph showing
many of the weapons
used by the Vulcan.
However, it does not show
the Yellow Sun, Blue
Danube or Red Beard
bomb casings.

restoration tasks, before each component was gradually returned to Bruntingthorpe for reassembly, prior to flight testing. However, the engineering task was only part of the restoration project. Most importantly, the necessary funds had to be found with which to finance the programme and despite a continuing trickle of money from donations and fundraising, the cost of restoring XH558 continued to climb steadily. Thankfully, the Heritage Lottery Fund eventually accepted an application for a grant, which effectively allowed the project to remain viable, but even this wasn't enough to get the aircraft to flight status. The entire project, which had been running for some seven years and cost $6 million, reached crisis point late in 2006. Literally at the last minute, it was saved by Sir Jack Hayward, who donated a further $500,000 so that work on the Vulcan could continue to flight test. Sir Jack commented: 'It should never have been allowed to stop flying. It's a lovely aircraft that will give a real thrill to the British public.'

Thankfully, his generous donation was enough to complete the project, enabling XH558 to finally fly again after having remained earthbound for more than fourteen years. After full restoration was completed, a series of engine runs was performed and on 18 October 2007, the mighty Vulcan leapt into the air once more, much to the amazement and sheer joy of thousands of enthusiasts. Getting the aircraft back into the air was a magnificent achievement, but the project still required much more money if the Vulcan was to keep on flying. Hopes of major sponsorship never translated into any substantial support and the project limped from month to month, reliant upon donations from the Vulcan's countless fans across the world. This support, together with income from display appearances, was sufficient to keep the aircraft in the air through the 2011 air display season but as ever, XH558's future is just as uncertain as it ever was.

Squadron Leader David Thomas, a former Vulcan captain, resumed his association with the Vulcan when XH558 returned to flight in 2007. Among the pilots responsible for displaying the newly restored aircraft, David was also one of XH558's last display pilots when the aircraft was still in service with the RAF:

The Ministry of Defence Participation Committee issued a list of venues that XH558 would be released to appear

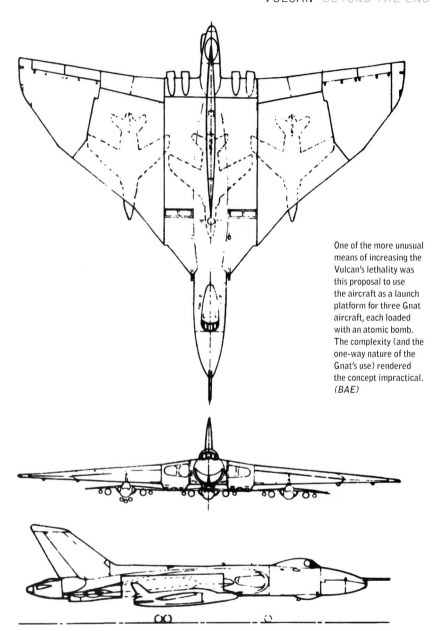

One of the more unusual means of increasing the Vulcan's lethality was this proposal to use the aircraft as a launch platform for three Gnat aircraft, each loaded with an atomic bomb. The complexity (and the one-way nature of the Gnat's use) rendered the concept impractical. (BAE)

at. The situation was slightly different back in 1992, as this was acknowledged as being the Vulcan's last year, so the Vulcan Display Flight was given some choice as to the show selections. Amazingly, although we obviously wanted to fit in as much as we could that year, we only

managed to add another two or three displays than normal, as we just ran out of crews. People were just not available away from their normal flying tasks. So a great deal of time was spent putting together a show programme for the season, making sure the aircraft was fully serviceable and that the crews were available at the right times and then we would liaise with each individual show venue, finding out exactly what they wanted and what time they wanted us to appear and so on. At Biggin Hill in 1992 for example, we flew out there on the Friday, and they used us as a static exhibit. Then on the Saturday we flew out to do a display at Locking, a flypast at Lyneham and then back to Biggin to do a display and land. That was quite a difficult one, as I had to fly the aircraft in a heavy configuration at Locking and of course the aim is always to have the aircraft as light as possible during displays, not only because the aircraft is then more manoeuvrable and therefore more impressive, but because she also uses less fatigue… and it also causes less fatigue for the pilots! Ten thousand pounds weight makes an incredible performance difference and we try to display with around 20,000lb of fuel, but at Locking I had 31,000lb of fuel. On the Sunday I launched early to do a short display and land, and then after a quick turn-round we took off again to fly to Cosford for another display and then on home to Waddington. In that way we flew two sorties, which means more ground work, but the actual flying element is much easier. It sounds fairly easy, but sometimes it was very difficult to tie three

different venues together on time. Some organisers are better than others at doing it. We always had freedom in deciding where we would stop and mount our displays from, but there would always be naturally imposed limitations such as flying hours and fatigue, which was always kept to a minimum.

Once we got to the venue, we always tried to get maximum exposure, so whenever possible we tried to park close to the crowd, in order to let everyone see the aircraft. But both Paul Millikin and I always preferred to be removed from any outside interference, however. People are very well-meaning and interested in the aircraft, asking lots of questions and so on, but about an hour before take-off I liked to get myself under control, calming everything down, thinking about the wind, working out how I'm going to fly the manoeuvres and things like that. So we always aimed to keep the spectators away from the aircraft at least an hour before take-off. That allowed me to get into the right frame of mind, so that I could fly the aircraft to the limit of its performance, but still have spare capacity to see what was going on around me. Obviously the last thing I wanted was to climb into the aircraft all hot and bothered, irritated and angry at someone maybe, or perhaps just distracted by something that someone might have said. It didn't always work like that though, and it's amazing how things could disrupt the flow. One of the Vulcan's problems was that it didn't have air conditioning, and sometimes you could be operating in cockpit temperatures of up to 130 degrees, so you got pretty hot. You always took cans of drink along to keep replacing lost fluid, but it always was a problem.

The amount of information we received from the display venue tended to vary quite considerably too. For example, taking Biggin Hill again, they were always very good, providing the material well in advance, creating no hassle. Other show organisers won't come clean until the last minute and obviously you need to know the time you're wanted on display, how long you've got to display, where the crowd and display lines are, and where the holding points are. Otherwise I expected the show organisers to already know what the display would be like, but things were kept flexible and, for example, where we usually included a touch-and-go, we would convert this to a low flypast when the runway was either unsuitable or didn't exist. But organisers knew our display sequence pretty well.

However, although we kept ourselves flexible, once we'd agreed a timing, I expected them to stick to it. If they came to me and said that we'd be ten minutes late, that would then create a knock-on effect right down the list of displays for that day, making things very difficult. So we insisted they stuck to their word, although in all honesty we always included some timing flexibility, but we kept that as an emergency back up, rather than allowing show organisers to go crazy. We would receive an instruction 'package' from each venue, with things like a drawing of the airfield layout, support services that would be available, who else would be displaying and a time schedule. We always flew to the clock, even on pre-show arrival days and we planned to arrive at each venue within a couple of seconds of our scheduled time, purely as a matter of professionalism. We didn't include any diversions, touch-and-goes, anything like that in our transit flights, the aim was always to go straight to the venue, fly a circuit to look at the airfield traffic pattern, and then land. The only exceptions were things such as the occasional flypast, not least at nearby Cranwell during their graduation ceremonies, and we would time our departure to include things like that.

For pilot continuation training we would fly specific dedicated sorties, often going over to Marham to run through a practice display. We had a 14-day currency

XH558 receiving a final touch-up after being re-sprayed at Kinloss, prior to becoming a dedicated air display aircraft. (BAE)

requirement and if we hadn't displayed within the preceding 14 days we would have to fly a practice display before flying before a show crowd. We always flew our display practices over Marham, simply because XH558 was actually a part of No. 55 Squadron and we had to fly there in order to be seen by our supervisors. It may seem rather odd that the aircraft was part of a Marham squadron but hangared at Waddington, however, one should bear in mind that Waddington was an established Vulcan base, where lots of technical support remained and where all the spares were kept. Hangar space was also available too. The aircraft was always flown clean, without any equipment, although our golden rule was to never separate ourselves from our personal baggage, so we carried that with us. Otherwise we transited as we displayed, to the clock, and with a light fuel load, to minimise flying time and fatigue. We usually carried two members of the ground crew with us so that there would be someone with us as soon as we arrived at a show site. We would often send a ground party ahead of us by road, but we carried people with us, just in case their transport broke down. We could then drop them off on a taxiway and let them guide us into our parking position. Most people these days are not familiar with Vulcans, and it's not a very manoeuvrable aircraft on the ground. One thing we had to watch was the organiser who stuck you in a slot that you couldn't taxi out of. If you didn't

XM651 is dismantled at Waddington. It illustrates some rarely seen details, such as the inner trunking of the engine exhaust and the flap/aileron actuating mechanism. *(Joe L'Estrange)*

have a towing arm with you, then you had a problem. It happened maybe once a year, and if there was any doubt we would take a towing arm with us by road.

I tended to become a little hardened to the whimpering of some show organisers who expected us to move heaven and earth to accommodate their wishes, but after so many years of display flying, we knew where the line was to be drawn and we'd do so much and then no more, simply saying that if we were messed around anymore we'd go home. And that had a very sobering effect on people! There were some shows where we came very close to just going home, but in the end the organisers saw sense; it's not a case of us being bloody-minded, it's just that when you have two or three shows to do in one day, you figure that if the organiser can't give you a take-off time within five minutes of a desired time, there must be something wrong with their ability and you can't disrupt maybe three displays because of a delayed take-off at just one place. Over the years we tended to display at the same venues, so there wasn't much that surprised us. However, you did see some incredible contrasts. For example, when we flew at Mildenhall we had 9,000ft of concrete and an enormous airfield. But after displaying there we went to Barton in Manchester, where there's about 3,000ft of grass and

the visual perspective is completely different. Instead of performing well within the boundaries of the airfield, you get a great urge to fly a really tight display, in order to stay within the boundaries of a much smaller airfield and of course it just doesn't work, and it's something you have to watch carefully. In a more conventional aircraft you could inadvertently stall the aircraft by trying to fly in a tightly confined space, whereas the Vulcan's very good as it just doesn't stall no matter how tight it gets. All the military shows we flew at were provided free, although the organiser had to provide the cost of accommodation, food, bringing equipment and so on. The civil shows had a blanket charge of something less than £2,000, a nominal fee, which obviously didn't pay for much.

It's interesting to note that towards the end of the Vulcan's display career, one show organiser simply stated that they would pay whatever the necessary asking price was, because they just had to have the Vulcan at their show. It's an incredible display aircraft, as it's a unique design, and XH558 was the only one of its kind. It flies very slowly, it's very manoeuvrable, it's big and it's noisy, quite unmistakable. A great deal of the pre-flight preparation was entrusted to the ground crew, but we still made a walk-round check, really just looking for the more obvious things. Personally I didn't regard the Vulcan as a lump of metal, but as something closer to an animate object, and each aircraft had its own characteristics. I tended to touch the aircraft, talk to her even, just to get myself together, to become at one with the aircraft. Sure you look at the tyres and hydraulic lines, but it's more to do with becoming part of the aeroplane. Sounds strange with a 120-ton aeroplane maybe, but that's how it was. Once inside the aircraft we ran through the whole pre-flight checks right from square one in complete detail. You could rush things, but that's no way to go into a display, and we'd always allow plenty of time. If everything went smoothly you could expect to go from climbing-in to getting airborne in maybe 35 minutes, but you don't want to erode your margins, and we'd aim to work with about 50 minutes to spare and then we could sit and hold at engine start, until the required time. It's an electrical jet, so if the aircraft had been standing out in the damp for any length of time we'd get silly little

XH558 back in the air in civilian hands – the last flying Vulcan. *(Tim McLelland collection)*

XH558 posing for the camera over the Lincolnshire countryside, shortly before retirement from RAF service. More than a decade later the aircraft returned to the air, externally unchanged but meticulously refurbished for civilian operation. (Tim McLelland collection)

electrical failures, especially in the navigation system, but luckily that wasn't really necessary for most displays. Since the Vulcan was dedicated purely to flying displays, we only lost just two displays, one because of engine intake cracks and one because the undercarriage failed to retract, and with only a minimal amount of fuel it would have been impossible to fly the display with the gear down, so I recovered back to Waddington. Problems were mainly of a minor nature. The vital things such

as the flying controls and engines never caused us any problems. It's only when the weather is bad that things like the navigation kit and the bombing system become important. It's amazing that back in the days of regular squadron service you'd have to drag the rear crew into the aircraft kicking and screaming, whereas now you couldn't keep 'em out! Certainly, if the rules allowed, you could have flown displays without the navigators on board, but you had to have the Air Electronics Operator on board as certain switch selections had to be made in the event of an electrical malfunction, in order to safeguard the integrity of the aircraft.

Basically there are two systems to start the engines. One is to use a ground air supply, to pump air into the engine. The other is to use stored air in high-pressure bottles contained inside the aircraft. We generally insisted on having a Palouste air starter at each display site so that we could use the internal rapid start system as a back up, rather than our primary means of starting the engines; another instance of not eroding your margins. Additionally, you can use one engine to start the others by cross-bleeding air to turn the other three in turn, the normal procedure being to start each engine directly from the Palouste unit. The internal rapid start system has sufficient pressure to make six individual engine starts, so there was always a great deal of redundant capacity in terms of engine start capability. The starting procedure was indicative of 1960s' technology and unusual by modern standards in that you would deliver air to the engine, let it wind up, then manually control the fuel flow into the engine before igniting it. So you started with a small fire, helping the engine to accelerate, and then you'd add more and more fuel until it was self-sustaining. Of course you could start all four engines at the same time with the rapid start system, and you could prepare the aircraft so that just one button needed to be switched to fire up everything automatically, but that was obviously not something we needed for display flying. There was more than sufficient thrust to get a good taxi speed with the engines at idle speed, but we would use a bit of thrust to gain a little inertia and then throttle back and use the brakes to keep speed in check. You can use differential braking to steer, but the Vulcan also has a nose wheel steering system using hydraulics in relation to the position of the rudder pedals. You can barely see the wingtips from the cockpit and they're a long way behind the main wheels, so when you make a tight turn you get what is called swept wing growth, and the wings seem to swing out much wider than you expect, but we were aware of the situation. At display venues you had to be very conscious of the problem, as there was often great pressure to put the aircraft into tight spots.

July 2008 and XH558 is back on the runway at Waddington after an absence of more than fourteen years. (*Tim McLelland collection*)

For take-off we'd run up to 80 per cent power and hold on the brakes, check that the engines are functioning correctly and go to full power as the brakes are released. You check that the engine acceleration stabilises at a predetermined rpm, which was dependent on air temperature. On a hot day we'd be looking for a minimum of 98.5 per cent rpm. Okay, the power isn't critical with so much in reserve, but if I didn't get that figure I'd obviously want to know why, as I might have an engine failure on my hands. In the take-off phase if you lose an engine you're likely to lose the adjacent one as well, which can be serious if you're flying slowly, or flying a display. Operationally we would practice three-engine take-off procedures as the aircraft has more than adequate performance with just two engines, and it has a climb-away capability even at a heavy weight on only one engine, but for display flying we always required all four to be functioning perfectly. XH558 has the Olympus 200 Series engines, whereas many Vulcans had the more powerful Olympus 300 engines and these aircraft featured a combat cruise selector restricting maximum power to the roughly the same figure as that attained by the less powerful aircraft like XH558. After some years in service, the aircraft with 300-Series engines had the cruise selector permanently wired up, in order to conserve engine life, which was degraded at full power, due to resonance inside the engine.

Normally we aimed to take off into a holding position, to give us time to settle down, but we often went straight into the display sequence. The rotation speed was usually 135kt, and that remained the same until the aircraft weight rose quite significantly. With no wind the take-off run was about 2,000ft. The display datum speed was around 155kt and even the tight turns were entered at that slow speed. You were able to manoeuvre fully at slow speed, and it always appeared to be close to the crowd because of its size, so the display was always impressive. Because the aircraft was essentially built to fly long straight lines, it has a very heavy feel when you're flying a display sequence, and we tended to use full control deflections. For example, in a steep turn we'd have full up elevator, and that gets very tiring. An 8-minute display is like 24 hours of normal work. It's physically demanding to fly a display in the Vulcan and despite the Vulcan's fighter-type control stick, we tended to use both hands in a steep turn. Another point to consider is the need to balance the adverse aileron yaw that is created by the Vulcan. If you roll quickly, one set of ailerons goes up, the others go down, and you start to yaw. So before you move the ailerons you must move the rudder to counter the yaw.

There's no finesse involved in Vulcan display flying. The only reason we used so much bank at the top of the turns was to bring the nose down more easily. The climb angle was very steep, and trying to bring the nose down with wings level would create a significant bunt, and the Vulcan isn't designed to fly negative-*g* manoeuvres, so we rolled the Vulcan on to its side and allowed the nose to fall through. The Vulcan's negative-*g* limit was zero, the positive limit being just two, so the secret of how we made the display look so impressive was to fly slowly. Modern aircraft can't perform well when they're close to their stalling speed, whereas it was no problem for the Vulcan. At the top of a tight turn the speed was even lower than the datum display speed. All the manoeuvring was done in a heavy buffet, which in a conventional aircraft would mean a deep stall, real trouble, but in the Vulcan we didn't have that problem.

Basically you cannot stall the Vulcan's wing. If you look at the stalling angle, the point where lift starts to decrease, it's 48.5 degrees angle of attack, but by that time the aircraft would have so much drag that it would be difficult to recover. What you actually get is a great deal of airflow separation over the top of the wing, so when we're manoeuvring we're sitting in very heavy buffeting but at a low speed, flying a big, flat plate through the air. The only stall warning as such would be a low speed indication and a very high angle of attack, but with a unique aircraft like the Vulcan, you could get out of that situation easily by just unloading the wing. There is so much thrust that you could quickly get into a situation where you could overstress the airframe though, so it literally requires just a couple of seconds at most to just unload the wing, get the speed back and then heave back into the deep buffet, because we control the aircraft speed by flying in the heavy drag area. That's why the aircraft display was so noisy, as we were just sat there with the engines roaring away, maintaining a minimum radius turn, using drag to control speed.

Our minimum manoeuvre height was 500ft, the level flypast at 300 and for a touch-and-go we'd hope it was zero feet! The top of the turns was around 1,600ft, sometimes a little lower. As you can imagine, there was quite a level of interest from the guys in the back, and the AEO called out heights, while one of the navigators called out speeds, especially if it went significantly high or low. It was very much a team effort, as when things start to go wrong, they go wrong pretty quickly, so a nudge from the rear crew about our speed or height was always very useful. As for other things going wrong during the display, we had very few problems. Once at a display over Barton we had an aircraft call short finals with an engine failure while I was flying a display, but I was able to reposition, and continue the display without creating a hazard to either his safety or mine. It was always our policy of not having any other aircraft flying over the airfield while we were displaying. You'd think that was pretty sensible, but many display organisers like to maximise their earning potential by having pleasure flights taking place during displays. But despite this, you'd see them flying as you were running in, which is very dangerous.

Touchdown speed was around 130kt and with the high nose angle you couldn't actually see the touchdown point, so you were looking some way ahead of you down the runway and you used your vision either side to judge your position. Close to the runway, the Vulcan sat on a cushion of air, so with the nose high, it was very difficult to have a bad landing. You allowed the aircraft to simply sink gently. If it was slightly fast it would balloon quite significantly. With the whole trailing edge acting as a flap, pulling the stick back would reverse the flap, causing the aircraft to smack on to the ground, so to stop an impact you pushed the nose down, although that would provide only a very temporary respite, because the aircraft pitches quite rapidly. So the easy way out of a difficult landing is to hold a nose-high attitude, put on power and go around again. Going down the runway with the nose held high, the aircraft remains quite responsive, but you reach a speed where you no longer have any control. It will sit there quite happily, but we tended to lower the nose at around 70kt. With short runways where we used the brake parachute, the nose wheel had to be on the ground in order to steer the aircraft

The final retirement of XH558 really did mark the passing of an era. It was tremendously sad for me and the rest of the Vulcan's crew. In the military you have to get used to losing loved ones sometimes, and the Vulcan was yet another loved one which we simply had to say goodbye to.

XH558 was the RAF's first Vulcan B2 and by co-incidence it was also the RAF's last. The very fact that so much money and effort has been put into returning XH558 to the skies illustrates the fascination and affection for the Vulcan that still exists to this day, even though the dark days of the Cold War (for which the Vulcan was created) are long gone. It is strange to witness the very evident public affection for a machine that was designed exclusively for the business of mass murder, but the Vulcan is a 'one-off' which, like the legendary Spitfire, has the ability to impress just by its very presence. By any standards the Vulcan was an outstanding aircraft, which more than fulfilled the promise of its manufacturer. Capable of delivering a megaton-range bomb into the heart of the Soviet Union, the Vulcan was at the very forefront of the West's striking power and undoubtedly ensured the credibility of Britain's (and therefore the West's) deterrent posture for many years. The Vulcan's adaptability, flexibility and sheer strength enabled the RAF to use the aircraft in a variety of roles for which it was never designed, but for which the aircraft was equally well suited. Certainly, it would be impossible to find a former member of the V-force who would offer anything but praise for the magnificent beast. The Vulcan was, and is, a true icon.

VULCAN PRODUCTION LIST

Prototypes
Contract 6/Air/1942/CB.6(a). Dated 6 July 1948

VX770:
Delivered August 1952.
Avon/Sapphire/Conway engines. A&AEE and manufacturer trials, suffered a mid-air explosion due to structural failure at Syerston 20.9.58 and was destroyed.

VX777:
Delivered September 1953.
Olympus 100 engines. Trials aircraft, converted to prototype B.Mk 2, making a first flight in this configuration 31.8.57. Further trials in new configuration before being used for non-flying runway trials with the RAE. Last flight 27.4.60. Broken-up at Farnborough 7.63.

Vulcan B.Mk 1
Contract 6/Air/B442/CB.6(a). 25 aircraft, dated 14.8.52.

1. XA889:
Delivered 16.3.55. Olympus 104 engines. A&AEE trials, Bristol Siddeley trials at Patchway. Struck Off Charge (SOC) 22.8.67. Withdrawn and scrapped at Boscombe Down in 1971.

2. XA890:
Delivered 27.4.56. Olympus 104 engines. A&AEE trials. RAE Farnborough and Thurleigh trials. Manufacturer trials. Radio and radar trials, blind landing trials and ballistics research. SOC 5.5.69. Withdrawn and scrapped at Bedford in 1973.

3. XA891:
Delivered 16.4.56. Olympus 104 engines. A&AEE trials. Bristol Siddeley trials at Patchway (Olympus 200 series), RAE trials at Farnborough. Manufacturer trials. Crashed on a test flight 24.7.59 near Hull due to electrical failure.

4. XA892:
Delivered 27.4.56. Olympus 104 engines. Manufacturers trials and A&AEE armament trials. Delivered to Halton for ground instruction (became 7746M) and scrapped in 1972.

5. XA893:
Delivered 18.5.56. Olympus 104 engines. A&AEE electrical trials connected with B.Mk 2 variant. Broken up at Boscombe Down in 1962, nose section transferred to 71 Maintenance Unit at Bicester. RAFM Cosford (8591M).

6. XA894:
Delivered 29.3.57. Olympus engines. A&AEE trials, engine development trials. Operated by Bristol Siddeley at Patchway, used as engine test bed for Olympus 22R as part of the TSR.2 trials programme. Destroyed during a ground fire while ground running at Patchway 3.12.62.

7. XA895:
Delivered 16.8.56. Olympus 104 engines. Converted to B.Mk 1A. 230 Operational Conversion Unit, Bomber Command Development Unit. A&AEE. Scrapped (Bradbury Ltd) 19.9.68.

8. XA896:
Delivered 7.3.57. Olympus 104 engines. 230 OCU, 83 Squadron, 44 Squadron. Bristol Siddeley test bed for BS100 vectored-thrust engine intended for Hawker P.1124. Partially converted for this role until fighter development was abandoned. Withdrawn during 1966 and scrapped at Patchway.

9. XA897:
Delivered 20.7.56. Olympus 104 engines. 230 OCU, A&AEE trials. Crashed during approach to Heathrow Airport 1.10.56 and was destroyed.

10. XA898:
Delivered 3.1.57. Olympus 104 engines. 230 OCU. Used exclusively by the OCU before being delivered to Halton 25.8.64 for use as an instructional airframe (7856M). Scrapped 1971.

11. XA899:
Delivered 28.2.57. Olympus 104 engines. A&AEE trials, RAE trials at Thurleigh, blind landing experiments. Autopilot development. Delivered to Cosford as an instructional airframe (7812M). Scrapped 1973. Nose section retained by Cosford Museum.

12. XA900:
Delivered 25.3.57. Olympus 104 engines. 230 OCU, 101 Squadron. Delivered to Cosford as an instructional airframe (7896M) 28.2.66. Withdrawn from use and transferred to Cosford Museum as last intact Vulcan B.Mk 1. Scrapped during 1986.

13. XA901:
Delivered 4.4.57. Olympus 104 engines. 230 OCU, 44 Squadron, 83 Squadron. Delivered to Cranwell as an instructional airframe (7897M) in 1964. Scrapped 1972.

14. XA902:
Delivered 10.5.57. Olympus/Conway/Spey engines. 230 OCU. Damaged in a landing accident 28.2.58. Engine trials (Conway and Spey) with Rolls-Royce. Scrapped 1963.

15. XA903:
Delivered 31.5.57. Olympus 101 engines. A&AEE, RAE Farnborough. Blue Steel trials aircraft. Delivered to Rolls-Royce as test bed for Concorde Olympus and Tornado RB199 engines. Experimental 27mm cannon fit at A&AEE. Last flight by B1 at Farnborough 22.2.79. Scrapped 1980.

16. XA904:
Delivered 16.7.57. Converted to B1A standard 1960. Olympus 104 engines. 83 Squadron, 44 Squadron. Damaged in crash-landing at Waddington 1.3.61. Disposed as instructional airframe (7738M) and later scrapped.

17. XA905:
Delivered 11.7.57. Converted to B1A standard 1960. Olympus 104 engines. 83 Squadron, 44 Squadron, 230 OCU, Waddington Wing. Delivered to Newton as an instructional airframe (7857M). Scrapped 1974.

18. XA906:
Delivered 12.8.57. Converted to B1A standard 1962. Olympus 104 engines. 83 Squadron, 44 Squadron, Waddington Wing. Stored at St Athan 10.3.67. Sold as scrap to Bradbury Ltd 6.11.68.

19. XA907:
Delivered 29.5.57. Converted to B1A standard 1961. Olympus 104 engines. 83 Squadron, 44 Squadron, Waddington Wing. BCDU. Withdrawn from use 3.11.66. Sold as scrap 20.5.68.

20. XA908:
Delivered 18.9.57. Olympus 104 engines. 83 Squadron. Crashed in Michigan, USA, 24.10.58.

21. XA909:
Delivered 1.10.57. Converted to B1A standard 1962. Olympus 104 engines. 101 Squadron, 50 Squadron, Waddington Wing. Crashed in Anglesey 16.7.64 following engine explosion.

22. XA910:
Delivered 31.10.57. Converted to B1A standard 1962. Olympus 104 engines. 101 Squadron, 230 OCU, 50 Squadron, 44 Squadron. Became instructional airframe (7995M) and later scrapped.

23. XA911:
Delivered 1.11.57. Converted to B1A standard 1962. Olympus 104 engines. 83 Squadron, 230 OCU Waddington Wing. Delivered to St Athan 2.2.67, sold as scrap 8.11.68.

24. XA912:
Delivered 2.12.57. Converted to B1A standard 1960. Olympus 104 engines. 101 Squadron, Waddington Wing.

25. XA913:
Delivered 19.12.57. Converted to B1A standard 1961. Olympus 104 engines. 101 Squadron, Waddington Wing. Stored St Athan 21.12.66, sold as scrap 20.5.68.

Vulcan B.Mk 1
Contract 6/Air/11301/CB.6(a). 37 aircraft, dated 30.9.54.

26. XH475:
Delivered 11.2.58. Converted to B1A standard 1962. Olympus 104 engines. 101 Squadron, Waddington Wing. Became instructional airframe (7996M) 20.11.67. Scrapped 7.6.69.

27. XH476:
Delivered 4.2.58. Converted to B1A 1962. Olympus 104 engines. 101 Squadron, 44 Squadron, Waddington Wing. Withdrawn from use 4.5.67, sold as scrap 21.1.69.

28. XH477:
Delivered 17.2.58. Converted to B1A standard 1960. Olympus 104 engines. 83 Squadron, 44 Squadron, 50 Squadron. Crashed in Scotland 12.6.63.

29. XH478:
Delivered 31.3.58. Converted to B1A standard 1962. Olympus 104 engines. Ministry of Aviation (inflight refuelling trials), Waddington Wing. Delivered to Akrotiri as instructional airframe (MC8047M) 3.69. Later scrapped.

30. XH479:
Delivered 28.3.58. Converted to B1A standard 1961. Olympus 104 engines. Waddington Wing. Delivered to Halton as instructional airframe (7974M), scrapped 1973.

31. XH480:
Delivered 22.4.58. Converted to B1A standard 1962. Olympus 104 engines. 83 Squadron, 44 Squadron, Waddington Wing. Delivered to St Athan 10.11.66, sold as scrap 30.9.68.

32. XH481:
Delivered 30.4.58. Converted to B1A standard 1960. Olympus 104 engines. 101 Squadron, Waddington Wing. Delivered to Cottesmore fire dump 11.1.68, scrapped 1977.

33. XH482:
Delivered 5.5.58. Converted to B1A 1962. Olympus 104 engines. 617 Squadron, 50 Squadron, 101 Squadron, Waddington Wing. Delivered to St Athan 13.10.66, scrapped 19.9.68.

34. XH483:
Delivered 20.5.58. Converted to B1A standard 1961. Olympus 104 engines. 617 Squadron, 50 Squadron, Waddington Wing. To Manston fire dump 3.8.67. Scrapped 1977.

35. XH497:
Delivered 29.5.58. Converted to B1A standard 1962. Olympus 104 engines. 617 Squadron, 50 Squadron, Waddington Wing. Withdrawn from use 17.5.66. Scrapped 1969.

36. XH498:
Delivered 30.6.58. Converted to B1A standard 1962. Olympus 104 engines. 617 Squadron, 50 Squadron, Waddington Wing. Became instructional airframe (7993M), later scrapped.

37. XH499:
Delivered 17.7.58. Converted to B1A standard 1962. Olympus 104 engines. 617 Squadron, 50 Squadron, 44 Squadron, A&AEE. Withdrawn from use 11.65, scrapped later at Bitteswell.

38. XH500:
Delivered 15.8.58. Converted to B1A standard 1959. Olympus 104 engines. 617 Squadron, BCDU, 50 Squadron, Waddington Wing. Became instructional airframe (7994M), to Waddington fire dump, scrapped 1977.

39. XH501:
Delivered 3.9.58. Converted to B1A standard 1961. Olympus 104 engines. 617 Squadron, 44 Squadron, 44/50 Squadron. Delivered to St Athan 3.11.66. Sold as scrap 8.11.68.

40. XH502:
Delivered 10.11.58. Converted to B1A standard 1962. Olympus 104 engines. 617 Squadron, 50 Squadron, Waddington Wing. To Scampton fire dump 1.68, nose section to Waddington for instructional duties.

41. XH503:
Delivered 30.12.58. Converted to B.1A 1963. Olympus 104 engines. 83 Squadron, 44 Squadron, Waddington Wing. To St Athan 6.12.66, sold as scrap 8.11.68.

42. XH504:
Delivered 30.12.58. Converted to B1A 1961. Olympus 104 engines. 230 OCU, Waddington Wing. Delivered to Cottesmore fire dump 4.1.68, later scrapped.

43. XH505:
Delivered 13.3.59. Converted to B1A standard 1960. Olympus 104 engines. 230 OCU, 617 Squadron, 50 Squadron, Waddington Wing. Delivered to Finningley fire dump 9.1.68, later scrapped.

44. XH506:
Delivered 17.4.59. Converted to B1A standard 1960. Olympus 104 engines. 101 Squadron, 617 Squadron, 50 Squadron, Waddington Wing. Withdrawn from use 10.1.68, sold as scrap 8.11.68.

45. XH532:
Delivered 31.3.59. Converted to B1A standard 1962. Olympus 104 engines. Last production B1. 230 OCU, 101 Squadron, Waddington Wing. Delivered to St Athan 17.5.66. Sold as scrap 8.11.68.

Vulcan B.Mk 2
Contract 6/Air/11301/CB.6(a). 17 aircraft, dated 30.9.54.

1. XH533:
First flight 19.8.58. Olympus 200 engines. A&AEE 26.3.59. St Athan Engineering Squadron (8048M). Sold to Bradbury Ltd as scrap 15.10.70.

2. XH534:
Completed 17.7.59. Olympus 201 engines. Manufacturers trials 4.3.60, A&AEE, 230 OCU 6.12.66. Manufacturer for storage 7.4.72. Converted to B.Mk 2(MRR) 8.73. Air sampling modifications. 27 Squadron 14.8.74, St Athan 7.4.81. Sold to Harold John & Co as scrap 16.2.82.

3. XH535:
Completed 27.5.60. Olympus 201 engines. A&AEE 27.5.60. Crashed near Andover 11.5.64.

4. XH536:
Completed 17.7.59. Olympus 201 engines. A&AEE 31.5.60. Waddington Wing 24.11.65. Crashed in Wales 11.2.66 during TFR trials.

5. XH537:
Completed 27.8.59. Olympus 201 engines. Manufacturer trials 31.8.60. 230 OCU 31.5.65. St Athan 14.2.78. Conversion to B2(MRR), air sampling modifications. 27 Squadron 8.5.78. Abingdon 24.3.83 instructional/exhibition airframe (8749M), scrapped 3.82, nose to Bournemouth Aviation Museum.

6. XH538:
Completed 23.9.59. Olympus 201 engines. Manufacturer/A&AEE trials 30.1.61, Scampton Wing 14.5.69. Waddington Wing 29.4.70, 230 OCU 21.4.71, 27 Squadron 3.12.73, 230 OCU 15.1.75, 35 Squadron 28.7.77, Waddington Wing 16.8.78, 35 Squadron 23.11.79, St Athan 11.3.81, sold to W. Harold & Co as scrap 31.8.81.

7. XH539:
Completed 30.9.59. Olympus 201 engines. Manufacturer/A&AEE trials 25.5.61. Blue Steel modifications. Withdrawn from use 12.71, to Waddington fire dump 7.3.72, later scrapped.

8. XH554:
Completed 29.10.59. Olympus 201 engines. 83 Squadron 10.4.61, 230 OCU 1.11.62, Firefighting School Catterick 9.6.81 (8694M), later scrapped.

9. XH555:
Completed 6.61. Olympus 201 engines. 27 Squadron 14.7.61, 230 OCU, manufacturer for fatigue tests, St Athan for structural integrity tests. Scrapped 1971.

10. XH556:
Completed 9.61. Olympus 201 engines. 27 Squadron 29.9.61, 230 OCU. SOC following undercarriage collapse 19.4.66, to Finningley fire dump, later scrapped.

11. XH557:
Completed 13.5.60. Olympus 201/301 engines. To Bristol Siddeley for engine trials 21.6.60. Fitted with Mk 301 engines in outer nacelles (one, followed by a pair), later fitted with four 301s. First B2 with enlarged intakes. Cottesmore Wing 6.12.65, Waddington Wing 8.2.66, Akrotiri Wing 19.4.74, Waddington Wing 15.1.75, 50 Squadron 3.81. Sold to Bird Group as scrap 8.12.82.

12. XH558:
Completed 30.6.60. Olympus 201 engines. 230 OCU 1.7.60, Waddington Wing 26.2.68. Conversion to B2(MRR) 17.8.73, air sampling modifications. 230 OCU 18.10.76, 27 Squadron 29.11.76, Waddington Wing 31.3.82. Conversion to K2 30.6.82, 50 Squadron 12.10.82, Waddington Station Flight 1.4.84. Allocation cancelled Waddington 14.11.84. Conversion to B2 during 4.85, 55 Squadron 9.85. Last Vulcan in RAF service. Sold to C. Walton and delivered to Bruntingthorpe, 23.3.93. SOC 23.3.93. First flight as G-VCLN 18.10.07.

13. XH559:
Completed 30.7.60. Olympus 201 engines. 230 OCU 24.8.60, St Athan 27.5.81, sold to Harold John & Co. as scrap 29.1.82.

14. XH560:
Completed 30.9.60. Olympus 201 engines. 230 OCU 3.10.60. Manufacturer 28.11.60, 12 Squadron 26.9.62, 230 OCU 29.11.63, Cottesmore Wing 23.8.65, Waddington Wing 10.4.67, Cottesmore Wing 2.2.68, Akrotiri Wing 15.1.69, manufacturer for storage 20.10.71. Conversion to B2(MRR) 1.2.73, air sampling modifications 27 Squadron 15.3.74,

Waddington Wing 25.3.82. Conversion to K2 15.6.82, 50 Squadron 23.8.82. Waddington Station Flight 4.84, Marham dump 29.11.84, scrapped 1.85, nose preserved (The Cockpit Collection, Essex).

15. XH561:
Completed 31.10.60. Olympus 201 engines. 230 OCU 4.11.60, Waddington Wing 7.8.67, Cottesmore Wing 8.5.68, Akrotiri Wing 19.3.69, 35 Squadron 6.3.75, 50 Squadron 4.9.81. Conversion to K2 4.5.82. 50 Squadron 18.6.82, Waddington Station Flight 1.4.84. Allocated 8809M 22.3.84. Delivered Firefighting School Catterick 14.6.84, later scrapped.

16. XH562:
Completed 30.11.60. Olympus 201 engines. 35 Squadron 1.3.63, 230 OCU 11.3.63, 35 Squadron 30.4.63, 230 OCU 19.9.63, Cottesmore Wing 1.8.65, 50 Squadron 8.3.66, Waddington Wing 10.2.67, Cottesmore Wing 24.4.68, Akrotiri Wing 15.1.69, Waddington Wing 9.5.75, 230 OCU 27.9.77, 35 Squadron 16.12.80, 9 Squadron 7.81, 101 Squadron 6.82. Firefighting School Catterick 19.8.82 (875851). Scrapped 1984.

17. XH563:
Completed 22.12.60. Olympus 201 engines. 83 Squadron 28.12.60, 12 Squadron 26.11.62, 230 OCU 5.3.65, Waddington Wing 6.8.68, 230 OCU 18.3.69, Scampton Wing 3.5.71, 230 OCU 7.5.71. Conversion to B2(MRR) 9.2.73, air sampling modifications. 27 Squadron 17.12.73. Allocated 8744M 31.3.82 for preservation at Scampton, scrapped 11.86, nose section to Bruntingthorpe.

Vulcan B.Mk 2
Contract 6/Air/11 830/CB.6(a). 8 aircraft, dated 31.3.55.

18. XJ780:
Completed 10.1.61. Olympus 201 engines. 83 Squadron 16.1.61, 12 Squadron 26.11.62, 230 OCU 16.8.63, Waddington Wing 10.10.67, Cottesmore Wing 6.12.68, Waddington Wing 18.4.69, Akrotiri Wing 12.1.70, Waddington Wing 17.1.75. Modification to B2(MRR) standard 31.3.76. 27 Squadron 23.11.76. Allocated for spares recovery 31.3.82. Sold to Bird Group as scrap 11.82.

19. XJ781:
Completed 20.2.61. Olympus 201 engines. 83 Squadron 23.2.61, 12 Squadron 29.10.62, 230 OCU 4.2.64, Waddington Wing 10.2.66, Cottesmore Wing 22.4.68, Akrotiri Wing 18.4.69. Damaged during landing, Shiraz, Iran 23.5.73. SOC 27.5.73.

20. XJ782:
Completed 2.61. Olympus 201 engines. 83 Squadron 2.3.61, 12 Squadron 23.10.62, 230 OCU 20.12.63, Waddington Wing 25.3.66, Cottesmore Wing 9.4.68, Akrotiri Wing 19.3.69, Waddington Wing 8.1.75. Modification to B2(MRR) standard 1.77. 27 Squadron 15.2.77. Flew last Vulcan sortie at Scampton 31.3.82. Allocated to Scampton dump 31.3.82. Reallocated to 101 Squadron 22.5.82. To Finningley for preservation 4.9.82 (8766M). Later transferred to dump and scrapped 5.88.

21. XJ783:
Completed 6.3.61. Olympus 201 engines. 83 Squadron 13.3.61, 9 Squadron 7.11.62, 230 OCU 28.2.64, Waddington Wing 3.1.66, Cottesmore Wing 22.3.68, Akrotiri Wing 15.1.69, 35 Squadron 16.1.75, 230 OCU 11.8.76, 35 Squadron 23.8.76, 617 Squadron 23.11.78, 35 Squadron 3.4.81. Spares recovery 1.3.82. Sold to Bird Group as scrap 11.82.

22. XJ784:
Completed 30.3.61. Olympus 201 engines. Refitted with 301 engines. A&AEE 29.3.61, 230 OCU 22.12.66, Akrotiri Wing 21.7.70, Waddington Wing 15.1.75, 9 Squadron 2.75, 44 Squadron 6.79, 101 Squadron 6.80. Spares recovery 10.9.82. Sold to Bird Group as scrap 8.12.82.

23. XJ823:
Completed 20.4.61. Olympus 201 engines. 27 Squadron 21.4.61, 35 Squadron 2.1.63, Cottesmore Wing 3.64, 230 OCU 11.5.64, Waddington Wing 1.11.66, Cottesmore Wing 29.4.68, Akrotiri Wing 5.2.69, Waddington Wing 17.1.75, 9 Squadron 2.75. Modified to B2(MRR) standard 3.77. 27 Squadron 27.4.77, 35 Squadron 2.4.81. Waddington Wing 1.3.82, 9 Squadron 3.82, 50 Squadron 4.82, Station Flight Waddington 4.1.83, sold to T. Stoddart 21.1.83, delivered to Solway Aviation Society, Carlisle 24.1.83.

24. XJ824:
Completed 11.5.61. Olympus 201 engines. 27 Squadron 16.5.61, 9 Squadron 25.2.63, 230 OCU 2.12.63, Cottesmore Wing 4.7.66, Waddington Wing 4.10.66, Cottesmore Wing 19.6.68, Akrotiri Wing 5.2.69, 35 Squadron 24.1.75, 230 OCU 14.2.77, 44 Squadron 10.79, 101 Squadron 7.82. Last Vulcan to leave Bitteswell after manufacturer's modifications 8.6.81. Delivered to Imperial War Museum Duxford 13.3.82.

25. XJ825:
Completed 27.7.61. Olympus 201 engines. 27 Squadron 28.7.61, 35 Squadron 4.2.63, 230 OCU 30.4.64, Cottesmore Wing 3.9.65, Waddington Wing 11.4.67, Cottesmore Wing 19.2.68, Akrotiri Wing 26.2.69, 35 Squadron 16.1.75. Modification to B2(MRR) standard 13.1.76. 27 Squadron 15.12.76, 35 Squadron 6.4.81, 101 Squadron 1.3.82. Conversion to K2, 11.5.82. 50 Squadron 25.6.82. Allocated 8810M 22.3.84, battle damage repair duties. Struck off charge 5.4.84. Scrapped 1.92.

Vulcan B.Mk 2
Contract 6/Air/13145/CB.6(a). 24 aircraft, dated 25.2.56.

26. XL317:
Completed 14.7.61. Olympus 201 engines. Blue Steel modifications. A&AEE 13.7.61, 617 Squadron 7.6.62, 230 OCU 24.4.74, 617 Squadron 1.5.74. To Akrotiri as 8725M for crash rescue training, delivered 1.12.81, scrapped 12.86.

27. XL318:
Completed 30.8.61. Olympus 201 engines. Blue Steel modifications. 617 Squadron 4.9.61, 230 OCU 22.5.72, 27 Squadron 31.1.74, 230 OCU 1.2.74, Waddington Wing 18.6.75, 230 OCU 5.8.75, Waddington Wing 7.11.79, 230 OCU 21.2.80, 617 Squadron 1.7.81. Last sortie by a 617 Squadron Vulcan 11.12.81. Assigned to RAF Museum 4.1.82 as 8733M. Transported to Hendon 12.2.82.

28. XL319:
Completed 19.10.61. Olympus 201 engines. Blue Steel modifications. 617 Squadron 23.10.61, 230 OCU 14.5.70, Scampton Wing 12.11.70, 617 Squadron 22.4.71, 230 OCU

19.9.72, 35 Squadron 16.10.78, 44 Squadron 1.3.82. Sold to North Eastern Aircraft Museum 20.1.83, delivered to Sunderland 21.1.83.

29. XL320:
Completed 30.11.61. Olympus 201 engines. Blue Steel modifications. 617 Squadron 4.12.61, 83 Squadron 6.71, 27 Squadron 9.71, 230 OCU 29.3.72. Flew 500,000th Vulcan hour 18.12.81. To St Athan 2.6.81. Sold to W. Harold & Co. 31.8.81 as scrap.

30. XL321:
Completed 10.1.62. Olympus 201 engines. Blue Steel modifications. 617 Squadron 11.1.62, 27 Squadron 1.71, 230 OCU 29.3.72, 617 Squadron 15.9.72, 230 OCU 11.10.72, 617 Squadron 13.4.73, 44 Squadron 8.6.76, 230 OCU 8.11.76, 35 Squadron 1.7.81, 617 Squadron 14.9.81. 35 Squadron 6.10.81, 50 Squadron 21.1.82. Delivered to Firefighting School Catterick 19.8.82 (8759M). Highest individual Vulcan operational flying hours (6,952.35). Later scrapped.

31. XL359:
Completed 31.1.61. Olympus 201 engines. Blue Steel modifications. 617 Squadron 1.2.62, 27 Squadron 3.71, 230 OCU 21.10.71, 35 Squadron 1.7.81. Allocated as gate guard at Scampton 1.3.81, but later dumped. Sold to Bird Group as scrap 11.82.

32. XL360:
Completed 28.2.62. Olympus 201 engines. Blue Steel modifications. 617 Squadron 2.3.62, 230 OCU 13.7.71. Waddington Wing 18.8.75, 230 OCU 21.10.75, 617 Squadron 5.12.77, 35 Squadron 31.5.78, 101 Squadron 5.1.82. Sold to Midland Air Museum 26.1.83, delivered to Baginton 4.2.83.

33. XL361:
Completed 14.3.62. Olympus 201 engines. Blue Steel modifications. 617 Squadron 15.3.62, 230 OCU 7.10.70, Scampton Wing 19.11.70, 230 OCU 30.11.70, Scampton Wing 5.4.71, OCU 12.5.71, 27 Squadron/230 OCU 14.1.74, A&AEE 7.8.75, 617 Squadron 3.9.75, 35 Squadron 3.8.77, 9 Squadron 13.4.81. Accident at Goose Bay Canada, 13.11.81.

Grounded 21.12.81 and placed on display at Happy Valley, Goose Bay 7.6.82.

34. XL384:
Completed 30.3.62. Olympus 201 engines. Blue Steel modifications including 301 engines. 230 OCU 2.4.62, Scampton Wing 5.8.64, Waddington Wing 23.3.70, 230 OCU 27.11.70. Heavy landing 12.8.71, allocated 8505M on 30.9.76 as escape trainer. Later transferred to crash rescue training as 8670M 29.1.81, and SOC 23.5.85.

35. XL385:
Completed 17.4.62. Olympus 201 engines. Blue Steel modifications including 301 engines. 9 Squadron 18.4.62, Scampton Wing 9.10.64. Ground fire at Scampton 6.4.67. SOC 7.4.67.

36. XL386:
Completed 11.5.62. Olympus 201 engines. Blue Steel modifications including 301 engines. 9 Squadron 14.5.62, Scampton Wing 16.8.65, 230 OCU 1.4.70, 44 Squadron 30.9.77, 101 Squadron 5.81, 50 Squadron 10.81. Delivered to Central Training Establishment at Manston 26.8.82 as 8760M, scrapped 9/92.

37. XL387:
Completed 31.5.62. Olympus 201 engines. Blue Steel modifications including 301 engines. 230 OCU 4.6.62, Scampton Wing 5.2.65, 230 OCU 5.7.72, 101 Squadron 10.1.73, 50 Squadron 8.75. To St Athan for crash rescue training 28.1.82. Sold to Bradbury Ltd as scrap 2.6.83.

38. XL388:
Completed 13.6.62. Olympus 201 engines. Blue Steel modifications including 301 engines. 9 Squadron 14.6.62 (Coningsby Wing), 230 OCU 19.4.71, 617 Squadron 15.9.72, 230 OCU 29.9.72, 617 Squadron 2.2.73, 230 OCU 14.5.73, 617 Squadron 1.11.73, 230 OCU 5.3.74, 617 Squadron 6.3.74, 44 Squadron 1.4.74. To Honington fire dump 2.4.82 (8750M). Sold to Swefeling Group as scrap 13.6.85.

39. XL389:
Completed 11.7.62. Olympus 201 engines. Blue Steel modifications including 301 engines. 230 OCU 13.7.62, Scampton Wing 20.5.65, 230 OCU 11.11.70, 617 Squadron 12.70, 230 OCU 7.4.72, 617 Squadron 30.6.72, 230 OCU 12.1.73, 617 Squadron 16.1.73, 9 Squadron 26.6.74, 44 Squadron 7.79, 101 Squadron 6.80. To St Athan 6.4.81. Sold to W. Harold 31.8.81 as scrap.

40. XL390:
Completed 19.7.62. Olympus 201 engines. Blue Steel modifications including 301 engines. First production aircraft with Skybolt hardpoints. 9 Squadron 20.7.62, Scampton Wing 27.5.65, 230 OCU 30.4.71, 617 Squadron 3.6.71, 230 OCU 31.5.74, 617 Squadron 4.6.74. Crashed during air display, Glenview Naval Air Station, USA, 12.8.78.

41. XL391:
Completed 22.5.63. Olympus 301 engines. Blue Steel modifications. A&AEE 22.5.63, BCDU 15.6.65, A&AEE 6.1.66, Cottesmore Wing 31.7.68, Akrotiri Wing 5.2.69, 9 Squadron 17.1.75, 101 Squadron 6.80. Selected for Black Buck modifications, but not used operationally. 44 Squadron 2.6.82. Sold to Manchester Vulcan Bomber Society 11.2.83. Delivered to Blackpool 16.2.83. Scrapped 1.06.

42. XL392:
Completed 31.7.62. Olympus 201 engines. Blue Steel modifications. 83 Squadron 2.8.62, 230 OCU 11.12.70, Scampton Wing 21.12.70, 230 OCU 12.1.73, 617 Squadron 15.1.73, 35 Squadron 4.1.82. Delivered to Valley for crash rescue training as 8745M 24.3.82. Scrapped 8.83.

43. XL425:
Completed 30.8.62. Olympus 201 engines. Blue Steel modifications. 83 Squadron 31.8.62, Scampton Wing, 617 Squadron 30.11.72, 27 Squadron 1.11.73, 617 Squadron 1.4.74. Grounded 4.1.82. Sold to Bird Group as scrap 4.82.

44. XL426:
Completed 7.9.62. Olympus 201 engines. Blue Steel modifications. 83 Squadron 13.9.62, Scampton Wing, 230 OCU 29.3.72, 617 Squadron 7.4.72, 230 OCU 28.6.72, 617 Squadron 4.7.72, 230 OCU 11.7.72, 617 Squadron 1.8.72, 230 OCU 13.4.73, 617 Squadron 16.4.73, 27 Squadron 6.2.74, 617 Squadron 21.2.74, 50 Squadron 5.1.82, 55 Squadron 1.4.84. Sold to Roy Jacobsen and delivered to Southend 19.12.86.

45. XL427:
Completed 29.9.62. Olympus 201 engines. Blue Steel modifications. 83 Squadron 2.10.62, Scampton Wing, 617 Squadron 9.69, 27 Squadron 3.71, 230 OCU 29.6.72, 617 Squadron 5.7.72, 230 OCU 25.9.72, 27 Squadron 4.1.74, 230 OCU 11.8.76, 27 Squadron 27.8.76, 9 Squadron 2.5.77, 50 Squadron 4.81, 9 Squadron 10.81, 44 Squadron 6.82. Delivered to Machrihanish for crash rescue training 13.8.82 as 8756M. Scrapped 1986.

46. XL443:
Completed 4.10.62. Olympus 201 engines. Blue Steel modifications. 83 Squadron 8.10.62, Scampton Wing, Akrotiri Wing 12.4.72, 35 Squadron 24.1.75. Allocated to RAF Museum 4.1.82. Later sold to Bird Group as scrap 4.82.

47. XL444:
Completed 29.10.82. Olympus 201 engines. Blue Steel modifications. 27 Squadron 1.11.62, Scampton Wing, 230 OCU 18.6.66, Scampton Wing 19.6.67, 230 OCU 5.4.71, 27 Squadron 11.5.71, 617 Squadron 9.71, 230 OCU/617 Squadron 19.7.72, 617 Squadron 18.12.73, 35 Squadron 31.5.78, 9 Squadron 6.4.81, grounded 10.9.82. Sold to Bird Group as scrap 8.12.82.

48. XL445:
Completed 19.11.62. Olympus 201 engines. Blue Steel modifications. 27 Squadron 26.11.62, Scampton Wing, Waddington Wing 30.9.66, Cottesmore Wing 18.4.68, Akrotiri Wing 15.1.69, 35 Squadron 16.1.75, Waddington Wing 16.6.77, 35 Squadron 1.10.77, 230 OCU 16.10.78, 35 Squadron 1.7.81. 44 Squadron 18.11.81. Conversion to K2 25.5.82. 50 Squadron 22.7.82. Allocated 8811M 22.3.84 for crash rescue training. Delivered Lyneham 1.4.84. Scrapped 1990, nose to N&SAM, Flixton.

49. XL446:
Completed 19.11.62. Olympus 201 engines. Blue Steel modifications. 27 Squadron 30.11.62, Scampton Wing, Waddington Wing 16.9.66, 230 OCU 28.12.67, Scampton Wing 18.4.72, Akrotiri Wing 31.7.72, 35 Squadron 16.1.75, Waddington Wing 24.5.78, 617 Squadron 31.10.78, 35 Squadron 4. .82. Grounded 1.3.82. Sold to Bird Group as scrap 11.82.

Vulcan B.Mk 2
Contract KD/B/01/CB.6(a). 40 aircraft, dated 22.1.58.

50. XM569:
Completed 4.1.63, Olympus 201 engines. Blue Steel modifications. 27 Squadron 1.2.63, Scampton Wing, Waddington Wing 17.11.66, Cottesmore Wing 19.1.68, Akrotiri Wing 26.2.69, 27 Squadron 4.7.74, 9 Squadron 23.11.76, 50 Squadron 6.79, 101 Squadron 9.81, 44 Squadron 8.82. Sold to Wales Aircraft Museum 21.1.83. Delivered to Cardiff 2.2.83. Subsequently scrapped, nose section preserved privately (Jet Age Museum).

51. XM570:
Completed 26.2.63. Olympus 201 engines. Blue Steel modifications. 27 Squadron 27.2.63, Scampton Wing, Waddington Wing 2.1.67, Cottesmore Wing 26.1.68, Akrotiri Wing 26.2.69, 27 Squadron 8.3.74, 35 Squadron 8.12.76, 230 OCU 28.2.77, 35 Squadron 2.3.77, 617 Squadron 4.9.78, 35 Squadron 31.10.78. Delivered to St Athan 11.3.81. Sold to Harold John & Co as scrap 29.1.82.

52. XM571:
Completed 20.2.63. Olympus 201 engines. Blue Steel modifications. 83 Squadron 22.2.63, Scampton Wing, Cottesmore Wing 20.1.67, Waddington Wing 3.7.67, Cottesmore Wing 13.9.67, Waddington Wing 15.12.67, Akrotiri Wing 19.3.69, 27 Squadron 3.1.75, 35 Squadron 9.4.75, Waddington Wing 16.6.75, 35 Squadron 3.11.75, 50 Squadron 15.6.76, 35 Squadron 15.11.76, St Athan 9.1.79, 617 Squadron 27.3.79, Waddington Wing 20.8.79, 617 Squadron 4.12.79, 101 Squadron 8.1.82. Conversion to K2 11.5.82. 50 Squadron 25.8.82. Waddington Station Flight

4.84. Allocated 8812M 22.3.84. Delivered to Gibraltar for preservation 9.5.84. Scrapped on site 89.

53. XM572:
Completed 28.2.63. Olympus 201 engines. Blue Steel modifications. 83 Squadron 28.2.63, Scampton Wing, Cottesmore Wing 5.4.68, Akrotiri Wing 19.3.69, 35 Squadron 24.1.75, 9 Squadron 2.9.81. Grounded 10.9.82. Sold to Bird Group as scrap 30.11.82.

54. XM573:
Completed 26.3.63. Olympus 201 engines. Blue Steel modifications. 83 Squadron 28.3.63, Scampton Wing, Waddington Wing 25.4.67, 230 OCU 15.2.68, Akrotiri Wing 26.6.70, 27 Squadron 17.4.74, 44 Squadron 9.3.77, 230 OCU 18.12.78, 9 Squadron 7.4.81, Scampton 22.5.82. Delivered to Offutt AFB, USA, 7.6.82, presented to USAF 12.6.82.

55. XM574:
Completed 12.6.63. Olympus 301 engines. Blue Steel modifications. 27 Squadron 21.6.63, Scampton Wing, 230 OCU 3.5.71, 27 Squadron 12.5.71, 101 Squadron 3.11.71, Akrotiri Wing 24.8.73, 35 Squadron 24.1.75, 617 Squadron 14.8.75. To St Athan 31.8.81. Sold to Harold John & Co. as scrap 29.1.82.

56. XM575:
Completed 21.5.63. Olympus 301 engines. Blue Steel modifications. 617 Squadron 22.5.63, Scampton Wing, Waddington Wing 28.7.70, Scampton Wing 27.11.70, 230 OCU 3.5.71, 617 Squadron 7.5.71, 101 Squadron 15.3.74, 50 Squadron 6.78, 44 Squadron 8.79. Sold to Leicestershire Air Museum 25.1.83. Delivered to Castle Donington 28.1.83. East Midlands Aeropark.

57. XM576:
Completed 14.6.63. Olympus 301 engines. Blue Steel modifications. Scampton Wing 21.6.63. Crash-landed Scampton 25.5.65. SOC 12.65.

58. XM594:
Completed 9.7.63. Olympus 301 engines. Blue Steel modifications. 27 Squadron 19.7.63, Scampton Wing,

Waddington Wing 24.8.72, 101 Squadron 6.75, 44 Squadron 5.77. Sold to Newark Air Museum 19.1.83. Delivered to Winthorpe 7.2.83.

59. XM595:
Completed 21.8.63. Olympus 301 engines. Blue Steel modifications. 617 Squadron 21.8.63, Scampton Wing, 27 Squadron 16.8.74, 617 Squadron 9.75, 35 Squadron 11.76, 617 Squadron 2.78, 35 Squadron 4.1.82. Grounded 1.3.82. Sold to Bird Group as scrap 11.82.

60. XM596: Not completed. Aircraft used for static fatigue tests at Woodford, in connection with low-level operations. Scrapped 1972.

61. XM597:
Completed 26.8.63. Olympus 301 engines. Blue Steel modifications. 12 Squadron 27.8.63, Coningsby Wing, Cottesmore Wing 18.12.64, Waddington Wing 18.4.68, A&AEE 29.11.71, 101 Squadron 8.73, 44 Squadron 9.75, 50 Squadron 4.76, 9 Squadron 5.79, 44 Squadron 10.81, 101 Squadron 7.82. Modified for Black Buck operations. 44 Squadron 1.7.82, 50 Squadron 24.12.82. Delivered to Royal Scottish Museum of Flight, East Fortune, 12.4.84.

62. XM598:
Completed 30.8.63. Olympus 301 engines. 12 Squadron 4.9.63, Coningsby Wing, Cottesmore Wing 11.64, Waddington Wing 9.4.68, 101 Squadron 5.72, 44 Squadron 8.75, 50 Squadron 4.78, 9 Squadron 10.79, 50 Squadron 10.81, 44 Squadron 6.82. Modified for Black Buck operations. Allocated 8778M 4.1.83, delivered to Cosford Aerospace Museum 20.1.83.

63. XH559:
Completed 30.9.63. Olympus 301 engines. 35 Squadron 1.10.63, Coningsby Wing, Waddington Wing 9.12.68, 101 Squadron 5.72, 50 Squadron 3.77, 44 Squadron 6.79. Delivered to St Athan 27.5.81. Sold to H. John & Co. as scrap 29.1.82.

64. XM600:
Completed 30.9.63. Olympus 301 engines. 35 Squadron 3.10.63, Coningsby Wing, Waddington Wing 3.5.68, 101 Squadron 8.73. Crashed near Spilsby following engine bay fire 17.1.77.

65. XM601:
Completed 31.10.63. Olympus 301 engines. 9 Squadron 5.11.63, Coningsby Wing. Crashed on approach to Coningsby 7.10.64.

66. XM602:
Completed 11.11.63. Olympus 301 engines. 12 Squadron 13.11.63, Coningsby Wing, Cottesmore Wing, Waddington Wing 24.4.68, 9 Squadron 12.75, 230 OCU 19.10.76, 35 Squadron 29.10.76, Waddington Wing 1.11.76, 101 Squadron 5.80. To St Athan 7.1.82. Transferred to St Athan Historic Aircraft Museum 16.3.83 (8771M). Scrapped, nose section to Bruntingthorpe.

67. XM603:
Completed 29.11.63. Olympus 301 engines. 9 Squadron 4.12.63, Coningsby Wing, Cottesmore Wing, Waddington Wing 18.1.68, 50 Squadron 8.75, 101 Squadron 12.80, 44 Squadron 7.81. Sold to British Aerospace for preservation, delivered to Woodford 12.3.82. Mock-up aircraft for K2 conversions. Intact at time of airfield closure 09.11.

68. XM604:
Completed 29.11.63. Olympus 301 engines. 35 Squadron 4.12.63, Coningsby Wing, Cottesmore Wing. Crashed near Cottesmore following loss of control during overshoot (engine compressor failure) 30.1.68.

69. XM605:
Completed 17.12.63. Olympus 301 engines. 9 Squadron 30.12.63, Coningsby Wing, Cottesmore Wing, Waddington Wing 16.12.68, 101 Squadron 8.73, 50 Squadron 5.79. Delivered to Castle AFB, USA, 2.9.81. Presented to USAF 8.9.81.

70. XM606:
Completed 18.12.63. Olympus 301 engines. 12 Squadron 30.12.63, Coningsby Wing, Cottesmore Wing 18.2.65, MoA 14.6.65, Cottesmore Wing 5.4.68, Waddington Wing

13.5.68, 101 Squadron 12.75, 9 Squadron 6.79. Delivered to Barksdale AFB, USA, 7.6.82. Presented to USAF 14.6.83.

71. XM607: Completed 30.12.63. Olympus 301 engines. 35 Squadron 1.1.64, Coningsby Wing, Cottesmore Wing, Waddington Wing 24.5.68, 44 Squadron 4.76, 9 Squadron 5.79, 101 Squadron 3.81, 44 Squadron 7.81. Modified for Black Buck operations. 44 Squadron 14.6.82. Withdrawn from use 17.12.82, allocated 8779M 4.1.83. To static display at Waddington 19.1.83. Displayed adjacent to runway.

72. XM608:
Completed 28.1.64. Olympus 301 engines. Coningsby Wing 29.1.64, Cottesmore Wing, Waddington Wing 23.2.68, 50 Squadron 4.75. To St Athan 6.4.81. Sold to Bird Group as scrap 2.12.82.

73. XM609:
Completed 28.1.64. Olympus 301 engines. 12 Squadron 29.1.64, Coningsby Wing, Cottesmore Wing 3.3.65, 230 OCU 7.8.67, Cottesmore Wing 1.10.67, Waddington Wing 8.3.68, 9 Squadron 9.75, 44 Squadron 4.76. To St Athan 12.3.81. Sold to W. Harold & Co. as scrap 31.8.81.

74. XM610:
Completed 10.2.64. Olympus 301 engines. 9 Squadron 12.2.64, Coningsby Wing, Cottesmore Wing, Waddington Wing 5.2.68. Crashed Wingate 8.1.71 following engine bay fire.

75. XM611:
Completed 12.2.64. Olympus 301 engines. 9 Squadron 14.2.64, Coningsby Wing, Cottesmore Wing, Waddington Wing 28.5.68, 101 Squadron 5.72. To St Athan 27.1.82. Sold to Bradbury Ltd as scrap 2.6.83.

76. XM612:
Completed 28.2.64. Olympus 301 engines. 9 Squadron 3.3.64, Coningsby Wing, Cottesmore Wing, A&AEE 5.3.68, Waddington Wing 4.4.68, 101 Squadron 5.75, 44 Squadron 7.81. Modified for Black Buck operations. 44 Squadron 23.5.82. Sold to Norwich Aviation Museum 19.1.83. Delivered 30.1.83.

77. XM645:
Completed 10.3.64. Olympus 301 engines. Coningsby Wing 12.3.64, Cottesmore Wing, Waddington Wing 15.12.67, 230 OCU 5.8.68, Waddington Wing 21.4.71, 101 Squadron 8.73, Akrotiri Wing 12.3.74, 9 Squadron 15.1.75. Crashed Zabbar, Malta, following explosion 14.10.75.

78. XM646:
Completed 7.4.64. Olympus 301 engines. 12 Squadron 8.4.64, Coningsby Wing, Cottesmore Wing, Akrotiri Wing 5.2.69, 9 Squadron 17.1.75, 101 Squadron 6.81. To St Athan 26.1.82. Sold to Bradbury Ltd as scrap 29.6.83.

79. XM647:
Completed 15.4.64. Olympus 301 engines. 35 Squadron 15.4.64, Coningsby Wing, Cottesmore Wing, Akrotiri Wing 26.2.69, Waddington Wing 15.1.75, 9 Squadron 1.75, 44 Squadron 9.79, 50 Squadron 9.81. Delivered to Laarbruch 17.9.82 for ground instruction (8765M). Sold to Solair UK 25.2.85 as scrap. Scrapped 1.3.85.

80. XM648:
Completed 5.5.64. Olympus 301 engines. 9 Squadron 6.5.64, Coningsby Wing, Cottesmore Wing, Waddington Wing 25.1.68, 101 Squadron 5.72, 44 Squadron 5.75, 101 Squadron 3.77, 9 Squadron 9.80, 101 Squadron 10.81. Grounded 10.9.82. Sold to Bird Group as scrap 8.12.82.

81. XM649:
Completed 12.5.64. Olympus 301 engines. 9 Squadron 14.5.64, Coningsby Wing, Cottesmore Wing, Waddington Wing 1 8.1.68, 101 Squadron 8.73, 9 Squadron 4.76, 101 Squadron 8.79. To St Athan 2.9.81. Sold to Bird Group as scrap 2.12.82.

82. XM650:
Completed 27.5.64. Olympus 301 engines. 12 Squadron 5.6.64, Coningsby Wing, Cottesmore Wing, Waddington Wing 20.12.67, 44 Squadron 5.75, 50 Squadron 1.77. To St Athan 28.1.82. Allocated 8748M 16.3.83. Sold to Bournewood Aviation as scrap 22.3.84.

83. XM651:
Completed 19.6.64. Olympus 301 engines. 12 Squadron 22.6.64, Coningsby Wing, Cottesmore Wing, Waddington Wing 24.4.68, 101 Squadron 5.72, 50 Squadron 9.75, 101 Squadron 9.79. Grounded 10.9.82. Sold to Bird Group as scrap 30.11.82.

84. XM652:
Completed 12.8.64. Olympus 301 engines. 9 Squadron 17.8.64, Coningsby Wing, Cottesmore Wing, Waddington Wing 24.12.67, 44 Squadron 9.75, 9 Squadron 10.81, 50 Squadron 10.82. Sold to Boulding Group 20.2.84. Dismantled and transported to Sheffield 7.5.84. Nose preserved at Welshpool, rest of airframe scrapped 2.85.

85. XM653:
Completed 31.8.64. Olympus 301 engines. 9 Squadron, Coningsby Wing, Cottesmore Wing, Waddington Wing 24.1.68, 101 Squadron 5.72, 44 Squadron 5.75, 9 Squadron 9.75, 101 Squadron 10.78, 9 Squadron 5.79, 101 Squadron 7.79. To St Athan 10.9.79. Dumped 18.12.80. Sold as scrap 28.7.81.

86. XM654:
Completed 22.10.64. Olympus 301 engines. 12 Squadron 26.10.64, Coningsby Wing, Cottesmore Wing, Waddington Wing 30.4.68, 101 Squadron 8.73, 50 Squadron 9.75, 101 Squadron 9.81, 50 Squadron 10.81. Grounded 29.10.82. Sold to Bird Group as scrap 30.11.82.

87. XM655:
Completed 19.11.64. Olympus 301 engines. 9 Squadron 23.11.64, Cottesmore Wing, Waddington Wing 12.1.68, 101 Squadron 5.72, 44 Squadron 7.81, 50 Squadron 8.82. Sold to Roy Jacobsen 11.2.84, delivered to Wellesbourne Mountford 11.2.84. Registered G-VULC 27.2.84. Re-registered N655AV 1985. Sold to Radar Moor 1992.

88. XM656:
Completed 11.12.64. Olympus 301 engines. 35 Squadron 15.12.64. Cottesmore Wing, Waddington Wing 2.2.68, 101 Squadron 9.75, 9 Squadron 12.80. To Cottesmore for display 9.8.82. Allocated 8757M, assigned to crash/rescue training. Sold to Bird Group as scrap 30.3.83.

89. XM657:
Completed 14.1.65. Olympus 301 engines. 35 Squadron 15.1.65, Cottesmore Wing, Waddington Wing 19.3.68, 101 Squadron 5.72, 50 Squadron 8.75, 101 Squadron 3.77, 44 Squadron 4.80. Allocated to Central Training Establishment 5.1.82, delivered to Manston 12.1.82. Allocated 8734M. Later scrapped. Last production Vulcan B2.

VULCAN SQUADRONS

(Vulcan B2 unless otherwise stated)

9 Squadron.
1 Mar 62 – 9 Nov 64. Coningsby
10 Nov 64 – 25 Feb 69. Cottesmore
26 Feb 69 – 31 Dec 74. Akrotiri, Cyprus
1 Jan 75 – 9 Apr 82. Waddington

12 Squadron.
1 Jun 62 – 16 Nov 64. Coningsby
17 Nov 64 – 31 Dec 67. Cottesmore

27 Squadron.
1 Apr 61 – 29 Mar 72. Scampton
1 Nov 73 – 31 Mar 82. Scampton

35 Squadron.
1 Dec 62 – 6 Nov 64. Coningsby
7 Nov 64 – 14 Jan 69. Cottesmore
15 Jan 69 – 15 Jan 75. Akrotiri, Cyprus
16 Jan 75 – 28 Feb 82. Scampton

44 Squadron.
10 Aug 60 – 21 Dec 82. Waddington (B1/1A until Nov 67)

50 Squadron.
1 Aug 61 – 31 Mar 84. Waddington (B1/1A until Nov 66, K2 from 82)

83 Squadron.
21 May 57 – 9 Oct 60. Waddington (B1 until Aug 60)
10 Oct 60 – 31 Aug 69. Scampton

101 Squadron.
15 Oct 57 – 25 Jun 61. Finningley (B1/1A)
26 Jun 61 – 4 Aug 82. Waddington (B1/1A until Jan 68)

617 Squadron.
1 May 58 – 1 Jan 82. Scampton (B1 until July 61)

230 Operational Conversion Unit.
Jul 56 – Jun 61. Waddington (B1 until Jun 60)
Jun 61 – Dec 69. Finningley
Dec 69 – Aug 81. Scampton

Wings and Bases

Coningsby (Mar 62 – Nov 64)
1 Mar – 30 Jun 62. 9 Squadron
1 Jul – 30 Nov 62. 9 and 12 Squadrons
1 Dec 62 – 16 Nov 64. 9, 12 and 35 Squadrons

Cottesmore (Nov 64 – Feb 69)
7 – 16 Nov 64. 35 and 9 Squadrons
17 Nov 64 – 31 Dec 67. 35, 9 and 12 Squadrons
1 Jan 68 – 14 Jan 69. 35 and 9 Squadrons
15 Jan – 25 Jan 69. 9 Squadron

Finningley (Oct 57 – Dec 69)
15 Oct 57 – 25 June 61. 101 Squadron
Jun 61 – Dec 69. 230 OCU

Scampton (May 58 – Mar 82)
1 May 58 – 9 Oct 60. 617 Squadron
10 Oct 60 – 31 Mar 61. 617 and 83 Squadrons
1 Apr 61 – 31 Aug 69. 617, 83 and 27 Squadrons
1 Sep – Dec 69. 617 and 27 Squadrons
Dec 69 – 29 Mar 72. 617, 27 Squadrons and 230 OCU
30 Mar 72 – 31 Oct 73. 617 Squadron and 230 OCU
1 Nov 73 – 15 Jan 75. 617 and 27 Squadrons, and 230 OCU
16 Jan 75 – Aug 81. 617, 27 and 35 Squadrons, and 230 OCU
Aug 81 – 1 Jan 82. 617, 27 and 35 Squadrons
2 Jan – 28 Feb 82. 27 and 35 Squadrons
1–31 Mar 82. 27 Squadron

Waddington (Jul 56 – Mar 84)
20 Jul 56 – 20 May 57. 230 OCU
21 May 57 – 9 Aug 60. 83 Squadron and 230 OCU
10 Aug – 9 Oct 60. 83 and 44 Squadrons, and 230 OCU
10 Oct 60 – 25 Jun 61. 44 Squadron and 230 OCU
26 Jun – 31 Jul 61. 44 and 101 Squadrons
1 Aug 61 – 31 Dec 74. 44, 101 and 50 Squadrons
1 Jan 75 – 9 Apr 82. 44, 101, 50 and 9 Squadrons
10 Apr – 4 Aug 82. 44, 101 and 50 Squadrons
5 Aug – 21 Dec 82. 44 and 50 Squadrons

Akrotiri, Cyprus (Jan 69 – Jan 75)
15 Jan – 25 Feb 69. 35 Squadron
26 Feb 69 – 31 Dec 74. 35 and 9 Squadrons
1–15 Jan 75. 35 Squadron

Vulcan Losses

XA897: 1 October 1956, Heathrow. Crashed during radar
　　approach
VX770: 20 September 1958, Syerston. Structural failure
XA908: 24 October 1958, Michigan, USA. Electrical failure
XA891: 24 July 1959, near Hull. Electrical failure
XA894: 3 December 1962, Patchway. Ground fire
XH477: 12 December 1963, Scotland. Crashed during
　　low-level training flight
XH535: 11 May 1964, near Andover. Crashed after entering
　　an uncontrollable spin
XA909: 16 July 1964, Anglesey. Engine explosion
XM601: 7 October 1964, Coningsby. Crashed on landing
XM576: 25 May 1965, Scampton. Crash-landed
XM536: 11 February 1966, Wales. Crashed on TFR trials flight
XL385: 6 April 1967, Scampton. Ground fire
XM604: 30 January 1968, Cottesmore. Engine failure
　　leading to loss of control
XM610: 8 January 1971, Wingate. Engine bay fire
XJ781: 23 May 1973, Shiraz, Iran. Crash-landed
XM645: 14 October 1975, Zabbar. Explosion following
　　undershoot landing attempt
XM600: 17 January 1977, near Spilsby. Engine bay fire
XL390: 12 August 1978 Glenview, USA. Crashed during air
　　display

V-Bomber Designated Dispersal Airfields

Class One Airfields (V-bomber bases):
Finningley
Coningsby
Honington
Scampton
Wittering
Cottesmore
Waddington
Gaydon
Wyton

Dispersal Airfields with ORPs for up to four aircraft:
Burtonwood
Bedford/Thurleigh
St Mawgan
Ballykelly
Filton
Kinloss
Shawbury
Cranwell
Middleton St George
Boscombe Down
Pershore
Leeming
Lyneham

Dispersal Airfields with ORPs for two aircraft:
Leconfield
Leuchars
Lossiemouth
Yeovilton
Llanbedr
Coltishall
Valley
Manston
Brawdy
Wattisham
Stansted
Elvington
Prestwick
Machrihanish
Bruntingthorpe

INDEX